# THE BITCH IS BACK

# THE BITCH IS BACK

Older, Wiser, and (Getting) Happier

*Edited by*
## CATHI HANAUER

*wm*

William Morrow
*An Imprint of* HarperCollins*Publishers*

The following are personal essays—creative works of narrative nonfiction based on the experience, point of view, and memory of the authors. In four cases, the author uses a pseudonym in order to protect or disguise herself and/or the people being written about. In several cases, names or identifying details have been changed—again, to protect the people or the identity of the people being written about—in a way that doesn't alter the meaning of the anecdote or essay.

HarperCollins books may be purchased for educational, business, or sales promotional use. For information please e-mail the Special Markets Department at SPsales@harpercollins.com.

FIRST EDITION

*Designed by Bonni Leon-Berman*

Library of Congress Cataloging-in-Publication Data has been applied for.

ISBN 978-0-06-238951-0

Excerpt from "Indian Summer" on p. vii from THE PORTABLE DOROTHY PARKER by Dorothy Parker, edited by Marion Meade, copyright 1944 by Dorothy Parker; copyright © 1973, 2006 by The National Association for the Advancement of Colored People. Used by permission of Viking Books, an imprint of Penguin Publishing Group, a division of Penguin Random House LLC.

16 17 18 19 20   OV/RRD   10 9 8 7 6 5 4 3 2 1

For Dan, still my favorite bastard

But now I know the things I know,

And do the things I do;

And if you do not like me so,

To hell, my love, with you!

—DOROTHY PARKER

Truth is the only safe ground to stand on.

—ELIZABETH CADY STANTON

# CONTENTS

# INTRODUCTION

About ten years ago, while on a paperback tour for my second novel, *Sweet Ruin,* I slid into my assigned aisle airplane seat and immediately became aware of the couple next to me in the window and middle spots. I'll call them Jack and Jill. Both were tall, blond, and attractive, if, like me, approaching middle age: He had the telltale extra pound or two in the gut, her face was slightly creased. Nonetheless, they had the distinct aura of two sixteen-year-olds newly in love. He teased, she giggled; he leaned over her to look out the window, her hand rested on his arm. As I sat—apparently on one part of his seat belt—he made a joke to me (but clearly for her benefit) about my not thinking him rude if he retrieved it. She laughed, he joked again, this time to her—"Hey, it was your idea for me to sit in the middle"—I joked back to them— "You guys want me to go somewhere else so you can have some privacy here?"—they both laughed—"Yeah, would you?"—and since the flight was packed and I couldn't actually move, we were off to a promising start for a writer always on the hunt for a good story. By the time we landed, I had theirs.

Jill was heading into her mid-forties, as I too was then. Unlike me, though, she had adult children (I had young ones), two young grandchildren, and a joyless, stifling, outdated marriage to—as you may have guessed by now—a man other than the one sitting next to her. She wanted to leave, and her husband knew that (and didn't want the same), but so far they hadn't divorced. Jack too was in an unhappy marriage. His wife hadn't wanted to have sex with him for years, though sometimes she did anyway, and he had cheated on her before; they had, he said, a "don't ask, don't tell" policy. Like Jill, he wanted to leave, but he had a ten-year-old son and didn't want to miss out on his son's childhood or pay alimony, especially when he'd funded his wife going back to school and, now graduated, she still hadn't returned to work.

Jack and Jill had met through their jobs. One thing had led to another, and now they were enmeshed in a full-blown affair, taking every chance they had to flee or hide out together. They spoke wistfully about when they might be with each other openly; she confessed that she cried sometimes when they parted, deciding she'd have to end this, as it was too hard to always have to say good-bye.

While they talked to me, they each ordered a drink from the cart, and then another, lowering the shade against the bright sun. Uninvited, she sloppily poured his beer into his plastic cup with about three inches of foam on the top, and they both cracked up, giddy with alcohol and lust, no doubt imagining the fun they'd have this week away from their spouses. At the end of the flight, I wished them good luck, and they promised to e-mail and fill me in on what happened.

Which they did. More about them in a bit.

• • • •

Several years before that—just about fifteen years ago, now—I conceived and eventually edited a book of essays called *The Bitch in the House: 26 Women Tell the Truth about Sex, Solitude, Work, Motherhood, and Marriage.* The contributors ranged in age from twenty-four to seventy-six, but the bulk of the book, and what ultimately made it a bestseller (and propelled me, to my amusement, into a person who can walk into my local bookstore and have the employees gleefully yell, "The bitch is in the house!") were the essays by my then-thirtysomething female peers, women juggling serious careers—careers in which they often significantly out-earned their boyfriends or husbands—while still, they felt, shouldering the bulk of the domestic, social, and parenting burden.

The overriding tone of the book was anger and dissatisfaction. Feminism, I posited, had opened the doors for the women of my generation to be educated and have careers on a level with men, to support ourselves and climb job ladders in our twenties, to fully anticipate fulfilling and lucrative professions in which we contributed a comparable or superior share of the family income, and to have the help, once we married and (especially) had children, of an *equal* domestic partner and co-parent in all of it. We picked sensitive, intelligent men who accepted and benefited from us as peers—intellectually, financially, and otherwise. But when the babies arrived, whether because they couldn't, because they wouldn't, and/or because society or we ourselves wouldn't let them, many of these men were not contributing what we working women perceived as their half. As a result, we were exhausted, disillusioned, resentful, and angry at our husbands. We felt guilty at work and guilty at home and much preferred sleep to sex. We were tired of "juggling" and running ourselves ragged, but there seemed to be no other way; with families that now relied on our income, careers that defined us, and few role models for how to "do it all," we had no choice but to carry on.

And so we did, but often not as graciously or contentedly as we wanted to or felt we should. We were "the bitch in the house"—the opposite of "the angel in the house" made famous by Virginia Woolf in a speech (a woman so selflessly devoted to her children and husband that if there was chicken for dinner she took the lesser pieces for herself; if there was a draft in the room, she sat in it).

And, as I learned from the response to the book, there were a lot of us "bitches" out there.

I published *The Bitch in the House* in 2002 and rode that wave for a while, and then I wrote and published the aforementioned second novel, *Sweet Ruin,* the story of a suburban couple with a young daughter in which the wife commits adultery. (I call it my midlife crisis novel.) And as time passed, as my own kids grew up and our family had a steadier income and life calmed down and I became, for the most part, much less angry, I began to think about doing a sequel to *Bitch,* something to reflect what happens later, after those frantic, demanding, exhausting years with work and very young kids and, sometimes, not enough money. But I wasn't sure exactly what it should be, so I filed away the idea.

Which brings me back to Jack and Jill on that plane, who I met during those relatively calm, less "bitchy" years. Their story didn't shock or surprise me; in fact, it was like a play-by-play slice of at least some of what I was seeing, hearing, and inferring around me at that time. The very night before, the mostly female audience of thirty- and early fortysomethings at the bookstore where I'd read from *Sweet Ruin* had, not atypically, vented the pent-up fears and frustrations they'd hidden and harbored for weeks, months, or years. My husband cheated, said one. *I* cheated, said another. I *want* to cheat, said a third. My husband and I rarely/almost never/ never have sex. I hate my husband. My husband hates me. Marriage sucks. You think so? Me *too*! (Yes, this was a room full of people who came to a reading of a novel about adultery. But still.)

Back at home, in my admittedly progressive, alternative town, even as someone well aware of the latest bleak marriage stats,* not

---

* Though close to 90 percent of Americans are still projected to marry at some point and for some duration, an increasing number of women are postponing marriage, if not forgoing it altogether. American marriage is at a record low, with, for the first time ever, the number of single women surpassing the number of married ones (51 percent versus 49 percent). Of the couples who do marry, 43 percent will divorce; 75 percent of those will

to mention someone who realizes that alternative communities like this one often fare "worse" with traditional institutions, I'd still been struck by the number of families in which the couple was now splitting up. Among my neighbors and peers and the parents of my children's classmates and friends, I was witnessing separations, affairs, divorces . . . flux and rebellion and disarray, almost all of it in that not-so-sweet spot of early midlife. I also was seeing the setting up of "alternative" arrangements—from separated couples "nesting" (taking turns living at the house so the kids don't have to move back and forth) to lesbians raising their new partners' ex-partners' biological kids—that, it seemed to me, had been virtually unheard of even a decade before. I saw formerly gay women hooking up with men; formerly straight women going for other women; baffled men left in the dust, often with joint (or more) custody of the children.

Some of us, of course, were still solidly married; more married couples than not, after all, stay together, for better and worse. But among my nonlocal friends, I saw more of the same flux I had seen here in crunchy Northampton, Massachusetts, affectionately nicknamed "the lesbian capital of the world." ("Where the coffee is strong and so are the women," reads a favorite local slogan.) Elsewhere, one close friend had recently left her twelve-year-long marriage and was now living happily with a much younger man. Four of my fortysomething female friends or acquaintances were having or had recently had affairs—two discovered by their husbands (both of

---

remarry, and of those, 68 percent will divorce again. Forty percent of American children now born to married or cohabiting parents will see these parents break up by the time they're fifteen. My sister, an economist, points out to me that if you looked at only the college educated, you'd get very different statistics. Nonetheless, unmarried mothers now have some 40 percent of the country's babies, with an increasing number of these mothers college-educated women in their thirties, forties, and fifties. And late-life divorce—also called "silver" or "gray" divorce—has become increasingly common, with people fifty and older now twice as likely to divorce as in 1990, and rates even higher among those over sixty-five. Sixty percent of divorces after age forty are initiated by women.

whom wanted the women to stay), two (so far) not; two of the marriages ending, the others so far continuing. Another female friend—who was her family's primary wage earner, as are most of my close friends—was miserable in her marriage, which she felt was unloving and unfair. She wanted out but couldn't see how to escape, with a consuming full-time job, a young son, and barely time to think, let alone initiate, pay for, and carry out a divorce.

On a recent date with a very social friend (I'll call her Aphrodite, so you remember her later), I told her my observations; she in turn told me first about her own struggling marriage and then about those of others she knew. "Maybe," Aphrodite concluded, "the problem isn't all of us, but *marriage*. Maybe we're all brainwashed to believe this is what we should be doing, when in fact marriage has outgrown its usefulness and now leads to more misery than happiness."

As if to echo her thoughts, galleys of soon-to-be-published books began to arrive at my door (as a writer, I am often sent books for review or endorsement) that bluntly stated the same thing. First came *The Marriage-Go-Round: The State of Marriage and the Family in America Today,* in which the author, Johns Hopkins sociology and public policy professor Andrew J. Cherlin, wrote, "What we have witnessed over the past half century is, at its core, the unprecedented decline of marriage as the only acceptable arrangement for having sexual relations and for raising children," adding, "In the space of a half century, then, we have seen the widest pendulum swing in family life in American history." Then came the hilarious and bitter *The Superior Wife Syndrome,* in which author Carin Rubenstein, who holds a Ph.D. in social/personality psychology from New York University, posited, "The fact that Americans view marriage as dispensable, and no longer compulsory, indicates that radical changes are taking place within the culture."

Magazines and the news media also trumpeted the trend. A *New York Times Magazine* cover story, featuring communities of women raising children together without husbands ("Two Kids Plus Zero Husbands Equals Family," it was titled, with the subtitle, "Many college-educated single mothers are setting up lives around other single mothers and all their children, with no role for men or romance"), appeared just one week after the magazine's cover story "What Is Female Desire?" in which one of the article's main experts concluded that "it's wrong to think that because relationships are what women choose, they're the primary source of women's [sexual] desire," and "within long-term relationships, women are more likely than men to lose interest in sex." In her *Atlantic* essay "Let's Call the Whole Thing Off," writer and comedian Sandra Tsing Loh described her decision, after having had an affair, to end her twenty-year marriage ("Given my staggering working mother's to-do list, I cannot take on yet another arduous home- and self-improvement project, that of rekindling our romance"). She wondered, "Why do we still insist on marriage? Sure, it made sense to agrarian families before 1900, when to farm the land, one needed two spouses, grandparents, and a raft of children. But now that we have white-collar work and washing machines, and our life expectancy has shot from 47 to 77, isn't the idea of lifelong marriage obsolete?"* In Tara Parker-Pope's piece "When Sex Leaves the Marriage," on the *New York Times* "Well" blog, she noted that 15 percent of married couples had not had sex within the past six months to a year. Though once you account for the fact that many people won't admit this—and then consider all of the above—it seems to me the percentage is likely considerably higher.

• • • •

Now, I knew that my generation of women expects and demands more from marriage than ever before, and, in some cases, perhaps

---

* See page 227 for Loh's new essay, "Living Alone: A Fantasy."

more than is reasonable or even possible. We want a best friend and a soul mate, a financial and domestic partner, someone who cracks us up, turns us on, makes us feel attractive and confident, stays faithful and sweet, and as a bonus can coach our daughter's basketball team and whip up homegrown basil pesto or grill an organic, cage-free, locally raised bird, possibly killing it himself—humanely, of course—with a spear made by an American company with union employees. We want hot sex and unconditional love, two things that not only aren't symbiotic but in fact have been diametrically opposed since the beginning of time. ("Romance only comes into existence," wrote Denis de Rougemont, "where love is fatal, frowned upon and doomed by life itself." "If there is such a thing as a good marriage," wrote Michel de Montaigne, "it is because it resembles friendship rather than love." "Where they love, they have no desire," wrote Sigmund Freud. "Where they desire, they cannot love." "Marriage has many benefits and values," wrote Susan Squire, "but eroticism is not one of them.")

But women of my generation also *contribute* more to marriage than perhaps ever before, or more accurately, contribute things that give us more power—namely, a big fat chunk of the income. And for that reason, we are a generation that, like no other, has the opportunity to make choices about our lives, from what kind of careers to have, to who and when to marry, to when, whether, and how to have children, to how much of our days—all, some, or, like so many of our own fathers, only evenings, vacations, and weekends—we spend raising them. And many of us now have the freedom to leave a marriage if it isn't working in a way that feels acceptable to us, if sometimes for a significantly less luxurious existence.

What's more, I now know that at that time—the time between Bitch 1 and Bitch 2, as I've come to call them—we were partway into a period of arguably the greatest sexual, gender, marriage, and relationship transition in history. Things that used to be fixed, or at least perceived as fixed—from gender roles to gender, sexuality to parenting—were now accepted to be fluid and varied, and for those with the means and the courage, much more about what we *wanted* than about what we were "assigned" at birth or even growing up. It had become a time when, not only in a town like my own progressive northeastern one but also in a growing number of places nationwide, a woman could marry someone of her own gender *or* outside it, or dress like a man, or *become* a man, or have a baby on her own without involving a man (only the sperm of one, which could be purchased online from a sperm bank). As was the case with a recent writer in a popular *New York Times* column, it might be the norm for a woman to sit down regularly to a cordial "family" dinner with her child, her child's father, her best friend, and her new, female, live-in lover, the last two of whom were one and the same—perhaps also with another friend who once had been male but now was female—all without at least some of the scrutiny or judgment of the past. Put another way, the political and the personal were merging in unprecedented ways.

• • • •

Which leads me to this book. Because now, finally, I began to figure out what the sequel to *The Bitch in the House* should be. I had seen friends and peers split from their spouses in midlife, and virtually all of them, after a devastating initial period—sadness, anger, pain, guilt, heartbreak—seemed happier and better off for it. I also had seen friends and peers stay married, as my husband and I had—including those who'd had one foot out the door just a few years ago. (Aphrodite, for example, now in her mid-fifties, had solved her earlier marital struggles and now seemed solidly in it for the long haul.) Some of us had done this in untraditional, innovative, or even what, not long ago, might have been considered "shocking" ways: open marriage, or living separately, or the wife making all the income while the husband does all the domestic work and child care. Others had improved their marriages partly by getting happier *themselves:* In many of the couples who stayed together, at least one spouse had gone on antidepressants or anti-anxiety meds—or discovered another way to "medicate" themselves and feel better, be it yoga, psychotherapy, gluten-free diets, copious travel, marathon running, liberal drinking, changing careers, claiming or building a room of one's own, adopting stray dogs, joining a chorus, taking up karate or painting or squash . . . whatever helped them grow and stay content and engaged.

Put another way, these women (because, admittedly, it was the women I knew and was interested in) had heeded the early midlife "call to awakening and action," as one friend phrased it—the necessity of connecting deeply to their lives and desires, as opposed to denying or becoming complacent, judgmental, bored, or all three. They had taken (or were taking) what was a prime time, and perhaps the last time, in their lives to significantly change themselves or their situation—at a time in society when just about any sort of personal or social change was possible—and had *made* that change; and they had done so in a way either profound and dramatic ("throwing off the broken ways and fighting for a new self/ life/identity," as another friend, who had just left her marriage, described it) or more subtle: often as simple as adjusting their expectations or finding a new appreciation for their lives. In short, they, *we*, "difficult" women, we thinking women, we women who finally have the opportunities and chutzpah to carve and design our own lives, had looked inward to see what was there and what was not, what we could live with or without, and what we still needed. And then we'd adjusted our lives and expectations accordingly.

I wanted this new book to incorporate these women and their myriad experiences, regardless of whether they had married or not, left their marriages or stayed, been faithful or had affairs; whether they'd become a parent or remained child-free; whether their husband had died or strayed, departed or stayed; whether they'd transitioned from one gender to another. How had we women—some, though not all, of us original contributors to *The Bitch in the House*—rethought or reconfigured our lives and come out in a more enlightened and content, less angry place? Our lives were not perfect, of course. Many of us were baffled by or worried about the rapidly changing financial, ecological, and technological world, beaten down by teenagers or health problems or tough economic times or just general wear and tear. Many of us were not, and never would be, wealthy enough to stop working hard and worrying about money. But we also were calmer, less frantic, less overextended—at least some of the time—with generally more self-confidence and control of our lives. We were more resigned in some ways, but also more self-possessed. And we were likely to have worked for and often achieved the life, or at least *a* life, that we wanted; to have taken the anger of those earlier years and used it to help us first figure things out and then get to a much better place. "If one has refused to budge through the midlife transition," wrote Gail Sheehy in her classic book *Passages,* "the sense of staleness will calcify into resignation. . . . On the other hand, if we have confronted ourselves in the middle passage and found a renewal of purpose around which we are eager to build a more authentic life structure, these may well be the best years."

How did we do it? How are we still doing it? What do we *think* about how we're doing it? That's the book you're holding. It's a book about choices—specifically, the choices today's bold, deep-thinking, impassioned women make as they approach and pass through midlife—and about what we might gain, and give up, with each choice. It's about the wisdom of *enlightened* middle age, and about happiness—real, informed contentment and happiness—and what that means, and how we get it and how we feel about it. It's about how today's strong, smart, courageous, and contemplative American women choose to age.

In it, you'll read about the most pertinent issues of midlife by many of the most interesting and talented women writing today. You'll read about divorce, affairs, perimenopausal/menopausal sex (and lack thereof), hormones, mood drugs, breast cancer. About the decision to have "work done," or not, on a middle-aged face, and about finally swearing off—or *not* swearing off—caring about being thin. About going from being the lesser to the primary earner in a marriage, and about being widowed (particularly as it pertains to sexuality), and about being with a much younger man, and about being married to a woman (when you're a woman too). You'll read about why some women stay or stayed married and others don't or didn't, about why some who once were married never would marry again, about one woman's marriage, at age fourteen, to a man her mother picked for her, and how, looking back on it after twenty-five years, that marriage fared. About a woman who, with her five sons in tow, fled an abusive husband, and how she feels about that decision, and the life it led to—and men in general—two and a half decades later. About a woman who asks whether we have a right, after many painful years, to say good-bye to a difficult parent, and how she ultimately answers that question in her own life.

What you won't learn in these pages—so I'll just go ahead and tell you—is that since the last book, three of the Bitch 1 contributors divorced, and five others married. The married include E. S. Maduro ("Excuse Me While I Explode"), to a physician who, happily, pulls his weight both financially and domestically (including with their two young sons), while she works hard herself as a psychologist; and Jen Marshall ("Crossing to Safety"), who eventually married Doug and moved, along with her publishing job, up to Massachusetts (though not to Riverboat Village!) to join him—

and is now the busy working mother of twin sons and a daughter. Catherine Newman ("Why I Won't Marry") nonetheless wed Michael shortly after writing her essay, for reasons having to do with health insurance; they now have a daughter as well as their son. Veronica Chambers ("Getting the Milk for Free") married the good guy from the end of her Bitch 1 essay, and you can read on page 179 about how, though she no longer "gives away the milk," she's learned to make—and expect—other marital compromises. Hazel McClay ("A Man in the Heart") also tied the knot with her true love from Bitch 1, and on page 105 you'll find her fifteen-years-later update on love versus sexual passion and how they play out in her marriage and her life.

You'll get updates on some of the other original "bitches" in these pages as well. What happened to Kerry Herlihy after she and her young daughter moved to Maine, leaving her (married) lover/baby daddy behind in New York? Or to Hope Edelman and her husband after she "released the dream of completely equal co-parenting"? Did Karen Karbo stay with her (much younger) boyfriend who succeeded her two ex-husbands, or Jill Bialosky reconnect with her husband after their baby was born, or Kate Christensen stop trying to be the perfect wife? Did Pam Houston end up adopting a baby? Was Cynthia Kling able to stay mysterious to her husband for another fifteen years? Or—so much for the husband—to *herself*?

You'll just have to read the book to find out.

When you do, I hope you'll find here a healthy variety of voices. Many of these women are, or at some point were, professional writers (i.e., people both inclined and schooled to think hard, dig deep, and present an interesting, organized story), but beyond that, they're no more alike than all businesspeople or all mothers or all dogs. Some of them are well-off, while others barely scrape by; some are naturally upbeat and outgoing, others more depressive and/or introverted. In terms of jobs, some are full-time editors or publishers who get up five days a week, dress professionally, go to corporate offices for traditional work hours, and manage or are part of large staffs, while others—generally the ones who make a living writing books—sit for hours alone in a library or studio or their own darkened houses until forced to come out into the world, slitty-eyed and blinking, to meet an editor or promote their new work or find a new story to write. Some teach; some write grants; some are poets; some write magazine columns. Some of them support an entire family with their writing, and some (though very few in this book) are mostly supported by their spouses. Debora Spar, though she's also published books and articles and essays, is the president of Barnard College in New York City. Sarah Crichton runs her own publishing imprint at Farrar, Straus and Giroux. Sandra Tsing Loh performs comedic monologues, onstage and on the radio. Kerry Herlihy is a high school English teacher. Kathy Thomas runs a housecleaning business. Cynthia Kling, among other things, is a garden designer. (She also teaches in prison—which she writes about here, on page 309.)

And that's just careers. The contributors live in cities and in sub-urbs, on college campuses and on ranches and in the woods. Some have children, others don't; some own houses, others rent. Some of them grew up in middle-class families; others decidedly did not. They range in age from thirty-eight to over sixty, and are white, black, Asian American, Indian American, and multirace. *The Bitch Is Back*—like its predecessor—is a book about women's choices in life and relationships, and it reflects the diversity of lives and rela-tionships we are honored to have. I hope you'll use it as a starting point for your own conversations—on and off the page, at readings and on social media, in book groups and in private discussions.

• • • •

Allow me to get you started:

. . . .

Fifteen years after *The Bitch in the House,* we "bitches" are—
yes—considerably older and wiser; we know what we're doing,
what we've let go of, and what we still need. But that doesn't mean
we allow ourselves to stagnate or not keep looking to improve our
lives and our psyches. ("The moment you say, 'I am satisfied with
that,' " said the yogi B. K. S. Iyengar, "you have closed the windows of your intellect.") We may be the generation of choice, but
in order for the privilege of choice to bear fruit, it requires evaluation, contemplation, *re*evaluation. Put another way, the world may
be our oyster, but oysters don't just sit around waiting to be eaten;
they're elusive and often deep and have to be located and plucked
and pried from their shells. We are women who want to live life to
its fullest, and we *can*—but only if we work to do that. And so we
should and will continue to ask ourselves what we want that can
be gotten without dissing or shirking those we love, and then we'll
continue to attempt to go get those things. We will continue to
try to improve our relationships and communities and world while
also taking space from them when we need to. If we're lucky, we'll
be able to do that for many more years. I, for one, think that later
midlife will be a fascinating and inspiring time. I know others in
this book would agree.

Read on. See if I'm right. In the meantime, here's what happened to Jack and Jill, my lusty but tortured plane seatmates, in
the end. After a couple of years dating Jack, and with his support
and encouragement—and with her full-time career to keep her
financially secure—Jill finally was able to leave her unhappy marriage. She hoped that Jack eventually would leave his too, but he
had always been honest about what he could give her, and divorcing, at least at that point, wasn't on the list. So after a long, fun but
increasingly painful time together—during which they fell deeply
in love but Jack still didn't leave his wife—Jill ended things; she

wanted more than an occasional partner and a relationship she had to hide. She has since traveled, gone to therapy, learned a ton about herself, and dated several men long-term, and while none of them was "the one," and she doesn't love dating in her fifties, she also says she has never looked back—at either the decision to leave her husband, or, as much as she still loves and misses him, the decision to leave Jack. "Nothing is as bad as staying in a marriage where you're made to feel 'less than,' " she says. "As for Jack, I wanted him 100 percent. If I couldn't have that, I had to move on."

Jack, for his part, is still married, and no longer has affairs. (Jill was his second.) After his time with Jill—exhausted from having conducted two relationships at once, one of them secret; his heart deeply bruised from how much he and Jill had to hurt each other in the end—he and his wife went into therapy. Their first therapist was useless. But the second was excellent, and, he says, "Something clicked for me. I realized I needed to either make the marriage work or get out." He still loved his wife; their main problem, he says, was that even when he got up at 5:30 every day to work long hours and make all the income, he still didn't feel appreciated by her. Plus, they both were stubborn, and they fought constantly about little things.

So he decided to try to change and to work on his marriage. "I stopped thinking I always needed to be right, stopped letting little things escalate and turn into a fight," he says. "If she nagged, instead of getting mad, I'd tell myself, 'Don't be an asshole. Just make her happy.' " He reminded himself that she was trustworthy, that she had stood by him all these years. And guess what? She noticed, appreciated his efforts, and began to reciprocate in kind.

What's more, she eventually went back to work part-time, which he says improved things more, helping to balance the relationship and making her less focused on little things or his flaws. ("It was good for her to get out of the house," he says. "And now, if I leave a sock on the steps, she's not around to notice it thirty times.") After ten years of "a very volatile time," Jack says, "I'm on the other side of it. I now have a really good marriage." And with their son soon heading to college, "we're starting to return to the way we were before he was born—doing things together, having fun."

Still, Jack doesn't regret his affairs. For one, he feels they probably saved his marriage, since they gave him "an escape valve" from the fights with his wife—a way to get out of the house and not focus on how angry he was. But also, he says, "Everything I've done has taught me something. Without the affairs, I don't think my marriage would be as good as it is. Because along with the fun times, the other relationships had their issues too, and they made me appreciate my wife."

So that's Jack and Jill in midlife: one married, one divorced, both a lot more enlightened than they were even when I met them on that plane ten years ago. Fifty-three is a long way from forty-three, which is a long way from thirty-three or thirty. The road is long, with hills and valleys, difficult and sublime. Come, travel a section of the middle of it with me—and twenty-five other remarkable women.

*—CH, February 2016*

# 1

# Me, Myself, and My Midlife Choices

## MY WAY OR THE HIGHWAY

*The only thing sweeter than idealism is the freedom gained after your ideals have been shattered.*

*—Anonymous*

# Five Crucial Things the Fifty-Three-Year-Old Bitch Knows That the Thirty-Nine-Year-Old Bitch Didn't (Yet)

**PAM HOUSTON**

*In "The Separate Equality of Our Perfect Chosen Paths," the final essay in* The Bitch in the House, *Pam Houston wrote about her struggle, at age thirty-nine, to decide whether or not to have a child. The essay ended with her opening up a book about adoption, suggesting she might well take the leap.*

*She did not. In the end, she chose to take different leaps and to acquire a different set of dependents and responsibilities—a decision she has never regretted. Fifteen years later, here she is to elaborate on what she's since learned, about herself and the world.*

## One: I really like (crave, need, require) being alone.

I was an only child. My father was fifty-three years older than me, and my mother lied wildly and erratically about her age, but let's be generous and say that when I was born she was forty-two. The woman who did the heavy lifting of raising me, a babysitter/fairy godmother named Martha Washington, turned sixty-two the year I was born. My mother was an actress and my father was a businessman/tennis player; they didn't have many friends with kids, and because my father was an only child and my mother and her only sister hadn't spoken for several decades, I met no aunts, uncles, or cousins. I made friends with the neighbor kids, and as I grew up and went to college and grad school, I cultivated friendships that have lasted a lifetime. I can't imagine a more devoted, more interesting, more various, more valuable gang of human beings than the ones who comprise my circle of friends, and in spite of the fact that I have mostly not been married and I never had children of my own, I always have somewhere to go for Thanksgiving, I always have someone to go on a road trip with, I always have someone to call in some long, troubled middle of the night.

What I have never had quite enough of since I was a kid, I have come to realize, is alone time. I love, for instance, to travel on my own, especially to a place I have never been before. If I had to quantify it, I would say that when I travel alone internationally—whether to Rome or Bhutan, Cuba or France—I probably have 50 percent more interaction with the place I am visiting, because I haven't brought my own community to serve as a buffer zone. But even when my destination is domestic and unsexy, there is a little thrill in not having to worry about anyone's good time but my own. I love being alone in the Denver airport, trying to decide if I have enough time to stop into Elway's for the Avocado Benedict, or standing outside on the car deck of the ferry coming back across Puget Sound at sunset to the lights of Seattle winking on, or walking across the Roberto Clemente Bridge on my way to a Pirates game at PNC Park. One birthday I bought two tickets to see Mavis Staples in concert and decided at the last minute to use one chair for me and the other for my coat. It was fantastic. There was no one sitting next to me who would want to leave early or who wouldn't love Mavis exactly as much as I do.

My favorite place of all to be alone is my ranch, my home, my 120 acres of tall grass and blue sage 9,000 feet above sea level near the headwaters of the Rio Grande. I'm not sure if this counts exactly, because to be alone at the ranch is to be in the company of two Irish wolfhounds, two elderly geldings (an American Quarter Horse and a Paso Fino), a bonded pair of miniature donkey jacks, four Icelandic ewes and a ram, and one aging mouser named Mr. Kitty. In summer, the ranch is a wildflowered, aspen-treed heaven on earth; in winter, there might be a pot of green chile chicken stew on the burner and a blue spruce fire in the woodstove, and when it dumps a foot or four, and the winds come behind the cold front and make the driveway impossible, even in the old reliable Toyota truck with the manually locking hubs, and I call my plow guy Randy and he says, "No point coming out there till it quits . . . how about Wednesday?"—I always think I will get my fill of aloneness. That maybe seven days between trips down the driveway, seven days of frustration with the Internet that is so slow it makes me long for the good old days of dial-up, seven days without being face-to-face with another person and using my voice only for the occasional work-related phone call, will be too much even for me. But it isn't. Nor is fourteen days. Nor even twenty-one. And when it is time to drive to the airport and head off to do a job in some shiny city, or to welcome my partner, Greg (who lives most of the year in California), or some friends back to the ranch for Presidents' Day weekend, I always find myself wishing I had just a couple of days more to myself.

It strikes me that I sound a little misanthropic, but mild misanthropy may simply be a thing intelligent women of a certain age grow into, because most intelligent women of a certain age have spent a huge percentage of their lives taking care of other people. Even childless, husbandless me. Or perhaps it is simply that I have learned at long last to like my own company, and to enjoy having nothing whatsoever between the world I am moving through and myself.

I wonder, given independent wealth, or the ability to do all my work from home, if I would get lonely here in three months, six months, even a year. I suspect not, as long as I had the company of a good dog.

## Two: Smart isn't the only thing.
## It might not be the biggest thing.
## It might not really be much of a thing at all.

Throughout my life I have had many insecurities, most of them having to do with my weight—my belly in particular, my face on occasion, my lack of "cool" from time to time. But one thing I have never been insecure about is my intelligence. It was measured, when I was young, and, accurately or not, proclaimed to be higher than that of a whole lot of people, and lower than another, smaller batch. I spent a lot of time trying to live up to the promise of that proclamation, trying to become, and then becoming, verbally agile, fast on my feet, and then using that quickness, in a lot of instances, to my great advantage.

I realize, when I say *smart and intelligent* and *fast on my feet*, that there are shades of different meaning attached to all three. But I have spent a lot of my life energy either being smart, or trying to get other people to see how smart I am, or trying to get smarter, as well as being utterly bedazzled by those smarter than me, without ever really questioning if I was getting a good return on that investment.

My animals don't give a shit about smart, for example, and they are the people I want to be around most of all. I have spent some percentage of my life in academia and have noticed that an awful lot of people in academia are brilliant, cynical, a little bit empty, and terribly, terribly sad.

And if smart isn't the big thing, I wonder what is. One is tempted to say wise, smart's older, calmer cousin. At fifty-three, I am finding it harder to pull up those banks of stored knowledge that were always at the ready in my thirties, so it is getting increasingly harder to sound as smart as I used to think I was. The Rolodex is wearing out, and since I can't always produce the facts, I have to go by feel or intuition. Maybe one part smart and two parts intuitive gets a person in the neighborhood of wisdom, and maybe wisdom is the reward for all that forgetting. Stay in the moment, the yogis are always telling us, and that gets easier when you can't remember where you were five minutes ago.

But kidding aside, I think what it comes down to is presence— bringing my whole self to whoever or whatever is right in front of me. Maybe the big thing is being all the way here.

## Three: I don't care what men think of me anymore.

This is the most surprising and most drastic change of all, and my sudden lack of interest in what a man, in what *any* man, thinks of me is such a profound and complete change from earlier in my life that I have to believe it is hormonally assisted.

For so much more of my life than I would care to admit, I thought I might die if some man or another didn't love me. Sometimes I was able to make them love me, and sometimes I failed to, and I'm a little chagrined to admit there are men on both of those lists whose names I could not recall right now with a gun to my head. I know I felt that way at one time because I have written books that are the records of those feelings. I have paid therapists and healers of all kinds thousands of dollars to help me cope with those feelings. But what not one of those people ever said to me is "Just hang in there, Pam, and make it to the other side of fifty, and those feelings will turn off like a switch."

The first question is why I needed these men to love me in the first place. The answer can only be one cliché or another. Because my father didn't? Because that is how the species perpetuates itself? Because I drank from the cultural Kool-Aid bottle that equates landing a man with winning some kind of prize? Even my mother, who was in as oppressive and soul killing a marriage as I know of, was very invested in my hair being parted on the side, in my wearing tummy-flattening underwear and shoulder pads (for crying out loud) so no one would see the real girl underneath. My mother had so many face-lifts that by the end of her life she couldn't close her eyes. I wouldn't have cosmetic surgery if I won it in a raffle and it came with a free two-week trip to the Bahamas. A woman is told in a million different ways that if she finds herself alone at middle age it means she is unlovable, unattractive, unappealing, unsexy. But what if it means she is independent, self-entertaining, free-spirited, and self-possessed?

The second question is, Where did all those desperate longings go? Down the dark disappearing rivers of estrogen and progesterone? Or did the life lessons accumulate to some critical mass where it finally sank in that men, by and large, demand more care and attention and daily propping up than dogs, and only the very best of them give a dog's worth of love back? Or is it the fact that I have been in a stable and sustaining long-distance relationship with a loyal and good-hearted man for eight years? Greg comes to Colorado in the summer and I teach one quarter a year in California, and we meet for a U2 concert in L.A. or a hiking weekend in Utah or countless other places his work or my work take us that we think we can turn into fun. He is a wonderful dog dad and I love his daughter very much and we are excellent at giving each other space.

Do I care what *Greg* thinks of me, you might be wondering, and I do, but I don't care *more* about what he thinks of me than about what other people of either sex that I admire/like/love think of me or than what I think of myself. What I am trying to say is that the caring has lost its obsessive, stick-a-knife-in-your-thigh-to-stop-the-pain quality. I spent years acting and not acting a million particular ways because I thought it was what a man wanted from me. Worse even than that was when I dimmed myself down from 100 watts to 60 because that was all they could take. When I think back on it, I can only shake my head in wonder. First I can't believe I did it. Then I can't believe how well I know that I will never do it again.

## Four: Wanting to stay alive is the world's most powerful motivator.

I've always been healthy as a horse. Until last year, when I went to the doctor and found out my blood pressure was 150/110. As the doctor was writing a prescription for the blood pressure meds, I asked her if I could have six months to right the ship. "No," she said, without looking up, so then I asked her if I could have three. "I'm writing the prescription," she said. "I won't be there to see whether you take the pills or not." I chose to interpret that as permission.

A week later, sitting at my kitchen table, I got an e-mail that provided a button to click for test results, and when I pressed the button it said, all in caps: HPV 16 EXTREMELY HIGH RISK CERVICAL CANCER>IMMEDIATE COLPOSCOPY AND FOLLOW-UP INDICATED, with language surrounding it that no human beings actually use. First I fainted—truly, out cold—right off my kitchen chair onto the floor. I came to when my dog William started licking my kneecap.

You can call the UC Davis Medical Center when something like this happens, but they'll put you on automatic hold and then drop the call after you have listened to twenty minutes of Muzak. It took me a good hour of raising my already high blood pressure by Googling "HPV cervical cancer" before I learned that it was much better to Google "HPV does not always lead to cervical cancer." Then I set about finding a doctor who would actually call me back.

Too much work, too much stress, too much eating on the run, and too many red-eyes. The ecosystem that was me was in trouble and there was suddenly nothing I wouldn't do for a second chance.

During the colposcopy, they took nineteen pieces out of me and sent them to the lab, but I didn't wait the two weeks for the results to change my life. The day I got the original e-mail I quit wheat, alcohol, sugar, and even (gulp) coffee and went on a strict version of the anti-inflammation diet. In truth I'd never eaten much bread or pasta and drank almost no alcohol, but sugar was hard and coffee was murder. The tests came back normal and negative. These were not two words I ever would have wanted associated with myself, but suddenly I couldn't get enough of them. For the first time in my life, I was sleeping eight hours a night. (Tossing the caffeine will do that.) For the first time since my river-guiding days I was walking a minimum of five miles a day, even if it was sometimes up and down airport terminals and hotel room corridors. In four months I lost fifty pounds. Then my hair started to fall out and my toenails started to fall off, because I never do anything halfway and if there is such a thing as getting healthy too fast I had managed to do it. So I backed off a little, but still felt the best I had in ten years. I have tried to lose weight all my life, but it turned out I'd just needed a better reason than that it would make my dead mother feel better about her parenting if I did.

Cutting the stress was harder. I tried to get better, sometimes, at saying no—and eventually I *had* to say no, because between the hiking and the sleeping there were not enough hours in a day for me to keep the workaholic's pace that had always been second nature. But I was done with unnecessary stressors. I closed my eyes and ears to all the ego-driven shenanigans at the university. I suggested to Greg that we stop rehashing the difficult past—his, mine, ours together. To my surprise, he enthusiastically agreed. I started getting down on the floor with the dogs a few times a day to rub their bellies and pet their perfect ears, and at least once a week we all sit on the porch together and watch the sun come up over the mountain.

I have to get cancer checkups every three months now, and a year and a half later I am holding steady at normal and negative. My blood pressure this morning was 117/75.

## Five: Generosity is its own reward.

A few years before he died, my father called and said, "You know, I was just getting ready to write my monthly check to the life insurance people, and it occurred to me that there is no scenario in which I am going to benefit from the $225 I am putting into this fund every month. So if you want the thirty grand after I'm dead, you're going to have to start making the payments."

I said, "That seems a little like betting against my own team in the Super Bowl just because I think they have a better defense."

"Well, it's up to you," he said. "I've probably put about nine thousand in there already. That ought to be enough to get me in the ground."

And we left it at that.

There was a purity to my father's selfishness that approached perfection. He was also the most unhappy person I have ever known.

When I was twenty-two years old, I had just come back from the Bahamas, where I had been working as crew on a high-end sailboat charter. I had spent six months spearfishing, sailing, and swimming in the most exquisitely colored water I had ever seen, combing deserted beaches, learning the names of hundreds of tropical fish, singing under the moonlight to the captain's guitar, and one lucky afternoon in Guana Cay, getting to go spinnaker flying off Jimmy Buffett's sailboat. I was breezing through Bethlehem, Pennsylvania, to see my parents on my way to another crew job on Lake Superior. My father eyed my tanned and muscled arms and legs, my bleached hair, the sea-air smile on my face that I couldn't seem to wipe off. He said, "Pam, one of these days you are going to realize that you spend your whole life lying in the gutter with someone else's foot on your neck."

*Maybe,* I thought, *but not anytime real soon.* And quite frankly, at fifty-three years old I have given up waiting.

Now I understand that what my father really suffered from (along with, perhaps, a lack of imagination) is a lack of generosity. And he wasn't simply stingy with his own money, time, and attention; he also seemed to begrudge every other person in the world every single good thing they got, even when that person's life bore no relation to his. He was a golf fan, though not a player, and I can remember him boiling with rage when a young Tom Watson won a first-place cut of the $280,000 purse in his first Masters victory. Why should Tom Watson have cashed in big for playing eighteen holes of golf when he, my father, had not? Years later, when I told my father about the advance W. W. Norton paid for my first book (a modest—even in those days—$21,000, but thrilling to me and my grad student budget), he shook his head and said, "You know, Wayne Newton is the highest-paid performer in the free world." Me, Tom, and Wayne, equalized in his mind as enemy because we all had received something that he had not.

My longtime babysitter Martha Washington (I would call her my nanny but that would misrepresent our socioeconomic bracket) took the time to teach me all the golden and golden-ish rules my father seemed to have missed out on. She taught me to write thank-you notes and hold doors for people and to offer my seat to anyone older than me on the bus. She taught me that *I'm sorry,* when said sincerely, can be the two most useful, most powerful words in the English language. And she taught me that if I was generous to others, they would often (though not always) be generous back.

It was only decades later, after I had dedicated the largest part of my life to teaching, that I came to understand the next step in Martha's lessons: that the good stuff about giving is the giving, regardless of what you do or don't get back. That the endorphin rush, the spring in your step, the feeling of peace, the good night's sleep—all that comes right inside the idea, the moment, the action of your own generosity. I know that for many of you, my latter-day realization is Humanity 101, but were my father still alive, there would be nothing on earth I could say to make him believe it.

You might be thinking that I don't have all that much occasion to be generous, spending significant periods of time alone not caring what the men think of me. But the largest part of my life I spend with students: in classrooms and conference centers, at loud raucous dinners that go on for hours, and on outdoor writing adventures where 24/7 I am the writing and kayaking/skiing/hiking/rafting guide. Three years ago I started a nonprofit—Writing By Writers—that builds creative communities in five states (and counting). Making and holding a space for my students' creativity is how I justify not only the time I spend at the ranch but also the space I take up on the planet. And as happy as I am with three solitary ranch weeks stretching out in front of me, I am perhaps just one tick happier welcoming ninety strangers to WxW's conference at Tomales Bay, California, knowing that five days later they will leave as colleagues, writing partners, and friends.

So maybe what the fifty-three-year-old bitch is striving for most of all is a life in balance, and the clarity and compassion (for myself and for others) that distills up out of such a life, like good Kentucky bourbon (which I no longer drink).

Am I there yet? Hell no. But I can see it out there in front of me like the rise of a new sun, shimmering.

# Vagina Notwithstanding

## JENNIFER FINNEY BOYLAN

W hat about Hardy?" I asked my wife just a few months ago, holding up a ventriloquist's dummy. "Keep, or throw out?"

Hardy was the surviving partner of a set of Laurel and Hardy dummies; by the time we came along, Laurel had headed out on his own. We'd been bequeathed Hardy by a family friend as a gift for our older son, Zach, when he was just a lad. But Zach *hated* Hardy, hated him as if we'd tried to give him a bag of venomous snakes as a present instead. He said Hardy gave him nightmares, and I guessed I could see why. What with the *schnurrbart/* mustache, the puppet did look a teensy bit like Mr. Adolf Hitler. And so Zach had banished Hardy to the back of a closet.

Which was where I found him, years later, as I prepared to pack up our home for good.

"Out," said Grace, answering my question.

"Yeah," I said, although I felt a little bad that Hardy was coming to the end of the line, being so redolent, even in his exile, of my son's early childhood. Still, when you pack up a house, you can't get sentimental over everything. It's heartbreaking, really, to part with things that connect you to specific moments of a vanished past. Zach was twenty years old now, a junior at Vassar; we didn't have that many of the toys and things that evoked his days as a tuba-playing, roly-poly child. I put my hand up Hardy's neck and blinked his eyes.

The puppet took his measure of our house. The books were in boxes. A pile of clothes for Goodwill was stacked up on the floor. The convertible sofa bed I'd slept on in grad school was being carried off to a Dumpster. There were some boxes piled up in the basement we could not bear to open; we knew we were better off not knowing. The bottom of one such box had torn open as Grace and I carried it out to the trash, spilling the dress she had worn to her high school graduation onto the asphalt driveway. "Oh, look at it," she said lovingly of the turquoise 1970s hippie gown. "Just look at it."

Hardy spun his head around, lamenting the state of our disassembled house. "Well, Stanley," he said. "This is another fine mess you've gotten us in."

"Out," said Grace.

• • • •

The house-moving was only part of a much larger stage of upheaval in our lives that Grace and I had christened Project Kablooey. Weeks before, our younger son, Sean, had departed for college, leaving us empty nesters. Simultaneously, after twenty-five years as a professor at the college I loved in Maine, I'd taken on a new position as the writer in residence at Barnard, in New York City. That had entailed finding a sublet and moving a ton of things down to Manhattan. Finally, we'd decided to go ahead with renovations at the house that had been our summer place, turning *that* into our primary Maine residence and selling the house that we'd raised the boys in. "If we're going to blow up our lives," Grace had said, referring to Project Kablooey, "we may as well go the whole hog."

It was not the first time our hog was whole. In 2000, after bearing the burden in secret for the first twelve years of our supposedly heterosexual marriage, I'd finally come out to Grace as transgender. Everyone always says the truth will set you free, but the people who say that have probably never seen the effect that revealing yourself as trans has upon someone you love. For years and years, I'd felt that the trans thing was my secret to keep, and that by keeping it I was shielding my wife and sons from harm. But just after New Year's, in the first year of the new millennium, I'd reached a point where I knew I had to be out with the truth. It felt, literally, like a life-or-death decision to me. And so I'd spilled the beans.

In the days and months that followed, sometimes it seemed like all we did was weep. For Grace, there were times when she felt she had no good choices at all. Either she could abandon the person she loved at the moment of her—my—greatest need, or she could stay with me as I went through a process that, almost by definition, would take the person Grace loved away from her. I'd stand there in my beat-up wig and abundant makeup and declaim, "But I'm the same person!"

Grace just shook her head. "In what sense?" she asked.

I'd given many hours of thought to the question of what I would do if the people I loved, and Grace above all, rejected me. At times I imagined starting over completely—moving to a new town, taking up a new profession. There was a little while when I thought about giving up teaching and becoming a nurse or a social worker or a minister. I wanted a profession in which I could help people whose hearts had been torn out, I guess. Being, as I was, something of an expert in the field.

After transition, though, I returned, for the most part, to the life I had known, in the spirit of that well-worn T. S. Eliot poem in which explorers arrive where we started and know the place for the first time. I realized there was nothing I liked as much as teaching college students; it was what I was wired for, and there was no point in taking up a whole different profession just for the sake of a fresh start. Grace, for her part, realized that there was generally no one whose jokes she liked as much as mine, vagina notwithstanding. And so we settled into our new life as two middle-aged women: not, to be certain, the lovers we had been, but, for better or worse, as the loving partners we had become. There were plenty of people, including the friend who had bequeathed us Hardy, who failed to believe that either Grace or I could be happy with the compromise at the center of our lives. But there we were, more than a decade later, together packing up our old house. It was, as Hardy himself might have noted, a fine mess.

• • • •

Then, against all odds, I won something called the Amtrak Residency. As one of Amtrak's writers in residence, I was given the opportunity to travel around the country on a long-distance sleeper train, writing and editing and—most important of all—looking out the window going *duh*. About half of my friends wrinkled their noses at this prospect, asking, "Who on earth would want to ride around on a train for two weeks?" The others sighed wistfully and said, "Oh. I've always wanted to do that."

One day I rushed into a room where Grace was rolling china plates into newspaper and triumphantly announced: "I've discovered the exact notes of a train whistle, at last! It's D sharp, F sharp, G sharp, B and D sharp."

She nodded lovingly, in the same way you might nod at, say, your son when he announces to you that he's *discovered a secret antigravity gun!* "It's a B major sixth," I added.

"I can see you're very happy at having found that out," she said.

"It is pretty cool," I said. I looked at the box she was packing. "Is there anything I can do to help?"

"Yes," she said. "You can make me a martini."

On Halloween, the night before the residency began, I spent the night playing rock and roll music in a barn with some friends. I played two songs that night, one of which was "Ghost Riders in the Sky" and one of which was not. The next morning I got up at 3:15, kissed Grace on the cheek, and slipped out the door with my suitcase. Ranger, the dog, raised an ear. "What are you doing?" he wanted to know.

It was hard to explain.

A few hours later, I was riding the Downeaster from Freeport, Maine, to Boston. From there I stepped onto the Lake Shore Limited and headed out to Chicago, and from there onto the California Zephyr to San Francisco. America rushed by my window, in all its cussed, contradictory charm.

We crossed the Sierras via the Donner Pass. Far below us was Donner Lake, where that doomed group of early settlers had become trapped one winter and their nightmare began. I looked out at the horizon, eating ice cream. I was reading James Stephens's *The Crock of Gold*, a scene in which the god Pan seduces the shepherd girl:

> *Come away with me, Shepherd Girl, through the fields, and we will be careless and happy, and we will leave thought to find us when it can, for that is the duty of thought, and it is more anxious to discover us than we are to be found. So Caitlin Ni Murrachu arose and went with him through the fields, and she did not go with him because of love, nor because his words had been understood by her, but only because he was naked and unashamed.*

• • • •

I had supper with many strangers during that cross-country trip—an Amish couple who did not approve of music; a man who owned his own storage-unit business; a young psychotherapist who was reading a biography of William James—but none of them resembled the great god Pan exactly, what with the cloven hooves. Still, I was not entirely immune to the melody of his pipes. In San Francisco I was met at the station by my friend Zoë, who plunked me down in the lobby of a hotel called the Rex and ordered something called a Moscow Mule. When we finished the first round, she ordered another.

"So what's the deal with your marriage?" she asked me.

"The deal, what do you mean the deal?"

"I mean, when you start teaching at Barnard and Grace is back in Maine, are you going to have an open relationship?"

"I don't *think* so," I said.

"Well, that's good," she said. Zoë was in the midst of a big divorce. "Whenever people say they're going to have an open relationship, what really happens is one person has an affair and the other person gets hurt."

"Yeah. I don't think that's in the cards for me."

"Still, you want to keep your options open," said Zoë. "I want for you what happened to me. One day my friend Mark kissed me, and just like that, my vagina went *whoa*."

I laughed. "That's sweet, that you want that for me," I said. "But I don't see that happening."

"But Jenny, don't you want more, sometimes? More than what you've got?"

I thought of a line from a movie a friend of mine had written. "Well," I said, "no one ever wants less."

A few days later, I took the Coast Starlight up to Seattle, then slipped onto the Empire Builder headed east through Idaho and Montana. In North Dakota, we passed through the "man camps" of the Bakken oil shale. There was a vast collection of mobile homes. Someone told me 1,200 men lived there. A guy standing by the side of the roadbed raised his hand as the Empire Builder passed by, and waved.

Later, Grace called me on the phone and gave me an update on Project Kablooey. The Sheetrock was up in the new kitchen. The chimney was done. "I love you," she said.

"I love you too," I said, and I meant it.

The supervisor of my sleeping car, Dennis, poked his head in the door a little later. He was a lovely Irishman who had the gift of gab, to put it mildly. Earlier, he had described the experience of being on a long-distance train this way: "Each trip is a microsociological experiment in its own right in that a host of disparate elements are tossed together in one sense against their will."

Now he wanted to make sure I was paying attention to the sunset. "Don't forget to look at everything."

I looked, and he was right. It was a world of wonders out there.

"It's phantasmagorical," Dennis said. His eyes twinkled, and I thought, *You know, Jennifer Boylan, that person there is not an unhandsome man.*

I went back to *The Crock of Gold*. Now Caitlin Ni Murrachu was leaving Pan and beginning a new relationship with Angus Og. "And she went with him not because she had understood his words, nor because he was naked and unashamed, but only because his need of her was very great, and, therefore, she loved him, and stayed his feet in the way, and was concerned lest he should stumble."

● ● ● ●

Thirty years earlier, long before transition, I'd stopped off at something called Lee's Mardi Gras Boutique, in New York, where I lived back then. It was like a mini department store for trans women. As I was purchasing a long blond wig, a businessman came up to me and said, "I love cross-dressing. Do you love cross-dressing?"

"Could be," I said. I didn't think of it as cross-dressing per se. I thought of it as the truth.

I'd lived on 108th Street and Amsterdam then, one floor above what might be politely referred to as an S&M dungeon. Barnard College and Columbia University loomed a few blocks north of my apartment, but I had almost no interaction with their world, which felt walled off and inaccessible. I remember one time trying in vain to gain access to the Columbia library, which the psychiatrist I was seeing had encouraged me to visit in order to learn more about transsexuality. But a guard at the entrance told me I couldn't go in, since of course I was not a Columbia student.

It was a cold, gray day, and I stood for a moment letting his words sink in. That library felt like a symbol of everything to me back then as a young, yearning artist—that there was a whole world waiting for me somewhere, if only I could learn to elude its gatekeepers.

So instead, in a vague attempt to cheer myself up, I headed toward the dark caverns of the Cathedral of Saint John the Divine, ducking in the huge doorway just as it began to snow outside. John Lennon had been killed the week before, less than a month after Reagan had been elected, and there was a biting melancholy in my heart, as if it was not clear whether the universe I lived in was the one in which I wanted to dwell. I sat there in a lachrymose trance. And then, unexpectedly, an organist at the cathedral began practicing for the following day's service. There, in that beautiful space, I heard the melody, performed in a set of variations for pipe organ, of John Lennon's "Imagine."

When the piece was over, I walked back out onto Amsterdam, my heart strangely lighter, open again. The city, in the interim, had been transformed by the snow into something crystalline and unrecognizable—a place out of Dickens, or maybe Tolkien. I felt, as I stood there on the steps of the cathedral, that things I had thought were impossible could in fact become real—that I would learn, in time, how to tell my story; that I would find the courage to come out as trans and begin to live an authentic life.

• • • •

After the Amtrak gig, I headed down to New York to get my office and our apartment set up. I was back on the Upper West Side, only two blocks from the place I'd rented in 1980. But now, three decades later, I was a middle-aged woman named Jennifer, not a young man named Jim, and I was set to begin an appointment as an endowed chair at Barnard named after a woman who once wrote, "It turned out that when my younger self thought of taking wing, she wanted only to let her spirit soar."

The S&M dungeon was gone, transformed into a ritzy apartment building with a doorman. I passed it one day en route to campus, where I was headed to do some research. When I arrived at the Columbia library, I showed the guard my ID. "Hello, Professor," he said, and he held open the gate so that I could walk in.

• • • •

I had been hoping that Project Kablooey would be complete by the time I headed to New York, but what with one thing and another, the construction on the new place was delayed. The mason had built the chimney, though. And Grace and I had spent an entire afternoon at a home supply store picking out toilets. It was surprising how many choices there were.

I can't say I'm any better at upheaval now than I ever was, although after all these years, I guess the process has become a little more familiar. A dozen years ago, Grace and I went through a kind of turmoil that few couples have to endure, and somehow we fought our way back to a place of stability and peace. Now here we are, with lots of the pieces of our lives still up in the air. It's unsettling, but I also wonder if true happiness requires more than a little kablooey now and again. It is good to come into the station, to be sure. But it's also necessary, now and again, to set out for points unknown.

• • • •

One morning on the California Zephyr—just weeks before my new teaching gig—I sat up in my sleeping chamber and looked outside. The clock read 4:30, and the world was dark. The train rocked from side to side, and the engineer blew the whistle. B major sixth.

I put on my terry-cloth robe and left my "roomette," a chamber that one of my companions in the dining car, a Texan, had described as "so small you couldn't cuss out a cat there without getting fur in your mouth." I slipped down to the observation car with my computer and a cup of coffee. I sat there, along with three or four sleepy others, and wrote for an hour or two as the skies turned pink above the Rockies. Dennis was right. It *was* phantasmagorical.

I thought about Grace and my boys, about the long road we had traveled, about the long road that lay ahead, about the strange blessings of turbulence.

The dawn came up like thunder. A woman sitting next to me started to sing "Here Comes the Sun." *Little darling . . .*

There was a beat as everyone in the car listened. Her voice was hoarse but sweet. Then we all joined in.

There we were, a bunch of complete strangers, our voices raised together in song.

# Gone Girl

## What I (Don't) Owe My Mother

**ANNA MARCH**

For three of the four years since I met my husband, Adam, we've traveled to Hawaii in late December. In the mornings, I swim in the balmy Pacific while he sleeps, and then we meet for breakfast: pineapple-orange-guava juice, macadamia nut pancakes. We linger and talk in the plumeria-scented breeze before beginning our days of relaxed work, grateful to be able to splurge on this annual luxury. Adam broke his back in a car accident when he was sixteen, and has been a paraplegic ever since. (He's forty-two now, and great.) My history is more complicated, but for now I'll just say that with Adam I found the love and happiness I had waited forty years for, and each year in Hawaii, we celebrate this.

So this particular January morning, as I emerge from my swim, my smile fades as I see Adam parked just off the beach, his face tense. "Your mother called six times," he says, extending the phone to me.

I grab a pink-striped hotel beach towel and take the phone, bracing myself. It won't be my grandmother; my mother would have other people to get attention from in that case: siblings, family friends. This is something to do with her, then—something she wants an immediate audience for, other than her husband of twenty-eight years, Bill, who has probably already rolled his eyes and continued with his day. I, her only child, am It—vacationing or not. I play the first voicemail. "I'm at the E.R.," squeaks her voice. "I think I've had a stroke!"

I turn to Adam. "I don't have to go home, do I? I don't. Please, tell me that." I know my words are selfish. But I also know this: I've earned the right.

•  •  •  •

Forty-six years before, when she was nineteen, my mother became pregnant with me during a fling with her older, married boss while her boyfriend, Martin, was serving overseas. She tried to abort me—she's told me this—but with abortion being illegal then, this was dangerous and difficult, especially for a Catholic teen living with her parents. In the end, she told Martin *he'd* gotten her pregnant, and even though the timing of my birth made it obvious she'd lied, he married her and kept her secret. I found out only in my twenties that I wasn't his daughter, when I called him for information for a medical form, and he said, "You won't need that from me. I'm not your father." Suddenly so much made sense. He had taught me to fish and play chess, had made me laugh and told me I could be a doctor or the president. But he'd also sexually abused me, starting, in my earliest memories, at age four, and continuing until I was nine: bringing me into his bed while my mother was at work to kiss me openmouthed on my mouth, run his hands over my body, put his fingers in places I hadn't even known existed.

•  •  •  •

I play the second and third voicemails now. With each one, my mother is more exuberant as, I assume, test results come in: "I had a stroke! I did!" I hand the phone to Adam—calm, sane, compassionate Adam, who will tell me if I'm being a jerk. He listens, shaking his head. "She's got a personality disorder. Who's happy they had a stroke?"

"Narcissists," I answer, and even though I know I'm right, and he is too—I have known for decades that my mother has real psychological problems—I still am grateful he says this; relieved to know that my skepticism and annoyance are not just me being the "ungrateful brat" she called me when I was ten, the "mean little bitch" at fifteen, but instead a valid reaction to her lunacy. I play the remaining messages. Then I pull on my sundress and sit down on the sea wall, first to face the phone calls to find out what actually happened, and then to perform the harder, newer part: the soul-searching that, among other things, will tell me if I need to return to frozen Delaware and my mother, or if I can stay in Hawaii with my husband.

• • • •

My mother didn't want me, but she still was my mother, dropping out of college to give birth to me. She fed and clothed me until I left home at seventeen; she paid my Catholic school tuition until eleventh grade, working two jobs. She bought me sports lessons and camp, took me to doctors, gave me birthday parties. She did not abandon me—at least not without leaving me with another adult. Even after I moved out, she sometimes helped me financially.

I'm not positive she knew of my father's abuse, but I vaguely remember her asking Martin about his behavior with me. Probably noticing I was kissing oddly, she asked me to demonstrate how he kissed me, and when I did—moving my head around, sticking out my tongue—she asked him why I'd said that. He claimed innocence, and she dropped it. When I finally told her about it fifteen years later, she said only "I didn't know." Maybe she didn't. But I'm convinced she wouldn't have confronted him anyway. He could have exposed my paternity (something she still doesn't readily admit). He also might have left us.

He did anyway, of course—when I was six. After that, though I still saw him some nights until he remarried three years later, my mother left most of my care to her parents, Auggie and Martha, who lived nearby in D.C., while she worked and often socialized afterward. I went to them after school and stayed through dinner; my mother picked me up at night and returned me at dawn, and my grandparents drove my carpool. I spent Sundays with them— church, cooking, family dinner. In many ways, my grandparents' generous love and stern guidance saved me.

But just before I started ninth grade, they retired to a beach town in Delaware, a few hours away. After that, my mother alternately screamed at and ignored me. She erupted over nothing, and if I fought back, she called her family or Martin and told them I was "out of control." When I was fifteen, after one fight (I'd forgotten to bring in the paper, maybe, or left a dirty fork in the sink), she begged her younger brother to come get me. So off I went to live with twenty-five-year-old Uncle Mark and his girlfriend, Pam, in their roach-infested apartment ninety minutes from school. My commute was a bus to a train to the carpool of a friend, who took me out of pity.

I liked Mark and Pam, but I was miserable so far from school and friends. Meanwhile, my mother had gone to Greece for a month, a Christmas present paid for by her boyfriend. (She was thirty-five, he sixty.) When she returned, I went home for junior year, determined to stay out of her way. I worked thirty-two hours a week at the Giant grocery store, paying my own school tuition. But my grades dropped, and then I got pneumonia and they dropped more. When I failed Latin, she seemed pleased: Now I *was* the "problem student" she'd called me for years. Around that time, she began pushing me to contact Martin and "work on getting your college tuition out of him," adding, "He's your problem now, not mine."

I stuck around until October of my senior year, and then I dropped out of school and escaped to my boyfriend, David, who'd been transferred by Foot Locker to a mall three hours away, in Virginia Beach. With no first and last months' rent to get an apartment, he was living in a dilapidated motel, and for eight or nine weeks I lived with him, chain-smoking and watching TV while he worked, too depressed to look for a job. The hotel clerk called us the "inter-race kids" (I'm white, David's black); we lived on his salary, $280 a week, and some weeks, after paying for our room and gas and our payday splurge at McDonald's, we had all of $50, or $3.50 a day, for food. I learned to live on peanut butter crackers and Coke, 7-Eleven hot dogs or soup, biscuits from KFC ($1.85 a dozen—fed us for two days). When we couldn't pay the hotel, we were locked out of our room, our stuff still inside. Then we slept in our car, or once, in the back of Foot Locker, using packs of socks for pillows.

I loved David, and he too saved me. But by then I'd internalized what my mother told me—I was hopeless, messed up, a lost cause—and for two decades after that, this was a self-fulfilling prophecy. I managed to graduate from high school on time (after returning to D.C. in January, I passed the GED in the spring) and, later, to complete two years of college, going sporadically when I could afford to. But I also had two failed marriages and two failed businesses (nonprofit arts organization and nonprofit consulting; both outfits folded). There were lies, bad health, heartbreak . . . those were not happy times.

• • • •

Sitting on the wall in Hawaii, I remember all this—times and situations I've replayed in my mind or in therapy. And then this: When I was thirty-seven, I left D.C. to live with my grandmother, by then eighty-two and alone, at her beach house in Delaware. Auggie had died a few years before, and, unlike for my mother, I felt deep love for Martha and also that I owed her something.

I stayed for two and a half years: cooking for her, keeping

house and scheduling her doctors, driving her to church and her hair appointments. We tried out lipsticks and listened to the Andrews Sisters; I learned to poach her eggs just right. It was both wonderful—the daily kindness and love, the chance to step back from my life and just *think*—and one of the hardest things I'd ever done; I had not been prepared to bathe her and wipe the intimate folds of her skin, to help her when she soiled herself. But I did it with love and even pride. Martha had raised six children before half raising me; she'd nursed her father for his final six years. I was happy to be able to give her what she'd given so many others.

Eventually I moved back to D.C., and then, a little later, back again to the beach, but to my own place. And in the next few years, living cheaply and purposefully, I rebuilt my life: found work doing grant writing and got financially stable, began running, adopted an emaciated old dog and nursed him back to health. I also—coincidentally?—at last found real love with a kind, stable man: the handsome and funny Adam.

I saw my mother once a week when I lived with my grandmother. After that, less, but we still had an occasional meal together, and I still felt some responsibility for her. Then, a year before the Hawaii trip, I traveled to Europe with her, Bill, and my grandmother. I knew it might be my gran's last chance to get away, and I thought—optimistically, stupidly—that we might all have fun together. Instead, my mother made a huge scene, screaming wildly at Bill and me in the line to board a ship. For the rest of the trip, I didn't eat with or talk to her.

On our return, with the help of a therapist, I finally came to understand: I would never make my mother proud or happy—or even really matter to her—because she wasn't capable of that; she would never treat me with simple kindness and respect. For a while, I grieved what this meant: Both she and I lost something enormous because of it, the opportunity for cherished love and real

connection. But after I stopped grieving, I set firm, finite boundaries, which I conveyed to her by e-mail. First, I would no longer
talk to her on the phone; for pressing business she could e-mail me.
Second, I would see her twice a year, for two hours each time—
once in May around her birthday (though not *that* May; it was too
soon), and once around year's end. She had Bill, her mother, her
siblings; she would not be alone. But she could no longer count on
me for regular help or companionship.

She e-mailed back: Could we meet in person to discuss?

No, I said.

As per plan, ten months later—just before Adam and I left for
Hawaii—I visited her at my aunt's condo in D.C. The house was
full (Mom, Gran, Bill, my aunt, one of Bill's grandkids), so, happily
for me, there wasn't time alone with her. There was talk of the
meal, the weather. I brought her a gift; she thanked me. As always,
she did most of the talking. She didn't ask how I was or what I'd
done the past months, but neither did she scream at or insult me.
Improvement already! I'd left for Oahu feeling victorious.

But now, less than two weeks later, things aren't quite so simple.
Staring at the vast blue sea, the toasted white sand, I wonder: Has
my mother *really* had a stroke? And if so, what happens now—to
her and to me?

• • • •

Here in middle age, so many of my friends are grappling with
what to do with and for our aging parents, our ill parents. What do
we owe them if they were good to us? How about if they weren't,
but are now? What do we owe a parent who's obnoxious but not
entirely without merit, who gets a D but not quite an F? Who's
obnoxious *without* merit—solid F—but because of a mental health
issue? Think of the panic attacks that befell even the mighty Tony
Soprano when he put his (bitter, narcissistic) mother in a (pricey,

respectable) nursing home. Where is the line between what our parents need and what *we* need in order to proceed with our lives?

What happens when we spend years in therapy learning that what's healthy for us is to stay away from a parent, to put distance there—and then suddenly they need us the way we once needed them? When things have reversed, and now they're the "children" and we the "grown-ups"? When does "not letting them get to us" turn into realizing we might have an obligation to take care of them as they once did (or didn't) us, and that, even if they failed—on some levels or all ("They fuck you up, your mum and dad," the poet Philip Larkin reminds us. "They may not mean to, but they do")—we *still* might need to take care of them? Refusing to deal with an aging parent, refusing to be loving and available instead of reserved and distant, makes you selfish or childish or worse. Doesn't it?

Or does it?

With my friends—an enlightened, compassionate, self-examined group, many from less than functional homes—there's a lot of talk about guilt when it comes to our parents. When I veer toward guilt about my mother, I examine what I'm feeling and it always turns out to be sadness. I would like to be able to do for her what I did for my grandmother: to take care of her in old age, even have her and Bill come live with Adam and me. We'd have morning tea together, family dinner at night, talk and laugh about our days. *But that's in a world where my mother is a different person,* I remind myself. Then I think about the terrified teenager she was when she got pregnant with me, by a man who surely should have known better than to fuck his nineteen-year-old clerk—and I realize I will never know the depths of her fear, anger, sadness. I'm filled with compassion for my poor young mother. But I also want to reach back to that teenage girl and tell her she should treat her baby as if she matters; that she's all that baby has. If she had worked harder to be a good mother to me—if she even did *now*!—I could be much closer to her.

But I can't reach back. And she isn't going to change, as some mothers really do. ("We were all bad mothers to some extent," a therapist said to me once. "What's important is how we deal with that in our child's adulthood. Do we apologize for it? Relate to our adult children with love and respect?" No and no, is the answer in my mother's case.) At sixty-six, unwilling to examine or see her part in her problems with me or anyone else, my mother has made her bed. And it took me decades to pull my life out of the horror show it had become—I won't say because of my mother, but certainly my childhood, from birth to adulthood, figured in.

And so, in Hawaii, after talking to my mother, then a nurse, then Bill (who admits he hadn't rushed to the hospital when she called; familiar with her hypochondria, he'd waited for confirmation that she actually was sick before he dropped everything); after relaying it all to Adam; after more pondering, and remembering what my various therapists taught me and what I vowed in Europe—a smart vow, made for the right reasons—I tell Bill I've decided not to return early. I'll be home in a few days, as planned.

"Good idea," he says. "No need for you to ruin your trip."

• • • •

I do, however, call my mother daily from Hawaii; at this point, it's a small price to pay. The second day, she tells me she'd like to retire but worries she and Bill can't afford it.

Years ago, I had told her I was trying to earn enough so that, when she was ready to retire, I could send her $1,000 a month. In the meantime, I said, I hoped she and Bill would map out how they'd otherwise support themselves for the rest of their lives. I suggested selling her house and buying a condo; finding part-time work; making a plan to cut back on expenses. There are checklists for this time in life, I told her; would she let me find her one?

No, she said.

So now, when she brings up retirement on the phone, I don't respond. I know she hasn't done the planning I suggested. But I also want to help her. I have the means now, and giving her money is something I can do fairly easily—not instead of spending time with her, because I wouldn't do that now regardless, but because I want to.

When we return from Hawaii, I go to her house. The stroke was minor, it turns out; she'd been discharged the next day. "That's great!" I say. "Sounds like you'll be fine."

She shakes her head. "My speech is slurred."

"Really?" I say. "You sound perfect to me."

Bill nods. "To me, too."

"Well, I'm *not*," she snaps. "I'm slurring my words. Horribly."

"Huh," I say, and then, in keeping with my vow not to engage, I take out my checkbook and write a check for $12,000. "I promised you this," I say, handing it over. "I hope it will help you retire. I'll do this every year, as long as we can afford to. But I hope you'll do what we discussed to set yourself up for the future, because I won't be able to see you more often or help you daily if something happens."

She doesn't respond.

"I would love to know you have a plan, Mom," I push. "Adam and I could hire a social worker to help you make one."

"I *have* a plan," she spits, finally. "I'm going to die before Bill."

I stifle my sigh. "Uh-huh. And if that doesn't happen? Or if he outlives you but he can't care for you?"

"Then I'll live with Rosie," she says, naming my aunt who, at sixty-two, has her own health problems.

"What if you need nursing care?" My mother is diabetic; the doctor had told me that while this stroke was minor, the next one might not be.

She shakes her head and turns away.

I rise from my chair. *Disengage.* "Okay, then," I say, in my calmest, coolest voice. "I'll see you in May. Good luck with your recovery."

•  •  •  •

For the next several months, Adam and I contemplate moving to Southern California. East Coast winters are increasingly hard for him in his wheelchair, and we've long talked of moving west. When I mention it to my mother in May, she says, "Good! I'll have a warm place to visit." Even my grandmother encourages us to go. Still, at first I struggle: no matter how little I see my mother, moving so far from her would mean truly turning my back—and while the rational part of me, the therapized part, knows this is okay, the emotional part still wonders: *Is this right?* Nonetheless, we continue planning to move, and one day we find a house. And suddenly, it seems, we're packing to leave.

When I have time to think about my mother, I feel myself inch toward that sad, fearful place, and I have to pull back, to do the internal reflecting I've done for so many years. I remind myself of the painful truths: My mother does not engage with me in appropriate ways. I don't have a meaningful relationship with her. I've been kind without much reciprocation that I can see. My questions are answered, then—at least until next time they arise. I owe my mother nothing.

•  •  •  •

In December—one week before Adam and I leave for California—I get another emergency call: My mother is being transported to the hospital for a possible heart attack. Bill has refused to come home from a charity food drive he's running, so she's called 911, and the EMTs have called me, no doubt directed by her.

"Adam!" I call out, and we stop packing, call the dog walker, head to the hospital ASAP.

On arrival, we learn there was no heart attack. In fact, they find nothing physically wrong, even though, hobbling around on her cane, my mother complains of vision loss, of terrible pain in half of her body. Perhaps she's being honest; I'll never know. Either way, there are hours of forms, examinations, drama. A nurse asks me if my mother is under psychiatric care, since it all seems "an elaborate acting out . . . not even an anxiety attack." Alas, no, I tell the nurse; she refuses anything of the sort.

On the way home—Adam drives, in our hand-controlled car— my mother chatters away: Bill is selfish, his kids are difficult, her sister is mean. I keep silent, my eyes on the road. Eventually, apropos of nothing, she announces, "I was an attentive mother." I'm not sure whether to laugh at the absurdity or howl with rage, but I keep my voice measured. "No," I say. "You weren't."

She is quiet after that. In her driveway, Bill waits to receive her. As we open the car doors, she begins to yell as usual, a high-pitched litany of words: "Come on in, I have stuff for you, it's been sitting here forever, are you coming? Is Adam?"

"Stop yelling, Mom," I say.

"I'm *not* yelling!" she yells, and Bill makes the mistake of meeting my eye and smiling, which turns her anger toward him instead, poor guy. But it's his turn; I've spent the day with her— though likely the last one for a long time. Maybe ever. "Good-bye, Mom," I say, getting out of the car. "I won't see you again before we leave for L.A."

She looks at me, at last silent, and then we hug tersely good-bye. And then I get in my car with my sweet, easy husband, and we drive—first back home to finish packing, and then, a week later, far, far away, leaving my mother and heading off into the sunny, beckoning second half of my life.

# Wrinkles in Time. Or Not.

## DEBORA L. SPAR

It was my friend who made me do it.

We set out for a short walk one morning, with her miniature dachshund and two rapidly cooling cups of coffee. Camille, as I'll call her, has a very fancy job, the kind that comes with gaggles of admirers and a hefty paycheck, and she's wildly good at it. She's also wildly smart, whippet thin, and carries a whiff of her original French accent, which always seems a grossly unfair advantage. We had no agenda except to walk and catch up, and so she caught me slightly off guard when she launched right into the topic. "So," she said directly, "what are we going to do about this menopause thing?"

I swallowed far too much coffee in a single gulp. "What menopause *thing*?" I asked. "I didn't know we had a choice in the matter."

"No," she said firmly. "It can be stopped. There are things you can do. Lots of things." She looked at me. "I know someone," she said. "A woman. She's great. Everyone goes to her."

Now she had me. Like most women in my liberal, feminist-leaning, highly educated peer group, I am ideologically opposed to intervening in such a natural and inevitable process as menopause. But like many of my peers, I am also a two-faced hypocrite—especially when it comes to parts of my own face that might well benefit from a twinge of artificial intervention. At just a dash over fifty, I hadn't yet reached menopause, but even the thought of drier skin, deeper smile lines, or a decreased libido could wake me in a cold sweat. So how, I asked Camille, did this particular sorceress work her magic?

"It depends," Camille said. "She starts by running all these tests. Figures out how old you are, mentally and physically. Then she prescribes whatever makes sense for you."

"Like what?" I shot back, quickly imagining the usual fare of broccoli, long walks, and just a teensy bit of red wine.

But no. "Hormones, of course," said Camille. "Estrogen to keep you from drying out. Progesterone to do whatever it is the estrogen needs to do its work. And testosterone. That's what keeps your libido alive and makes your brain not go senile. Plus calcium and vitamin D and a bunch of other stuff." Camille had already signed on for most of the hormones, and was interested in trying whatever else the menopause doctor might pass her way. Her parents were in their eighties already, she reasoned, and yet quite healthy. Why not do whatever it took to keep her age in check too?

Why not, indeed. When I tentatively mentioned her routine to a doctor friend the following week, she smiled knowingly. Sarah is a decade younger than Camille and me, smug still in her flat stomach and unjowled cheeks. But everyone takes testosterone, she said. Everyone should. "Just a little dab every day," she confided. "It's great for your energy. You just need to make sure to get the dosage right."

And then she proceeded, as she does every six months or so, to shoot a few jabs of Botox into my brow. I winced at the pain and tried not to cry.

• • • •

Aging, to be sure, is no great fun for anybody. It slaps us all with the same unpredictability, randomly sprinkling a smattering of gray hairs here, a bout of cancer there. Age is one of the few forces (along with weather, maybe, and bingo games) that care nothing about your race or social standing, or how well you fared on your SATs. It will get us all, and it won't be pretty. But middle age, like many things, falls particularly hard on women, coming as it so often does with the double or triple whammy of menopause. BOOM! Your skin sags and your belly grows. POW! Your teenage children disdain you and your reproductive days are through. Your hunky husband is still considered attractive—"distinguished"— while you can no longer entice even a second look from the guy at the 7-Eleven. Now what do you want to do with the rest of your life?

I know. Any self-respecting feminist would cringe in her sensible shoes. Because women, of any age, are not supposed to be valued for their looks or reproductive capacities. We aren't supposed to depend on the gaze of men to furnish our self-image or on the making of babies to boost our self-esteem. And as we age, we are supposed to become wiser and more generous, treasuring our wrinkles as the laugh lines of life. I love this idea. I wish I could embrace it.

In fact, I probably wish it even more than most women. Because when I am not fretting about my brow lines or commiserating with my equally agitated friends, I am president of a women's college, one of the top schools in the country for educating women who want to leave their mark on the world. What horrible lesson am I conveying to my students if I focus even the briefest bit of attention on my worry lines or my suddenly morphing into middle-age body? What message am I sending if I treat aging as anything but a natural process, the inevitable bookend to the puberty that each of them so recently survived? A few years ago, a woman leaped up after a lecture I had given on the problems of perfection and lambasted me for my (brown, curly, totally nondescript) hair. "How could you?" she scolded. How could I *what*? "How could you stand in front of us, in front of your students, talking about the pressures young women face to look like some perfect ideal, and still dye your hair? How can you set such an unconscionable example?"

The first answer is easy. Because maybe I feel that my hair is *my* business. Because maybe I believe that not every bit of personal style needs to carry a political statement. And because maybe gray hair makes me feel old, and coloring my hair seems a relatively painless way to make that feeling go away—so painless, in fact, that nearly all the women I know do it, save for those lucky few blessed with that fabulous natural white that doesn't come from a bottle. And I'm not talking just about Manhattan, where I live, or even, increasingly, in academia, where I work. Count the heads of Congress, if you must, and you'll see that Clairol crosses the aisle with shocking consistency. Nancy Pelosi, at seventy-six, a deep mahogany brown. Michele Bachmann, sixty, chestnut brown. Even Elizabeth Warren fights from the left with a coif that has grown distinctly blonder over time.

The second answer, though, is more complicated. As I said, almost every woman I know—wealthy or working class, fashion model or stay-at-home mom—colors her hair in some way, whether from a box or at a pricey salon. On top of that, these days, at least in Manhattan (and L.A. and London and even Paris, I suspect), many women will quietly confess to a shot of Botox from time to time, or a dose of filler to soften their smiles. (And even if they're not confessing, the data betray: More than 6 million Americans had Botox treatments in 2013, up 703 percent since 2000.) It's after that point that things get dodgy. Face-lifts. Brow lifts. Liposuction. Estrogen. Progesterone. Testosterone. Is it all a slippery slope to some kind of Kardashian hell? Or, like Propecia and Viagra—age-fighting interventions that men use and rarely take much crap for—simply elements in a modern medicine chest, there for the picking? When, for women of a certain age, does intervening with our faces and bodies become a choice, and when an obligation? And how do we think about drawing the line?

• • • •

When I was twenty-one, I underwent breast reduction surgery, reducing my embarrassingly large chest to something that could at least fit inside a cardigan. Although there was some medical rationale for the procedure, the overwhelming reason was that I was sick and tired of every man on the planet being unable to look above my neck. Their fault, I know, not mine, and symptomatic of the baggage, both physical and psychological, women are forced to carry around with them. But once my own baggage was surgically removed, I felt amazing—lighter, prettier, healthier. Was this an indulgent move on my part? Maybe. Have I regretted it over the past thirty years? Not for a single moment. I had a problem, or at least what felt an awful lot like a problem, and I made it go away. Far be it for me, then, to cast aspersions on anybody's tummy tuck.

When it comes to aging, though, I'm torn. Because technically, aging isn't a problem at all. Like menopause and receding hairlines, it just *is*. Mother Nature has it in for us all, reducing us to shriveled frames and crepey arms en route, eventually, to dust. Does a little face-lift along the way constitute treason or just a reasonable accommodation? I truly don't know. What I do know, though, is that for women in certain professional or social circles, the bar of normal keeps going up. There are virtually no wrinkles on Hollywood stars, of course, or on Broadway actors; ditto for female entrepreneurs or women in the media. There are few wrinkles on the women in Congress and even fewer on Wall Street.* CEOs, bankers, hospital executives, heads of public relations firms and publishing houses, lawyers, marketers, caterers . . . certain

* I think you are allowed to have wrinkles on the Supreme Court. I have no idea why.

standards of appearance have long been de rigueur for women in these positions, from being reasonably fit and appropriately dressed to sporting attractively coiffed hair and manicured nails, but more and more these standards now also include being nearly wrinkle-free. A renowned professor and author of several acclaimed books tells the story of her own literary agent saying to her loudly, in the middle of a meeting, "J———, you need Botox!" Even Gloria Steinem and Marlo Thomas, two icons of feminism now in their eighties, share not a brow crease or ounce of fat between them. Just saying no—to chemical peels and lasers, fillers and Botox, even going under the knife—becomes harder and harder under these circumstances, even if no one wants to admit that it's so.

What's more, as with so many issues that surround women and beauty and aging and sex, there's a paradox today that seems to strike women of the postfeminist generation with a particular force. In the bad old days—before women worked outside the home; before anyone lived much past their reproductive years; before there was Restylane and Juvéderm, Radiesse and Sculptra—the idea of halting aging or fading its tracks was only a fantasy, the stuff of Ponce de Léon and the fountain of youth. No one actually *did* anything about it, much less worried about the moral implications of doing so. But today, women facing the onslaught of middle age are armed with both an arsenal of age-fighting implements and a feminist-inspired philosophy that disdains using them. It is a trivial dilemma, perhaps, but a painful one nevertheless. If a woman with some degree of professional success brags about or even comments upon her fabulous new filler or face-lift (When's the last time you heard a movie star tout her plastic surgeon? Or a leading executive thank her dermatologist?), she risks being derided as a traitor to the cause, someone silly enough to have spent the time and money to subject herself to an unnecessary, possibly dangerous, procedure. By the same token, if that same woman ignores the process of aging and eases more honestly into her inevitable wrinkles and jowls, belly fat and gray hair, she is liable to stand out as an anomaly within her personal and professional circles. In political science, we would refer to this as a collective action dilemma: Everyone's better off if nobody Botoxes, but once anyone starts, it gets harder and harder to pull back from the practice.

And so instead, an entire generation of feminist and postfeminist women—the very same women who stormed the barricades of the American workforce, planned their reproductive destinies, and even got their partners to occasionally fold the laundry—are now engaged in an odd sort of collective self-delusion. Everyone (at least in certain high-profile or professional circles) is doing it, and very few are confessing—which in some ways is even more disturbing than the surge in the surgeries themselves. Because not only are we nipping and tucking and suctioning and hormoning, but we're also (a) feeling embarrassed about it, and (b) lying. Neither of which was really the point of women's liberation.

• • • •

In South Korea today, one in every five women has had cosmetic surgery done, most to achieve the rounded eyes and larger breasts of Kpop idols.

In Brazil, even young and working-class women regularly invest their disposable income in tummy tucks and the country's signature "butt lift."

And on a sleeting night on Manhattan's Upper East Side, I sidled into a friend's annual Christmas party. The room was packed, as it always is, with a particular subset of the city's elite—the power women of a certain age, mostly from media and politics. The men wore Hermès ties and as much hair as they could muster. The women were uniformly thin and dressed in either black or red. A Clinton was spotted and appropriately fawned over. I stayed for a while and mingled, gulping some wine and making hosts of hasty promises that had something to do with lunch and the New Year. Then my friend Elise pushed me toward the exit, where our husbands were waiting. Like my doctor friend Sarah, Elise is about a decade younger than me; she's also Nordic, smooth-skinned, and built like a ballerina. "Did you see that room?" she said, smiling and rolling her eyes. "Every other woman there was over sixty and yet there wasn't a wrinkle to be found! They all looked great," she acknowledged, "but, God, so similar!"

We ducked into the car and started heading back to the West Side. In the darkness, she grabbed my arm. "Promise me that we'll never do that," she said.

"Do what?" I asked, pulling my own red dress more tightly around me.

"That plastic surgery thing," she said.

I demurred, mumbling quietly, "Come back and see me when you're fifty."

• • • •

The next day, bleary-eyed, I left my apartment at 6:25 A.M. and headed downtown to the dance studio on West Twenty-Sixth Street that has become like a second home to me. It smells, as my daughter describes it, like peonies and sweat, and beats with the sound of adulterated hip-hop and the laughter of twenty-four-year-olds. I have absolutely no business being there. The trainers, as you would expect, are lithe and gorgeous. Two are recent Rockettes. One just finished a tour with the Las Vegas production of *Mamma Mia!* They all have vaguely Australian accents and leggings to die for. Not only are they all young enough to be my daughters, but on some days, when attendance at the dance cardio class is sparse, I am pretty sure that I am older than the entire class combined.

But I go. Not only regularly, but religiously, racing downtown for a 7 A.M. workout or squeezing in an evening class before a formal dinner. I go so frequently that my husband jokes that I have become worse than an addict, dragging not only my own tired bones to the studio again, but also those of any friend I can manage to ensnare. In my more honest moments, I think I understand what I'm doing: trying—like my husband, who refused to acknowledge the shoulder that wouldn't move for six months; like my friend Michael, who insists on playing competitive tennis with men thirty years younger than him—to defy age. Trying to pretend that if I kick my legs high enough and hold my plank long enough, the years will somehow be held at bay. Most days, though, I just try to drown it all out and pray that the ear-splitting beat won't be too embarrassing for me to dance to.

One day, though, in the middle of a complicated grapevine/ jumping-jack thing, I felt a cramp in my foot. A bad cramp. I should have stopped. But the music was blaring, the lithe ones around me pumping away, and so on I went. The next morning, I couldn't put any weight on my foot. Or the morning after that. Or really the entire next week, when I nevertheless slung on some sandals and limped several miles around London with my husband. I hobbled on that foot for about six months, still walking around the city as much as I could; still jumping (and wincing) through several cardio dance classes a week. Finally, the doctor who removed a totally unrelated small cyst from that same foot insisted that I go see an orthopedist.

He was thin, as I guess the sports medicine folks usually are. Young. And figured me out in about ten seconds flat.

Gently he pressed my foot and gauged the reflex that nearly sent me flying off the examining table. He pressed again, and again, apologizing for the pain with a wry smile as he also cast a not-so-subtle glance at the three-inch heel I had just removed from that foot.

He looked at the chart, at me, and again at my shoe.

"So," he said finally. "You're a runner, right? And you take these, what, dance classes?"

I mumbled a yes, noting that I ran only a little bit these days, and that I was trying to stick with the low-impact classes.

He wasn't impressed. "You injured that foot, what, six months ago? And you haven't stopped running or dancing?"

I mumbled some more.

He looked again at my shoe. Then at my chart. Finally back at me.

"You're, like, a college president," he said slowly. "Right?"

I nodded.

"You're an idiot," he pronounced. "Do you have any idea how badly hurt your foot is? Do you have any idea how much worse you've made it by treating it that way?"

I knew, I guess. I know. But all I could do was curse him (under my breath, and totally unfairly) for being so right, and so young.

We made a deal of sorts, the young doctor and I. I had the MRI and stopped running and made promises about the dance class that I knew I would break. I sadly moved my highest heels to the back of my closet. (Yes, I'm fifty, but I like heels. I always have, and I refuse to stop liking them now.) I rigged up a little splint for my office—an ice bag wrapped in a dish towel and supported by my recycling bin. And as I hobbled unceremoniously around the halls, I proclaimed my new lower-the-bar goal: to limp gracefully into the sunset each night.

Four weeks later, I was back at the studio on West Twenty-Sixth Street, ice pack, bad foot, and all. I'm sorry, Dr. Steinberg. I know you're right. But we all have lines we must draw, foolish things we do to defy age or at least enjoy the youth that remains. Some people (mostly men, I would wager) go bungee jumping. Some drive fast cars or ridiculously wide motorcycles. Me, I'm going down to bad show tunes, smelling of peonies and sweat.

• • • •

If, that is, I go down at all. Which, in case it's not obvious by now, I don't plan—college president or not, feminist or not, left-leaning academic or not—to do without a fight. And so, on a recent cold winter's day, I placed a call to the menopause doctor. She was in Palm Beach on vacation—which I suppose made sense—but she agreed to talk to me anyway. I expected her to be slick and glamorous-sounding, to slip swiftly into marketing mode and begin selling me on the virtues of stopping age. But instead she was thoughtful and smart, interested in discussing menopause and how American medicine regularly misdiagnoses and overdiagnoses a range of so-called feminine ailments. I asked about her patients, expecting to hear of celebrities and social butterflies. But no, she said, those were rare. Instead, the women she saw fell into two distinct groups: professionals who wanted to keep their energy levels stable as they entered older age, and recently divorced former beauties hoping to recapture their youth. The first group, she said, intrigued and excited her. The second made her sad.

• • • •

Sometimes—yes—I do wish I could say that I am entering the midpoint of my own middle age with appropriate grace and wisdom; without grueling exercise regimens or a shot here and there to keep myself looking smoother than nature alone might dictate. Sometimes I regret that I don't seem to be turning into one of those feisty older women who welcome each laugh line as a memory of joy. (I presume these women exist; I have never actually met one.) But obviously I do fret—about my gray, about the inevitable sags and wrinkles, about the dawning realization that my heels will need to shrink. Again, part of my concern no doubt stems from being a professional woman in the high-powered and image-conscious environment of New York City, but another part, and a part of many women's concerns, I suspect, runs deeper. It stems from millennia of knowing—either through biological pathways or societal norms—that, like it or not, beauty matters. Physical attractiveness *does* confer influence, and has since the days of Cleopatra and Helen of Troy. Beauty gives women a tangible power, whether to turn heads in the street or earn millions of dollars by selling products—songs, clothes, magical potions, or diet pills—that promise to sprinkle some fairy dust of this beauty on less fortunate souls. We deny the power of beauty at our peril, which is why its inevitable passage is so poignant and so hard.

In trying to rationalize my own choices, though—to myself, to my daughter, to my students, even to the critics at my lectures—I have come to only one firm conclusion. And that is not to pass judgment. If a middle-aged movie star feels she needs to rearrange her face to maintain her career—or even just to feel prettier—who am I to criticize? If a working-class woman in Brazil wants a butt lift to boost her spirits, why should I disdain her choice? Instead, I'd like to think of cosmetic intervention—or any age-defying intervention, really—as akin to skydiving or bungee jumping. Do it if you wish, for whatever reason you want. Do it at your peril. But try not to feel bad or embarrassed about it. Because these pleasures, after all, like those of youth itself, are bound to be fleeting. So try, at least—as long as you're on it—to enjoy the ride.

# What's Love Got to Do with It?

## I'm Havin' My Baby

**LIZZIE SKURNICK**

did not plan for *The Real Housewives of Orange County Reunion* to be what finally made me sure I wanted to be a mother, but there it is.

For those who don't know the Real Housewives franchise, its stars are wealthy women unequaled in their greed and vapidity, unstinting in their self-regard, and often really mean to each other. I love it. And I especially love the reunion episodes, in which the cast members sit around in ball gowns and rehash the last season, periodically abandoning their positions on the couch to break into fisticuffs.

My breakthrough occurred about halfway through. There was an altercation between particularly bitter enemies, a gang-up involving husbands and gossip and dinner-party side-eye. But suddenly someone brought up one of the women's children, and they all paused in their vitriol. They sighed. They smiled. One congratulated the other on her parenting.

I had always thought that when I made the decision, I would think, *I want a child.* But I surprised myself. Instead, it was *I want to be a mother.*

• • • •

At thirty-seven, I hadn't known if I wanted a baby. In my early twenties, I thought I did; as a corporate assistant, I had walked through the halls of Time Warner carrying stacks of Xeroxes like a pregnancy. But the parenting part was still hazy, and by the time I reached twenty-five, the urge had passed.

I wanted to get away from my New York boyfriend, throw dinner parties, sleep with lots of people, be friends with lots of people. I wanted to teach, work, write. I wanted to see what happened.

And I did. My writing, in particular, filled me with a bold, delirious joy. A series of poems I wrote holding a pen on the steering wheel as I drove got me fellowships at Yaddo, in Prague, in Wyoming. I wrote a book of poetry, a mystery novel, ten books for teens, dozens of book reviews.

I think this is when I'm supposed to say I neglected men in favor of work. Or that this whole time, I was looking for a good relationship with a man that never happened. But it never felt that way to me. I can't explain it better than to say I wanted *privacy:* privacy to write, to read, to become a happy person, fully cooked. There also was my as-yet-unsolved depression, which I'd had since puberty. Often it was difficult enough to tolerate myself, let alone another person.

Ten years later, I had medicated and therapized the depression into submission. I had a book-stuffed one-bedroom apartment in Jersey City and a circle of fascinating and devoted friends. The members of my family were no farther than a few turnpike stops away. I was proud of the work with my name on it, and I even managed to have really good—if spectacularly expensive—health insurance.

In my early thirties, I had loved to get in a spangly dress, do something glamorous, and come home at two in the morning. But by a few years later, all I could think about on weekends was exiting the Seventy-Ninth Street subway stop with a stroller, heading with my baby to the kid-friendly Museum of Natural History. It didn't seem to make sense to be doing anything else.

This didn't mean, however, that I wanted to get married.

I have never entirely equated romantic love, or even couplehood, with having children—to the point that I am somewhat perplexed by people who do. Not only did I not have someone I wanted to marry, I wasn't sure what I would want from the marriage if I did. (On the other hand, living with all my mom-friends within a one-block radius—now, *that* I could get behind.) I worried about the intrusion into my life and work, and the obligation to give another adult such a massive amount of my headspace. There's a Philip Roth novel in which one character tells another that you shouldn't marry unless you feel lucky—greedily lucky—that you get to have this person to yourself for the rest of your life. That seemed like a lovely way to think about marriage—and if I ever meet such a person, I'll think about it too.

• • • •

I told my family I was going to try to get pregnant on my own, without a partner, before I actually did. This turned out to be wise. My father, a local politician, after telling me in a concerned yet startled voice how hard parenting was, finally delivered a shaky joke: "I won't be able to show my face at the council meetings!"

"Well, Dad," I said, "I'm very happy about my decision, and I hope you can be happy for me too."

This may have been my first real act as a parent—a blithe indifference to what anyone else thought about my future child and me. I was equally confident in the face of my mother's strained smile and obvious great effort, which lasted into my second trimester, to assure me I *was* doing the right thing. And though I sobbed, I also was firm when my sister-in-law, in the early months of my pregnancy, asked that I not tell my seven-year-old nephew the circumstances of the birth. "This is going to be my son's story!" I said. "Not something he's supposed to be ashamed of, that I'm going to hide. I'm *happy* about how he's coming here."

Was I in a practical position to have a baby? Not particularly. I was a freelance writer—successful by this point, but freelance is freelance (and writing is writing)—and an adjunct college instructor with a master's degree in (yes) poetry. I was not exactly flush. But I reminded myself that, after all, most of the people who have babies in the world aren't wealthy—and people with regular jobs get fired too. Many of my friends had been supporting their husbands for years. My father was eager to be a manny, as he had with his other grandchildren, and my parents would help with money in a pinch, even if I didn't want them to have to. I wasn't going to make such a fundamentally human decision on the basis of money. I knew how to work hard. I would make it work.

. . . .

If you have a uterus and some sperm and you're fertile, you can have a baby without anyone needing to preapprove. This was lucky for me. Some of my friends have created entirely bespoke babies using surrogates and purchasing eggs and sperm or both, but a baby like that ran, I knew, into the six figures. And a single forty-year-old in a one-room apartment is not a great candidate for adoption. As for fostering, I know people who spent years trying to get custody of a child from parents in and out of jail for drugs or abuse—sometimes losing in the end. Too heartbreaking for me.

I found the sperm emporium California Cryobank through my gynecologist. (I was too dumb to know that at thirty-nine, most women go straight to a fertility clinic.) My gynecologist had checked my levels of follicle-stimulating hormone (FSH), which helps control the production of eggs by the ovaries, to see if I was a good candidate for intrauterine insemination (IUI). Happily, I was. IUI is basically a fancy turkey baster that uses a catheter to sneak past the sperm-killing cervix. It costs about $500 out of pocket, which is great, because in vitro fertilization (IVF—try to keep track of the acronyms), the next rung on the fertility ladder, runs into the thousands—and only fifteen states mandate that insurance cover fertility procedures. (And states don't, as my insurance representative actually said to me, necessarily include in the definition of infertility, "don't have a man.")

Donor sperm is also in the comparatively reasonable range of about $700 a vial, and finding a donor online is not unlike shopping for a dress on J.Crew. On the website California Cryobank, baby pictures of the donors rotate in a slideshow on one of the site's pages, while the search box, adorned with a jaunty sperm, allows you to boil down your donors using any number of factors, from height to hair color to years of education to religion.

Once you click on a choice, you get his headline ("He's a One-Man Band"), a descriptive paragraph ("This blue-eyed blondie is a talented musician and composer"), and a celebrity look-alike (my donor's was Adrian Grenier). For an extra couple of hundred dollars, you can drill down more: voice interviews, personality tests, even favorite poems.

I know women who chose a donor for his height, or to get a different race from their own, or because he looks like their existing children. I have friends who bought each donor à la carte, trying a different one each time. I know people who have used sperm from former boyfriends or from male friends who don't want children; I have friends who, as lesbian single moms, have chosen a gay donor who would be their co-parent. I have friends who have, in passing relationships, used the time-tested method of Accidentally on Purpose.

I thought I was open-minded, but as I rejected and unclicked, I found out the ways I wasn't. I rejected businessmen, who made me picture cheap loafers. Musicians made me think of flakiness and pot. Baptists were too credulous for this atheist. I wanted an "open" donor, one my child could contact later, so there was no dramatic mystery at the center of his or her life. I didn't want one who was married or had children of his own. ("So conceited!" one friend summed up.) I wanted one with reported pregnancies; my eggs were both aging and untried. And I seemed to veer toward scientists, mathematicians, and engineers. I'd provide all the depressive artistic genes he needed by myself, thank you.

I also crowd-sourced my sperm to make sure I wasn't missing something. One friend checking out my choices got so into it that she made it to the shopping cart before she remembered she wasn't buying sperm for *herself*. My brother the computer programmer immediately unclicked anyone who wasn't a scientist. And a male friend pointed out that one donor I had "favorited" was fat. "I don't mind fat," I said. "Someone five-foot-ten and two hundred and twenty pounds is unhealthy," he said—exactly the kind of thing I wouldn't have noticed.

Donor 13038 ("Loves Science and Singing") was the first one I saw that I liked, and the one I ultimately chose. I liked that he rode around on a bike made of salvaged parts. (He builds things!) I liked that he had traveled to every continent except Antarctica. (He has get-up-and-go!) Given the chance, he would meet the engineers of the pyramids at Giza. (Finally, someone who did not want to meet Thomas Jefferson.) I liked that he never described himself as "laid-back."

He also had something I hadn't even realized I wanted: He was racially and ethnically mixed—and even better, they were all (Colombian, Mexican, white European) races and ethnicities I didn't already have. I am a white-looking black person (mother black, father white), a secular Jew from my dad's side, who has been told

"I don't think of you as a black person" by white people about six million times, which I hate. I had agonized over whether to use a white or black donor, or a Jewish donor. But what was I going to do—choose a black donor so the child would be *genuinely* black? Risk diluting my crucial percentage of blackness with a white donor? I considered using Asian or Indian sperm—but you can't make race not a factor by choosing a different race.

Let's be clear, though: I know you cannot pick your child like you pick your sperm. I knew that geniuses produce doofuses; rage-mongers, peaceniks. He could emerge terrible and odious, with a high, funny voice and a mole-riddled face.

But my worry was different. I was afraid my child would not feel as "real" to me as the children of "normal" families: the ones where the parents meet cute or have a great-grandmother's sepia photo. As of yet, I had only a bill for $4,290 (six vials of sperm, plus fees, minus discounts) and a cryopreserved sample in a lab in California. But as I went on, I began to believe that those couples just had more mystical grist for their child's story. After all, a married couple's decision-making can consist entirely of one person rolling over and saying, "Wanna try?"

Does the human brain have the ability to ascribe mystical meaning to anything, or is any child's conception beautiful and mysterious? Because 13038 felt magical to me. When I gave my credit card number to the California Cryobank representative to buy him, my scalp prickled. And when I tracked my ovulation, I was suffused with joy as a line, full and red, appeared alongside the control. I wasn't pregnant—just ovulating! But I exulted nonetheless.

And it did not escape me that the cardboard box containing 13038's sperm tank was exactly the size and heft of a newborn. I know this, because I carried it twenty blocks down Park Avenue to the Thirty-Third Street PATH station on the day before my first insemination. On the train home, I couldn't bear to put 13038 on the floor. I was sure that, had my fellow riders known what was in there, someone would have offered me a seat.

. . . .

I'd always had an idea that there were certain tribes in which the gaggle of women handled the pregnancy, birth, and aftermath, while the men went hunting or sat around chewing whatever it is men chew. My gaggle appeared immediately: My friends and family muscled in on every part of the whole thing.

The night before my first IUI, a friend with three children who lived three hundred miles away simply showed up to stay over. She passed me off to two other friends at the gynecologist's, who sat with me as the sperm crept up. I took my first pregnancy test at a Korean restaurant with a friend who went out to Duane Reade to buy it because we couldn't stand the suspense. (That one was negative.)

I was talking to my brother on the phone when I found out I was pregnant. It was only my second try, and I wasn't expecting much. I had just peed on the stick when he called, and as we spoke, I looked on in astonishment as the second line began to form.

"Oh my god," I interrupted. "I'm pregnant! I just did a test and it says I'm pregnant!"

"Whoa," said my brother. "Congratulations!"

When I announced my pregnancy on Facebook ("I'm pregnant! With a BABY!"), the Likes tumbled in, and presents began to arrive: a hand-knitted cap and booties from a high school friend I hadn't seen in twenty years; jars of spiced pickles from a blogging buddy; and, after I posted a craving, lemon-poppy-seed muffins from a "Friend" in California.

Today, you could hand me a newborn in an alley with half a cracker, and I'd be fine. But then it made all the difference to know that, in fact, I wasn't doing this alone. BabyCenter.com—from which I received extremely valuable weekly e-mails on the food-related size of my fetus (lentil, lemon, gourd)—estimates that a baby's first year costs $10,000, half of which is gear. If I spent a dime on gear, it is only the fault of Amazon Prime. A best friend provided me with her son's stroller, crib, changing table, two carriers, and at least forty bottles. Another gave me her son's old co-sleeper, and yet another an unused car seat. A neighbor left a nearly new Quinny stroller out on the street. Friends gave me everything from old carriers to tricks for making your jeans fit with a rubber band.

My parents, after that shaky start, had gotten entirely on board. They readied a nursery at their house, insisting I stay with them for the first few months, indifferent to my feeble stabs at independence. ("Those Indian grandmothers, they come over for months!" my father assured me.) My best friend agreed to be my birth partner. I had a doula, a psychiatric team monitoring my meds, a gynecological team monitoring my fetus, a prenatal yoga coach. It's a wonder I had any time to lie in my bed, prop *Wolf Hall* on my belly, and eat chocolate pudding by the pack.

Still, during my pregnancy, I carried around phantom husbands. You will not be surprised to hear that one was supremely unhelpful. He fought with me about getting a baby boy circumcised. He looked at me sideways when I asked him to go out and get me a tuna fish sandwich and a strawberry shake. He didn't like my blackout shades.

But the other husband I had to admit I missed, and missed deeply. One night, as I sat at buybuy BABY filling out the registry form, waiting for a friend who was going to tell me what to buy, hot tears ran down my face. Here I was, alone, and why? What had I done wrong? Would anyone ever love me or want to take care of me? Yes, I had opted to do this alone, and I would do it again the same way; yes, I had not craved marriage, and there had been no one in my life I had been (remotely) willing to marry; yes, I had so many devoted friends in my life helping me. But still, none of that meant I couldn't feel horribly alone.

The staff looked on, concerned. They asked if I needed some water. I was embarrassed, until I realized: There was no way I was the first weeping pregnant woman they'd ever seen. Married or not.

• • • •

My contractions started as I sat on my nephews' bunk beds, talking to my mother and sister-in-law about how you know your contractions are starting. That night, my parents stayed over while I bounced on an exercise ball in the living room, excitedly tracking the contractions with an iPad app and texting my doula.

At 4:30 A.M., we headed to the hospital to avoid rush hour. I called my birth partner to come up from Baltimore. ("Are you *sure*?" she said sleepily.) The doctor sent us home—I wasn't dilated enough yet—and we wound up at my cousin's place nearby, where she put me in the guest room to doze. "My water might break," I warned. She handed me towels. "It's so exciting!" she said.

Downstairs, I could hear my birth partner, my cousin, and my parents kibitzing and roaring with laughter. My water broke. (Yet again, I was excited: The first time you're in labor, it seems miraculous each time the thing that's supposed to happen actually happens.) I gathered up the towels, went downstairs, and sat on the heap to join the conversation. There was even pastry and coffee—a fancy brunch, except for the lady in labor.

The rest of the day seemed to simultaneously last five minutes and ten hours. One minute I was at the hospital doing deep knee bends with my birth partner and discussing whether or not you could still wear boot-cut jeans. (No.) The next I was on the table, surrounded by a small crowd: my mother, my birth partner, my doula, my doctor, two nurses, a crowd of interns, and a pediatrics team in the back to make sure the baby did not have gills from my antidepressants. (He didn't. He was absolutely fine.) They cheered each push, like regulars at a bar. It took eighteen minutes for my son, Javier, to fully arrive into the world.

Hours later, my baby, my birth partner, and I were alone, waiting to be brought to our room. The delivery room was like an abandoned airplane hangar, machines of dubious use half pulled out from their positions. Outside, the East River's lights ticked in the distance.

"Ugh," my partner said. "I'm so tired."

There was a pause. We burst out laughing.

"Now I know what the father feels like!" she said.

• • • •

People say it's impossible to understand parenthood until you have kids. That was definitely true for me—at least the first week. My son would be in my lap and I would look around, panicked, wondering where he was. At four in the morning, I would stagger into my parents' room and ask if one of them could rock him for an hour while I tried to sleep; then I would pop my head up every other minute to make sure they were keeping him alive.

Like many American moms, I had no paid maternity leave and couldn't afford to lose my job—or jobs, in my case. In the hospital, while I was shifting the baby on my boob, a bound book galley filled with errors was sent out from a publishing imprint I run, prompting a hysterical call and an e-mail from the author that I read from my hospital bed. An editor blithely gave away a magazine column I write to another writer, prompting a hysterical call and an e-mail from *me*. I sat at my parents' ancient computer, my baby strapped firmly to my chest, watching videos on side-boob nursing so I could work while he fed. Russia, I had read, clocked in with 140 days of fully paid maternity leave—and Iceland had such generous child care benefits that women began having babies in college. I was not jealous of other parents, but I was jealous of women with "parent states."

One midnight, I raced to the bathroom to pee as he screamed. He had been screaming for hours. I had signed on to create an entire person and then take care of him forever, all by myself. *This,* I thought, *was a terrible mistake.*

But then we sat down in our rocker. His eyes were black and bottomless, and he looked, in my arms, for all the world like he was holding on for dear life. We stared at each other for hours.

*Are you my person?* his eyes seemed to ask.

"I'm your person," I said.

• • • •

I had worried throughout the pregnancy that Javier would feel foreign to me—half my face, half a stranger's face. But from the moment he was pulled out of my belly and the looping cord was cut, I had a happy realization: He was just *himself.*

And the face I was worried would be half a stranger's has become the one I love to see on his three half sisters, the other children of the donor. We five co-moms (two a lesbian couple), from all over the country, met through California Cryo's donor registry. After trading pictures and messages on Facebook, we went away on our first trip together, now a yearly event. Around the kitchen table, we talked about why we had chosen the donor. (I hadn't even remembered that he sang karaoke!) We listened to his audio interview and laughed at how the staff member was obviously flirting with him. We talked about the ways the children looked like one another, and how excited we were that they could have relationships in the future. We found we had all been calling them just *brother* and *sister*, without the *half*. Before the trip, I had been thinking of having another baby so Javier could have a sibling. After the trip, I felt like he already did.

I spent the first year with Javier working with him strapped to me, and taking him with me to meetings. In our second year, he has traveled across the country with me on work trips. When we're home, he goes to day care four days a week and surprises me with the letter B or number 3. He spends Fridays with his aunt and grandparents (who mess up his sleep training and feed him cookies), has Saturday dinner with his cousins, and does bedtime reading sessions and park trips with my ex. (He also has an extremely loyal Facebook following.) He is a perfect city kid—well behaved at restaurants, well traveled, and terrified at the sound of the wind in the trees.

• • • •

Once you report a pregnancy to California Cryo, you can buy something called a Keepsake Packet, a hard copy and DVD of everything about the donor. I bought 13038's, and immediately wondered how to make sure it would stay intact for Javier when and if he wanted to learn more about his dad. Should I keep it in a bank vault? Copy everything to the cloud? Publish it in a hardcover book with the enclosed DVD?

Then I remembered: Javier can actually meet his father. He knows his sisters already. He'll have pictures of his childhood, his maternal relatives, and his many friends. Where I grew up in the 1970s and '80s, people thought it was exotic—and, often, awful—to be half-black and half-white. Where we live today, in Jersey City, lesbian couples in which each mother carried a baby from a different donor are not rare, and his peers come from every type of family—long married, divorced, spermed, single parent, mixed race, atheist, devout—and live in a range of environments: crappy apartments, vast houses, abroad. Here, now, Javier's story is closer to the norm.

Given the frequency with which, hearing about how I had Javier, people say, "Good for you!" or "That's so brave," my story still is not as commonplace or "normal" as it always has felt to me. But my first, spontaneous answer to them hasn't changed: I recommend it.

# The "Other Woman"— Then and Now

**KERRY HERLIHY**

*Fifteen years ago, in "Papa Don't Preach" in* The Bitch in the House, *Kerry Herlihy wrote about starting a casual affair in New York, where she lived, with a "six-foot-tall black married man we'll call Michael"—chosen as much for his unavailability as for his good looks—and about then leaving him, many months later, age thirty and very pregnant with his child, for Maine, where her parents lived and would help her with the baby. She had Michael's blessing and joy about their child, but no commitment that he would be involved—nor did she expect one. "I have moments when I want him to be there," she wrote. "But I remember that when I chose to have my daughter, I chose him as well, married and all."*

*They continued to talk often, and after their daughter was born Michael visited them occasionally, but mostly he "loves us from a distance," Kerry wrote. In the meantime, she thought, "Perhaps I'll be the quintessential girl of the new millennium who, after years of juggling children, job, sex, and scandalizing partners, finally figures out how to do it all. If so, I'll let you know."*

*Here's how it played out.*

When I left Brooklyn in a U-Haul—eight and a half months pregnant, no money for New York rent, headed north to my parents' house in Maine—I accepted my status as the other woman. I didn't offer Michael an ultimatum. I didn't hope he would beg me to stay. It's not that I hadn't imagined him leaving his wife or thought of us together, making dinner and playing with our new baby, but I never believed that he would abandon the life he had lived for so long.

Almost two years before, when I'd slept with Michael for the first time, I'd had a reckless bravado and a hunger for the next adventure. This adventure happened to present itself in the form of Michael, a beautiful, older black man at my workplace—married, yet seemingly free to roam.

Michael was a counselor for a nonprofit that assisted men and women who had been in prison. When I first met him, during orientation, I checked out the muscles under his tight black T-shirt and the spear-shaped metal pendant hanging from his neck, and imagined him naked. After that, every day, as I walked down the corridor to his office, I made up an issue so I could talk to him. The conversations led to flirtation—innuendos about "jungle fever"—which led to a proposition: If I slept with him, he said, knowing I still wasn't fully over my last relationship, I could call him any name I wanted. I thought I had nothing to lose.

Looking back, I try to remember what I felt as that supposed one-night stand bled into a full-blown affair. Under the memories of weekly trips to pay-per-hour New Jersey motels and bathroom quickies in East Village bars, I also remember his cavalier dream about a New York City loft, filled with morning light, where we would make beautiful babies. In the early days, I could not see his words as anything but empty, as he made his way home to his wife and daughter hours later. When I became pregnant soon after, I could just make out the lines of the fantasy he had whispered. I wanted part of that domestic, serene, sunlit life, even if it was without him in it.

. . . .

Hours after our daughter was born in Maine, I called Michael in New York and told him we had a beautiful girl. "The universe makes no mistakes" is all I remember him saying. After that, from the basement of his Harlem brownstone, where he worked out daily, he would call me and check in—find out if we had walked along the ocean that afternoon, or whether I had made it out of my pajamas by noon; fill me in on the New York scene. In her first six months, he saw our daughter twice, when I visited the city. Each time, he told his wife he was going out of town, then picked us up at the airport in his family's car and stayed with us at a friend's apartment. Snuggled with our daughter on a futon, he marveled at her features. It was hard not to get attached to this idea of our own family, now that we had a child.

However, there was a serenity to my life in Maine, three hundred miles away from Michael, right along the ocean, with only a few year-round residents nearby. I was a freelance editor as well as an intermittent substitute teacher. When I had a deadline or a day at school, my mother watched my daughter. When I wasn't working, I walked the beach with her, consumed with watching her shift in tiny yet miraculous ways: a new laugh, a grip around a finger, a lifted head.

At night or on weekend mornings, I had Michael's voice, snuck into the edges of his day. He listened when I told him I felt I was outgrowing the wild, carefree girl he had known in Brooklyn. I told him this scared me and wondered out loud what it would mean for us. He said he didn't know, but we'd figure it out. In spite of our limited expectations, we had grown something strong in these shadows, outside the radar of most of our friends and family.

I found a power in our secrets, and I had no desire to move on or date other men. And I knew I was a fixed point in Michael's orbit, even if I was the distant star.

When our daughter was six months old, after I had decided to settle in Maine, Michael got tired of his double life. He called me to tell me he had confessed everything to his wife. He told her he had been cheating on her for most of their twenty-four-year marriage with more women than he could count. He had been seeing me for a long time now. I was thirty: twenty-four years younger than he, twenty-three younger than she. I was white. I had gotten pregnant and had his baby. We lived in Maine. He planned to keep seeing us both.

His wife was furious, but still wanted to try to make the marriage work. She wanted to go to counseling, but he refused and moved to a smaller one-bedroom apartment in the Bronx later that month. She came to his apartment and banged on the door, wanting an explanation for why he had hurt her so much. I heard her through the phone lines, and it filled me with fear.

When the ten-page letter arrived from Michael's wife, I read it, though I knew it would do neither of us any good. It pointed out how I would suffer for taking what was not mine, said I had no right to have a baby born of so much sin. When her phone calls began to wake me up at 5 A.M., I wanted nothing more than for Michael to take it all back, to tell his wife he had made a terrible mistake. I was willing to let him go so my daughter and I could return to our peaceful walks, so I wouldn't have to jump every time I heard an engine rev—almost able to see this woman peering through the crack of a window. I saw the aftermath of what it meant to be a wife to a man who did not want to be a husband. It was a lesson I couldn't forget.

I didn't believe Michael and I would survive as a couple after he left his wife. I was comfortable as *the* mistress, but I wasn't so sure I could be a member of a pack of other women. Although he had told me when I was still in New York that he didn't see other women then, I couldn't know for sure, though he'd had no reason to lie to me at that point; but I don't remember worrying about it, because I knew he wanted to be with me more than with anyone else. Now, though, while I could be cajoled into phone sex, I was no longer the lover a subway ride away who would have sex all night and then sweetly kiss him good-bye, no strings attached—and so, whenever the phone calls grew less frequent, I began to worry. I wanted him to want me as he had when we began our affair, when the idea of our bodies together made everything else in his world fade away.

But I knew that after Michael moved to the Bronx, there were multiple women who competed with me. He referred to them vaguely, in cursory descriptions. My friend in the Bronx. My Puerto Rican friend. My married friend. My widowed friend. These declarations did not shock me, because he had never been monogamous. And he assured me it was just sex, that he still spent most nights alone, but when I called and heard the click of his voicemail, I imagined some woman's underwear in a heap on his floor, her bare legs entwined with his, his sweet moans in her ear. I pretended it did not bother me, that this was what happened when you fell in love with a married man who was not faithful, but if I had focused on it too much, it would have broken me when I needed to feel like he loved me the most.

In contrast to the man Michael was, I kept imagining the man I needed, or would need, in my life and my daughter's: a Saturday soccer coach, a dependable weekend date, someone to shovel the driveway of the houses I rented during the endless winters. There were moments Michael kept alive my new fantasies that he could be that kind of partner. During one visit, I snapped a picture of him holding our daughter before she could walk, her chubby cheeks pushing against her thick hooded sweatshirt, both of them smiling as they squinted into the sun. That's where I saw the father he could be: patient, sweet, attentive. I remember kissing him at the bus station, thinking we could somehow make this work after all.

And in fact, the women in Michael's life faded away about a year after he left his wife—not because I wanted them to, but because Michael discovered that without the need to sneak around, so did his need for other lovers. Soon after, he told me he might come to Maine once a month, suggested we could try this family thing. I listened with the phone balanced between my shoulder and chin, straining to hear while frantically vacuuming the bedroom, wondering if I might break out in hives. After picking fights with him over girlfriends he no longer had, I told him I wasn't ready to change my life.

• • • •

The idea of commitment made me think of being a wife, which had always made me think of being trapped and static—whereas the idea of a mistress, in contrast, meant there was freedom to continually see what unfolded. I could focus on the next encounter with Michael and know that at any point, I could leave. I had room to change my mind, to bail out if I needed, no questions asked. In the beginning I wanted a hot lover, then I wanted a baby, and then I even wanted Michael around more, but I never wanted the traditional husband. I always felt the freedom to choose in my relationship with Michael, even in my most uncertain moments. By sharing him, hard as that was, I also learned that his love was not finite, that he really could love me and his wife and even someone else too. I could not have learned that lesson from the vantage point of a wife, under the weight of expectations. Our path was not direct or neat, but felt like the one that worked the best for us.

. . . .

In the years after our daughter was born, we built our relationship, even our family, across the distance. Eventually Michael did visit Maine every month or so. And our daughter and I visited the Bronx, going to the same sixth-floor apartment where he moved after he left his wife. Our daughter got to experience her father's neighborhood, which was almost entirely black and Hispanic. She and her father would walk to the corner bodega and then, later, through Harlem. She would hold his hand and hear women tell him they really could do something with her hair. But she also got to retreat to the woods and beaches of Maine and grow up in its quiet. She continues to find a part of herself in places where both her mother and her father made their homes.

And as far away as Michael was, he also helped me parent when I needed him. When our daughter, at age ten, spiked a fever of 106 and I thought she'd have a seizure from the heat in her head, I called him from the bathroom, my voice and hands shaking, and told him I didn't know what to do. "Put her in the tub, not too cool. Breathe. You've got to hold it together. I'll be there as soon as I can." I mopped her damp curls, prayed for the fever to break, and reminded myself that I had done this alone for years, that I didn't need Michael to come for every crisis. But he took a week off from work to take care of her. They played Monopoly and ate Popsicles, watched *The Real Housewives of New York City.* He gave her medicine for the pneumonia in both her lungs, ordered her to rest even when she rolled her eyes. When I came home most afternoons that week, I would find them on the sectional couch, napping, heads almost touching, her fingers resting inside the crook of his elbow. When it was clear our daughter would fully recover, Michael returned to the Bronx.

As the years went by, my friends would tell me they wanted a part-time husband like I had: one who would visit, listen to what they had to say, clean the house, have sex, and then go home. Michael and I would talk about the irony of these women, some of whom had condemned me a decade ago. Anyway, I suppose we could have continued our relationship like this for a long time. We certainly both were happy with the arrangement.

· · · ·

Looking back, I should have seen the signs: the fatigue, the talk of retirement, the desire to move to Maine. Even when he couldn't go to our daughter's dance recital that he had flown in to attend, and we ended up at the E.R. that night with him in what I assumed was severe gas pain, I did not panic. As the third doctor approached to examine him, I waited for the man to apologize for the wait, to tell us that an enema or a double dose of milk of magnesia should do the trick. We would tell him about the recital Michael had missed that afternoon, and Michael would say no big deal, he'd catch tomorrow's matinee. But again, I didn't read the signs: the dim lights, the extra questions about Michael's pain level and comfort, the doctor's eye contact with me. Even when he said softly, "I have some bad news," even when I took Michael's hand, I still thought he'd tell us Michael just had a bad virus, or maybe, at worst, an obstructed bowel. Instead he said to Michael, "The scans show you have several masses. The one coming off your small intestine, from what we can tell, is the size of a football. It looks like it may have started in the pancreas. It looks like it is probably cancer. I'm so sorry."

And Michael, who had not seen a doctor for decades, simply nodded and said, "I suspected as much."

I looked back at the doctor and Michael and wondered what the hell was going on. How could Michael, who biked ten miles just yesterday, have masses throughout his body? When the doctor said, "I'll give you and your wife time to talk," I wondered if he meant me. Then I lay my head on Michael's chest and sobbed. He stroked my head. "Are you sure you are ready for this?" he said, and for the first time in all the years of my life with him, I felt as if I would finally have to make a choice.

• • • •

Michael was moved from the E.R. to the cancer floor; he was tested and prodded and eventually told he had twelve to eighteen months to live. He called his estranged wife and adult daughter in New York to give them the news, and although he told her not to come, Michael's daughter immediately flew to Portland. My daughter and I went to get her at the airport: It was the first time we'd ever met. She carried a backpack and wore leggings and an oversize T-shirt, her hair in a natural Afro. Although she was close to thirty, she seemed young to me. We hugged awkwardly and talked about Michael's current condition. In my car, we made small talk, pretending I was not the woman who broke up her family, pretending her father would be fine and back in New York at his job in a few weeks. Pretending we could return to the boundaries we had drawn for so long.

But his daughter wanted Michael to return to New York with her—she argued that Memorial Sloan Kettering is world renowned for its treatment, and I could not disagree—and later that afternoon, a hospital worker entered the room and announced that a woman had called saying she was Michael's legal wife. The woman wanted, the worker said, glancing at me, a psychological consultation for Michael, because she thought the cancer may have metastasized to his brain, as he was making "questionable choices, clearly not in his best interest." I tensed, but Michael just laughed. He looked at me and said to the messenger, "This is my partner. I want to be here if she'll have me. Some people don't like that."

He turned to his daughter. "This hospital is my choice," he said gently, and though he could have been referring to the doctors—he had told her he liked the bedside manner of the staff in Maine; he had called them his "road dogs"—when she got up and walked out of the room, I knew she realized it meant more than that. Later, when I talked to her, I tried to reassure her I wanted the best care for Michael too, that we both loved him. She nodded hesitantly, then asked me to help her convince him to return to New York. I told her I'd try. In the end, my efforts were halfhearted and Michael dismissed them impatiently. I still believe she felt betrayed by my failure to change his mind, but it was the best I could do in the moment. After all, I wanted him to stay.

Eventually Michael came home, and for the first time, that home was in Maine with me and our daughter. As his cheekbones started to become more prominent, as he stopped walking the dog, stopped taking out the trash because he no longer could lift the bags, he told me he wanted us to get married, and he began to plan our wedding. He'd like it simple, he said, on the beach where my cousin was married five years before, where we'd bodysurfed the summer waves during his visits up here over the years. He wanted me barefoot, he said, maybe in a vintage Carolina Herrera dress. For his part, he'd play it casual in Tommy Hilfiger, open collar, white bucks.

• • • •

He told me this fantasy before the July sun rose one morning, as we lay in bed, before we knew whether pain would overwhelm him that day. He kissed my forehead and I closed my eyes and felt his soothing touch, absent of the frenetic lust we had had for so long, and I wondered: Is this what it feels like to be married? For all intents and purposes, we *were* married: in sickness and in health. But he had to divorce his wife to officially marry me, and the lawyer told him he'd need to go back to New York to do that. And that couldn't happen now; there was no way he could make the journey.

So instead we watched my father, only five years older than Michael, remarry three years after my parents divorced. Michael sat in the first row, sweating in the outfit he had picked out when he'd had energy days before. He had on his new white sneakers instead of his favorite wing tips because his feet were too swollen for the shoes. The cane I'd bought leaned next to him.

That morning, when he'd wanted to take more medication than prescribed so the pain wouldn't catch up to him while he was out, I'd reminded him of the dosage and he'd turned to me and snapped, "You have no idea what it is like to be in my body." So I'd shut up and handed him the liquid morphine, like a good wife, and he'd placed the drops on his tongue, closing his eyes as if saying a prayer. It worked. He made it through the vows, sweating profusely under the hot sunlight but still holding my hand and smiling for the photographers. During the reception, Michael napped in a quiet corner in the back of the room, and finally we got in our car and waved our good-byes. We didn't discuss the toll it had taken on him. Instead, I reached over and rubbed the top of his head, felt its smoothness, remembered how I used to feel him between my legs, how we used to pull over at a rest stop to jump in the backseat. That seemed like forever ago now; I'd been so young. Another life had replaced it, and despite its sadness, its loss, there was also something beautiful about this life we had just begun.

A week after my father's wedding, while I slept on a mattress next to the hospital bed, Michael died in my bedroom. In the hours before dawn, I bathed him and dressed him in the outfit he had picked out a few days before: a black spandex shirt, black jeans, a teal blazer with a turquoise print pocket square, and his crisp white sneakers. I sprayed him with his favorite Tom Ford cologne and waited for our daughter to wake.

When I met with the funeral director, he told me we would have to wait four days to have Michael cremated because his wife or daughter had legal claim over his body. During the wait, his wife called Michael's job to ask that I not be invited to a memorial service, filed papers with a court in the Bronx, and was named voluntary estate manager. She sent me a list of things she wanted returned to her, but his ashes were not one of them.

Michael's boss called me and told me I was welcome to come to the memorial service, and I decided to go with our daughter. I was worried that his wife would show up and make a scene, but neither she nor their daughter attended. My daughter and I were given seats in the front of the room, and when the line of young men began to talk about Michael, they looked directly at us and told us they were sorry for our loss. It felt strange to be so publicly acknowledged by people who also loved him—but also, somehow, right. And I wondered what a life not necessarily as his wife but perhaps as his partner would have felt like out in the open.

• • • •

When I picked up Michael's ashes after the memorial service, I couldn't believe he fit into a container so small. I had expected the box to feel like he had returned to me, but instead it just felt heavy in my hands. Still, even in that moment, with all the grief that surrounded me, I knew I'd had his unconditional love; and in the end, I'd gotten to live a life with him that felt true to both of us.

I placed the container on the passenger seat and kept my right hand on top of it as I drove, folding my fingertips around the plastic cover. Taking him home.

# Dirty Work

## KATHY THOMAS, AS TOLD TO CATHI HANAUER

started working the day I turned sixteen. I'm almost sixty now, and I can count on one hand the number of days I've missed, other than a few when each kid was born. For the past eighteen-plus years, I've cleaned houses. Once, I had to cancel an afternoon client because I almost passed out cleaning that morning—severe bacterial stomach infection, probably caught from scrubbing a toilet—and the homeowner, a doctor, made me go home. Other-wise, never. It's a money thing, yes—in my jobs, no work equals no pay—but it's more too. Working saved me. It gave me power and pride at times when I had none. It still does. So even though it's getting harder, I can't imagine stopping.

I was married for fifteen years. I worked throughout. In fact, I mostly supported us. I left the bastard—Angelo—three times. The third was in 1989, during Hurricane Hugo. He would have killed me if he'd caught us, but guess what? He didn't. Maybe I should thank the rain for that, but I'd rather thank myself. I'm six feet tall, I can stretch a dollar, and I don't take any crap from anyone now—male or female. It wasn't easy for me to get the hell out of Angier, North Carolina, but I did, and for twenty-six years, I've been free. We all have.

By "we" I mean me and my boys: Gelo (Angelo Jr.—I call him *Gee*-lo), Jermey (my own spelling), Derrick, Billy, and Troy. Gelo was fourteen when we left. He sat up front with me, holding Troy, three, on his lap. The others were in back. Two were barefoot; we'd left too fast to grab shoes. I was still in my Burger King manager uniform. We'd tied wire around the passenger door handle; otherwise it flew open.

Their father was a charmer. Dumb as a bag of rocks, but he could dance, he could play pool. I was seventeen when we met, waitressing nights at a truck stop. I'd work 11:00 to 7:00, go to high school till noon, then home, sleep, and back to work.

Angelo came in one night with eight women. He was twenty-four. I was dating sailors, because that's what you did in Portsmouth. Nothing serious, but we had fun. I lived with my mother, stepfather, and two little sisters. My real father I met only once; my mother married him at fifteen but left when I was six months old. An alcoholic, six-foot-six, green eyes. That's who I look like.

My stepfather was okay. He knocked me around when I was twelve or thirteen, but I threatened him with a fork. My mom took his side and told me to leave, so I went to my grandmother's that summer. But my parents moved, so I had to go with them. Every time they moved, I had to switch schools.

So Angelo came in to the truck stop that night, dripping with women. Soon we were dating. You had to be twenty-one for the clubs, but with him, they didn't card me. His brother was a musician. My mother let me go because she thought it was cool we saw live music.

Around then, my stepfather left my mother. My sisters were five and three; my mother didn't work. "Does Angelo want to live with us and pay rent?" she asked me, so he moved in. I'd been a virgin, but so much for that. My mother found out and threw us both out.

We went to Orlando. Rented a trailer, got restaurant jobs. I turned eighteen there. But his father had cancer, so we went back, moved into my grandmother's apartment with her. She was the first female public bus driver in Richmond, Virginia, married five times. I loved her.

She was cooking at a truck stop and got me a job waitressing. Angelo painted houses. Soon I was pregnant. I guess I was happy. I mean, *he* wanted a kid, not me; I never liked kids. Funny, because I raised five of 'em—six, with my grandson. After Gelo was born, we traded off working and watching him. Angelo would get bored with one job, quit, find another. I mostly worked nights. I wasn't using birth control, because the pill cost $32 a month. A week's groceries. And of course Angelo didn't use anything.

One day, I'm leaving for work, and Gelo, who's sitting on the floor—he'd just learned to sit up—starts crying. And his father smacks him in the face, so hard he somersaults over his toys. Angelo had hit me before, but never the baby. The next day, when he left for work, I packed up Gelo and drove to my grandmother's. That's the first time I left him.

Angelo showed up later yelling at me to come home. But I found a nanny job in Virginia Beach, a half hour away, and two days later, Gelo and I headed there.

The job was great. Nice, professional people, nice house, yellow Chevy I could use. They had a baby Gelo's age, and I swam with the boys in their pool. But one morning I got sick. Yup. Pregnant again.

The family didn't mind. But Angelo begged me to come back. And guess what? I did. Unbelievable to me now. But I was young and sick, and he had that power over me. He made me feel I was fat and stupid and no one else would want me. Once, he burned all my clothes. He was a sick son of a bitch, with low self-esteem. But also, back then, down there, it wasn't unusual to smack your wife around. And I felt sorry for him. He'd had a rough childhood; I wanted to make up for it. Still, after he hit the baby, I don't think I'd have gone back if I hadn't been pregnant again.

I had Jermey when Gelo was thirteen months. And though Angelo didn't hit Gelo again till much later, he was never nice to Jermey.

I started work again within days. Angelo worked on and off. We fought, and he'd beat me up, but he didn't touch my face, so there was no evidence. The neighbors would call the cops, but I'd cover for him. I had nowhere else to go. There were no shelters there then.

And it wasn't always bad. We had our good times. Sometimes he cheated on me, and I'd say to the woman, Good! Take him! But he always came back. And soon enough, I was pregnant again, with Derrick.

My grandmother would watch the youngest while I worked—11:00 to 2:00, then 5:00 to 10:00. Dock's seafood. Famous people came in: Walter Cronkite, Roy Clark. I could make $200 a day, eat really well. I got pregnant with Billy then. I was twenty-six.

One night, a coworker showed me pictures of Angelo at a bar with some girl. She was nineteen; he was thirty-three. Seven months pregnant, I went to the bar and threatened her, then told him he had twenty-four hours to get out. The next day, she came to collect him. I went down and beat the shit out of him with a broom; took a few whacks at her, too.

He left for a week, then came back. "I love you, baby," he'd say. "I'm gonna change. You'll see." He used mind control on me. You can't understand until you've been there. But also, when there's no one to help you, you want to believe people will change. You have to.

We lived then in the top of a two-family home; my grandmother was downstairs. We had two rooms and a bathroom, but no kitchen. Billy slept with me and Angelo, the other three boys in the other room. I cooked with a hot plate and an electric frying pan, washed dishes in the bathtub. You do what you have to. Finally we moved, to a cute house—$150 a month, and chickens out back. But no hot water. Angelo worked on and off, painting houses, security guard. I worked nights.

We moved again. He was beating me often; I always had bruises.

So one day I packed the car, got the kids from school, and drove a bunch of hours to Charlottesville, Virginia, a big college town. Within three days I had a job, a babysitter, and a rented farmhouse. The kids went to Sunday school; the church helped with furniture, food. I don't even know what church. Baptist? Didn't matter. We were poor but safe. Angelo couldn't find us.

But pretty soon the pastor tells me, "You can't raise four boys alone. They need their father." All the sweet-talking men, so sure they know what you need. He guilted me into calling Angelo, and the bastard came and got us.

Within a year, I was pregnant with Troy. I was *so* mad. Billy was almost four. I was thirty. I couldn't believe I had to start over. I wanted an abortion, but our medical care was from the state, and they wouldn't give me one "without a reason."

I was sick the entire pregnancy. My water broke at work. I ignored it. Finally Troy was born, by C-section. Now he slept with me and Angelo, the four older boys had the second room, and Angelo's mother had the third. She was uneducated, and Angelo moved her in and took half her social security. He and I were fighting like dogs. Then *he* left, this time. Took $200 from our bank account and disappeared.

I was so happy! We all were. He'd been strict and abusive toward the boys. I hoped he was dead. But three weeks later, he calls from North Carolina. "Come, baby," he says. "I'm making good money. We'll have a new beginning."

It was great down there, I admit. A small town, the first time the boys weren't in the minority, being white, at their school . . . and they were athletes and made friends fast. I worked at Hardee's, then Burger King. Angelo painted houses. We had a great sitter, a sweet old lady who'd hold Troy while he slept. And then Angelo says, "I don't want to work six days a week. I'm quitting."

Here we go again. Eventually I found him a job at my work. Night auditor—like a janitor. Four hours a night, 11:00 to 3:00.

Well, you can't give a leopard new spots. One evening he comes home from somewhere and starts beating me, worse than ever before. With his fists and also this thick metal bar. He hit me all night. I didn't resist, because it would have made things worse. The kids were crying. I yelled at them to get in their rooms, so he wouldn't hurt them too.

I had a busted lip, bruises all over. But I went to work the next morning—5:00 A.M., because I was opening. "I fell out of my truck," I told people. They knew I was lying. One friend offered to have her brothers kill him. "Let me think about it," I said. But I had guilt. Yes, *guilt*! That's domestic abuse. They make you feel you deserved it.

But a few days later, he starts beating up Jermey. I grabbed a boot with a thick heel and went crazy on him. Bloodied his nose, broke his finger . . . and got him off my son.

After that, I knew I had to go again—this time for good.

• • • •

I picked a night, not knowing the hurricane was coming. September 1989. Angelo got to work, and I left for home, as always. Got Gelo, drove back to work—twelve minutes—and dropped him at a pay phone nearby, in the rain. "Stay here, and when you see Dad come out, call me," I said.

I drove a 1967 Plymouth Valiant, stick shift, bought for $100. Back home, I emptied the boys' dressers into the trunk, then put Troy, Billy, and Derrick in the car. Jermey was gone—I didn't know where. I went back for Gelo. The phones had gone dead from the storm, but Angelo was still at work. We couldn't find Jermey, so I drove to a motel twenty miles away.

The next day I called home, and Jermey answered. He was in bed, terrified—school was canceled, the wind was raging, Angelo was home, plus he thought I'd left him. I said, "I'm coming back for you!" and he said, "Mom, Dad's on the extension." I hung up, then drove an hour each way, with the kids, to pick up my paycheck from the corporate office. Finally, when we saw Angelo leave for work, I got Jermey.

I wasn't scared at that point; too much adrenaline. We drove on back roads, just in case. The older boys were upset to leave their football equipment, but they knew we couldn't risk it. And once I realized what I'd done, I was terrified he'd come after me.

We headed north, because a woman at work had family in Canada who would help us if I made it there. We ate Subway for days; I had a buy-five-get-one-free card. Two nights in motels; otherwise, we just drove. But the car overheated every 100, 150 miles, despite the rain. We'd have to stop, wait, put water in.

On Sunday, September 24, 1989, I pulled off the interstate into Northampton, Massachusetts, as the radiator cap blew off—we heard it ping against the hood. I let the kids play in a park for a while, then put water in the car and prayed we'd get to the closest Motel 6, a half hour away.

We did. And there was a shelter nearby, in Greenfield—the Family Inn—that happened to have an available room with six beds. The welfare office helped us get there. I had less than $100 left, a broken car. But the place was full of kids. And locked, so no one could get in.

Still, I watched for him for months. But he didn't find us. He kidnapped my sister in Virginia just after we left—she was fifteen, with a new baby—and made her drive around with him, trying to figure out where I was. She didn't know, and he finally released her. Then he drove to my sister in Maryland, waited outside her condo till her husband came out with a shotgun. Told her he'd kill us all, then himself, when he found us.

After six weeks, I rented an apartment under section 8 housing. People helped us with clothes, food, jobs, furniture: Community Action, the Family Inn, the United Way. But I always worked. I turned thirty-three five days after we arrived. And my new life, *our* new lives, had begun. No one would treat me that way again. Not now, not ever.

• • • •

In January, with financial aid, I started at the local community college: school during the day, work afternoons, nights, and weekends. The boys were in school, Troy in day care. After school, the older ones watched the younger.

I studied for two and a half years, got associate degrees in criminal justice and liberal arts. I wanted to be a probation officer for troubled kids, but they said I needed two more years of college, at a school farther away.

So I worked at Howard Johnson's, for years—waitressing, supervising, night manager. Then, briefly, in a saw-blade factory. Boring job, shitty pay. Finally I worked for a cleaning company—the Joy of Cleaning. Ha. But I like to clean.

We cleaned five days a week, seven hours a day. We worked in two-person teams, and because of my HoJo's experience, I was the supervisor. It wasn't hard, but it paid $8 an hour—barely minimum wage. Eventually I called a few customers and said, "I'm starting my own business, less than he charges. Are you in?" They said yes.

That's how Cathy's Cleaning Crew started (a friend already had Kathy's Cleaning Crew, so I used a C). I started with five houses. Now, with one helper, I clean twelve a week. Takes about two hours per house, plus travel, so maybe thirty-five hours total. In eighteen years, I've missed only that half day I got sick. I lost forty pounds from that stomach infection. I got better, gained the weight back, and now have type 2 diabetes.

On Saturdays, I'm a personal care assistant for a neighbor. I take her shopping, and Mass Rehab pays me $10.50 an hour. That's fifteen to eighteen hours a month. The cleaning pays about $40 an hour, but my helper gets $15 and then there's gas, car payment, insurance, supplies . . . so maybe $20 after that. The first year of the business, I got audited—because I made less than before. That kills me, when there are corporations making billions.

At one point, around then, I went to night school for microeconomics. Four nights a week for a year and a half. I finished Part 1, but you couldn't get the degree without Part 2, and Part 2 wasn't offered.

I'm used to the cleaning now. But my body is failing a little, and that's scary. I have very little saved. I can't afford to stop.

• • • •

The boys mostly did great up here, thanks to sports. They're all well over six feet tall. Gelo is six-nine. The Thomas boys were known for basketball. They all graduated from high school, and most had at least some college. Gelo got a full ride to the University of Maine, though he finished closer to home. Now he teaches elementary school phys ed, runs a basketball business, and coaches high school ball. He's married with two kids, owns two houses (rents one out). Jermey has a house too. He works at a wholesale distributor—physical labor, great money. Derrick, thirty-seven, works with me, also some for Gelo. He lives at home right now. Taking a sabbatical.

The younger two, different story. Billy was the smartest of all, good-looking, fun . . . everyone loved him. But when he was twenty-three they found a tumor on his pituitary gland. They removed it, but his pituitary stopped working, and he went from happy-go-lucky to a mess. His hair fell out; the drugs made him a zombie. His work and marriage suffered. Eventually, he OD'd: eighty-six sleeping pills. He was twenty-eight, with a three-year-old. Now Caleb is nine. I have him two days a week after school.

I also have Braedyn, Troy's son, who's six. I've had weekday custody for almost three years now; his other nana has weekends. Both of Braedyn's parents have issues!

I don't have sympathy for Troy, because I believe in mind over matter. He has an easy life—his mother houses and feeds him, takes care of his kid. He works at a sandwich shop. How hard is that? All he has to do is decide he's not doing drugs anymore.

But I do sometimes think part of his problem is never really having had a father. And I was gone sixty, seventy hours a week here, working, going to school. I thought making money was the best I could do for them. But he didn't have a steady male role model.

And it's not like I couldn't have had men in my life. I had three marriage proposals here. I said no. Once you've lived with an abusive husband, it's hard to find someone you feel comfortable enough to live with, to give up your power. But I've had good boyfriends. One guy, Kurt, was great—sweet, had his own business . . . he didn't need me, but he wanted me. And most men don't have the intimacy with their kids that a woman has, but this guy did. I loved that.

After a while Troy started calling him Dad, his daughter calling me Mom. That made me nervous. I told him we needed to chill. I didn't really mean it, but this other girl pursued him, and he got her pregnant and married her. They had a son, then split up. Now his daughter sees Troy and says, I wish your mom had stayed with my dad.

I think maybe it was a mistake to lose him. I didn't need a man, but the boys could have used one. Troy, at least. Not their father, though. Not that jerk.

After Kurt, I didn't date seriously for five or six years. Then came Ed. Nice, handsome, but *so* boring. Never knew about anything happening in the world, on TV . . . all he knew was his Harley. I told him, Go spend $200 on your damn Harley and see if it keeps you warm at night. He'd come over for dinner. It was like having another child.

I quit both alcohol and men twelve years ago. I don't need a man—especially now, with my sex drive gone. So many women think if they don't have a man, they're nothing. But you need to be a whole person to invite someone into your life. You need to believe this person can help you do what *you* want—not "complete" you. An abused woman is not a whole person; if she was, she wouldn't put up with that shit. It took me escaping Angelo and starting over—with nothing—to believe in myself, to get strong.

I'm not lonely. Honestly, I've never had the time or the privacy. Once, just once, I lived alone for five months. I loved it. I painted Troy's room six shades of purple. (In another house, I painted palm trees all over the kitchen!) Now, in my two-bedroom house, Derrick has one room, Troy's on the couch, and Braedyn's in with me. I have a driveway and a yard. I have over a hundred plants, inside and out. They're one of the rare things here that's mine, even though I paid for everything. If I owned a house, I'd be in a magazine for my flowers. That'll never happen, though. I'd have to double my income *and* have two sons cosign with me.

But Braedyn's friends love this house. I treat them like my own children. I'll put a kid in time-out. My kids were raised with corporal punishment, home and school. Braedyn is my chance to do better. He told someone the other day, "My life began when I came to Mee-Maw's." That's me. He's a good kid. I'm bored when he's gone. But with the boys, the work, clipping coupons (I'm OCD about saving money) . . . I'm lucky if I get six hours of sleep.

Sometimes I ask myself, When will my life get easier? It won't.

I'm not angry, though. Or sad. Or happy, for that matter. It's just life. If Troy would straighten up, I'd be happy. But my work keeps me sane. It's my "physical therapy."

I went on antidepressants once, for about a month, after Billy died. The doctor said it would help my mood, help me lose weight, maybe help me stop smoking. It did nothing. And I don't mind smoking anyway. It's better than drinking, and it doesn't hurt anyone except me. I don't buy the stuff about secondhand smoke— although I did cut back when I got Braedyn. But everyone deserves some pleasure in their life.

Massachusetts is okay, though full of liberals. I'm a registered independent. I loved Jimmy Carter—he gave a shit—but I sometimes vote Republican, because I don't like the government telling me what to do. Don't tell me I have to wear a seat belt. It's my life. Yes, the shelter helped me, but I got out and never went back. I know women who go in and out without good reason. People mostly take the easier road if they can. The woman I help on Saturdays is my age. She gets SSI disability, but she walks to CVS, and she's not stupid, so surely she can do *something*. She has cable TV, an air conditioner. But it's easier for the government to give people money and forget 'em. I have a problem with that. That, and them choosing *me* to audit. But yes, I still have section 8 housing. I claim between $8,500 and $9,500 a year. And I have a dependent.

But it's not like I think everything Republicans say is the Bible either. Of course women should have a choice about abortion! But that doesn't mean someone should have three or four of them.

I believe in heaven and hell, and I raised my kids to believe there's a God, but that person can do only so much, and then it's up to you. If you do something bad, it'll come back and bite you in the ass. And hard work is good.

But I don't know how much longer I can clean houses. If I start collecting Social Security at sixty-two, I'd get $725 a month. My car payment alone is $300 a month, not including $70 for insurance. And Braedyn's only six. I'll be dead before he's raised. I'd better be. I don't want to live to more than seventy, because I don't want to be taken care of. If I get to that point, hand me the sleeping pills.

I've been up here twenty-six years, so I guess I'm staying. My life has always been chaotic. But I'm very strong mentally. That's my biggest strength. And I'm not afraid of anyone. Not since I got away from that bastard. He did eventually figure out where we were. He called once, after six or seven years. I answered, and he said, "Kathy." I felt only rage. I said, "What the hell do *you* want?" He wanted to wish Troy happy birthday. I said, "It's ten o'clock on a school night. He's asleep, you stupid son of a bitch." Then I hung up. He died two years ago, and I celebrated. Someday I'll go piss on his grave. But for now, I've got too much to do. Work, and otherwise.

# 2

# Sex, Lies, and Happy(ish) Endings

## BECAUSE THIS AIN'T DISNEY, DOLLS. IT'S LIFE.

*Love and lust are inseparable parts of a larger whole for some, while for others they are irretrievably disconnected. Most of us, however, express our eroticism elsewhere in the gray areas where love and lust both relate and conflict.*
—*Jack Morin,* The Erotic Mind

# The Coming of Age
## Sex 102

**SARAH CRICHTON**

As my marriage of thirty-odd years was exploding in a spectacular fashion, I said to my therapist, "Well, one good thing is going to come of this. I'm going to have a sex life again."

I hadn't planned on saying this. I'm not sure I was conscious of even having thought it. But out it came. "You know why?" I said.

"Because you like sex," he said.

"Yes."

"Oh, for Pete's sake," says my friend Mary. "I am so sick of aging women who boast about how much they still like sex."

Believe me, I am not boasting. But when you did enjoy something (like a sex life) and someone (like your husband) took it away from you (when? only the assiduous journal keepers among us ever record the final fuck), you do have a hankering to get it back in your life.

Let's paint this picture: You are no spring chicken. In fact, you are in spitting distance of sixty. Over the years, your husband has taken to accepting work that takes him farther and farther from home, and longer and longer to complete, until one day he just doesn't come back. "Sweets," he writes, "got to see a man in Bratislava. Wi-Fi spotty; will try to Skype soon." He never does.

The man in Bratislava turns out to be a Czech boutique owner in her thirties. But let's get back to me.

My world collapses. But in short order I get something extraordinary: a handsome widower who is ready to be happy again. He will woo me with flirty e-mails and surprisingly thoughtful gifts. He will call me his "sweet angel," but of course he's not the only one being saved. And there will be sex. I want to say a lot of it, but then my teenage self looks down on me with a cocked brow. Okay, fine: There will be *plenty* of sex.

But before there can be sex, there are—there must be—The Preparations for Sex.

• • • •

The handsome widower lived in one state, I in another, and we met in a third, at a dinner party (thrown by a mutual friend). He was ten years older than me—so, getting on in age and a bit stooped, but still lean, and I could tell he liked sex by the way he kissed my cheek at the end of the night, and he could tell I liked sex, he later said, by the way my hand lingered on his back as he proffered that kiss.

He sent me an e-mail. He would soon be passing through town, he wrote. Would I be interested in dinner and a play? This was exciting stuff! No longer young, not yet divorced, and already I was being asked out.

"You will not sleep with him on the first night," my friend Stella told me firmly. I was camped out in her apartment, in exile as my future ex-husband, back from God knows where, took over our home to sift through thirty years of belongings, ferreting out what he wanted in his new life.

Stella and I go way back. She knew me in the reckless seventies, and she was a step ahead of me now, because, while her long relationship had ended a few years ago, she was in love again. She had both old and new wisdom to share.

"I don't care how much you drink," she said, "and you can kiss him—kissing's fine, kissing's good—but that's it, Sarah."

Wait. What was she saying? That it's my inclination to be a slut? That I—

"I'm saying you're not ready yet."

Ah.

What Stella was saying was that women's bodies that have not connected for some time with other bodies lose the physical memory of sex. And she was surmising: *The last time you had sex was before you went through menopause, and here you are on the other side of the great divide, and your body probably needs some help getting ready for what it is you think you may want to do.*

But I knew Stella was wrong about me. Here's why: I happened to have had a gynecologist appointment that very week. "I've met a man," I told my doctor. She poked around, and she smiled. "You are good to go!" My doctor is on Park Avenue; she's fancy. You should have seen me sashay down the street that afternoon. *Lookee here! My husband may have gone walkabout, and I may be postmenopausal—but, baby, I am good to go!*

"Really? That's what she told you?" Stella looked askance. "Huh. She's wrong."

I was offended. What did my friend know about the inner workings of my body? Maybe other women go dry. Maybe a lack of visitation causes *their* muscles to lose a lusty spring, whereas mine—

I visited myself that night, if only to prove my friend wrong, but . . . Oh. Whatever readiness my gynecologist had found eluded me. Where my hand landed, where once it had been as inviting as Gauguin's Tahiti, was now as . . . well . . . I'll tell you many things, but I won't tell you that. But it was frighteningly clear that even if I was determined to sleep with a near-stranger on a first date (and at my age, why the hell not? At what age do you no longer have a reputation to protect?), even if I was willing to throw my body down, I was not, at this moment, ready to receive guests.

When had the welcoming port to my being pulled up the plank? Where was I when this happened? Asleep? Alone, at least. That much I know. I was alone when it happened.

Oh, the degradations of inattention! It isn't so much time that does us in, I think, as being ignored as time glides along. Toward the end of my marriage I had begun to feel like a wife in a 1950s comic strip. "Let's see if he notices this haircut!" "I wonder if he'll comment on my new glasses!" There was an upside to this, of course. There are some changes you'd prefer no one monitor. "You look fine," my husband would say, in part because he wasn't looking.

Now I stand in black underwear before a full-length mirror, and I *do* look fine. The misery of recent years has inadvertently served me well. The lack of an appetite has slimmed me. The highlights to hide the hair shocked gray are "pizzazzy," says my mother-in-law. (She's southern. And yes, technically she's my *ex*-mother-in-law, but not in either of our hearts.) It startles me, this body, simultaneously young and old, smooth and loose, taut and round. The wear of six decades is inescapable: I am crisscrossed with scars, peppered with moles. But the spirit and the power of my younger self, the twenty-eight-year-old woman who could feel heads turn as she walked by, is still very much present, in the long legs, the broad shoulders, the narrow wrists that I have always loved because they are the only parts of me that ever seemed petite. If I spotted this woman striding down a French beach in a bikini, I would marvel, "Look at that attractive older woman, so comfortable in her own skin!" (Okay, maybe not marvel. But note affirmatively, I like to think.)

If my date with the handsome widower goes well, there will likely be another, and eventually the time will come when all these scars, these imperfections and more, will be exposed. And you know what? That will be fine. "Really," says a friend, "by the time you take your clothes off, men are so grateful to have you naked they don't care *what* you look like." I will bank on that too.

• • • •

I am a good student. If I'm dreaming of having sex in this new older body, I will learn how it works, and how his works as well. On the AARP website I call up "How Sex Changes for Men after 50" and find this: "It becomes less like the Fourth of July, and more like Thanksgiving." That's not really the fun I had in mind, but it's a hell of a lot better than the postmenopausal kicks promised on a popular woman's site: "We do wacky things, wear purple, or join Red Hat Societies."

I don't want to be wacky. I want to have sex.

I go to WebMD and mayoclinic.org. I am ill prepared for the horror of it: *vaginal atrophy, thinning tissue, penetration pain* . . . Dear God. Maybe it's too late for me. Maybe this is not to be.

"Poor Cinderelly!" says the sad little mouse in the Disney movie. "Cinderelly not go to the ball." It is a very poignant moment. But you know what happens next? The other little mice and bluebirds of happiness spring into action—and they save Cinderella.

In my story, it is the Sisterhood of the Still Sexually Active that rushes to my aid. I started to write "the small Sisterhood," but really, you rarely know who among your friends is sexually active. And what is "active"? Every wedding anniversary or every Sunday? As my marriage came unglued and I shared intimate truths with dearest friends, they offered me glimmers into their lives, and I was dazed by the spectrum of behavior. Some long-married friends were having sex faithfully—once a week, even twice, and more on holiday—while others who I'd assumed led lively lives turned out not to have been intimate in decades.

"There's absolutely no norm," I said to my therapist.

He nodded.

"I mean, the only norm seems to be that you either think you're the norm or fear you're not."

He nodded again. "And the norm changes."

Yes. What was normal for my body forty, twenty, even five years ago isn't now. Will this new body like what it once liked? Will it respond as it used to? What if I'm now just . . . a cuddler? And this new body of mine will engage with a sixty-eight-year-old man. What if *he*'s just a cuddler? So much is unknown.

The Sisterhood steps in with practical wisdom. They debate lubricants, weigh in on waxing. (Friend one: "At our age, Brazilians are a seriously bad idea." Friend two: "Brazilians can be a fun change of pace.") If my goal is to return to an easy state of play, I need to consider hormone replacement therapy. My friends demystify this low-dose, local estrogen and break down the differences between tablets, creams, patches, rings. To get me started, a beloved buddy offers me spare sticks of Vagifem, much as she used to slip me Percocets in the old days. "Amp up!" she says. "It will take weeks, even months, but you'll get there, girl!"

* * * *

I have my date. It goes swimmingly. He worries I haven't ordered enough dinner and feeds me meat off his plate. He leans in at the punch lines of the play, and afterward, dazzles me with magic tricks at a bar as we sip limoncello, which I pretend to like. At the end of the night, in a subway station in Times Square, we embrace and promise to see each other again.

"Stella!" I exclaim as I get home. "I need new underwear!"

"I wouldn't worry about that. At our age, you don't spend a lot of time prancing around."

Oh.

"But there is this other matter we haven't discussed."

In essence, what Stella asks is this: You are thinking of entertaining again; you are ready to invite a gentleman caller into, let's say, your private chambers. If (to keep the euphemism rolling) he shows up at your door with a large piece of furniture, hoping to move it in, will there be room for it?

That night I visit myself again, this time in order to explore dimensions.

Damn.

Stella can read the dismay on my face the next morning, but as always she takes matters in hand. "This is completely solvable. Just get out your vibrator—"

My vibrator.

Her eyes widen. "You don't have one?"

I glare across the room. I am sick of having to learn about what once came so naturally. And if Stella evinces a scintilla of pity, I will pop her.

Of course, looking at it objectively, this is not punishment. I'm not being ordered to run laps or lift weights. It is simply being suggested that if I want to get key muscles back in shape, stretched and toned, after a long period of disuse, then there's a method (masturbation) and a means (a vibrator).

But which vibrator? I am, as I've said, a good student who appreciates homework, and I am not an impulse shopper. So I do my usual when shopping for any piece of equipment: I log on to ConsumerReports.com. But alas, their V listings cover only vacuum cleaners and video game consoles; there are no vibrators here.

I Google, I Yelp, and I finally hit the mother lode at Babeland, a women-friendly sex shop, which has not only a snappy and informative website but an actual brick-and-mortar shop not far from where I live. I can do my research online, in the privacy of my own room—and then shop locally!

I study the Customer Pick reviews, peek at the "luxury vibrators," quail at the strap-on cocks, narrow my choices, then head to the store. Within minutes, its supremely knowledgeable saleswomen exhaust me: I don't want to discuss what I'm "looking for in a vibrator." I grab the cutest of the bunch. Barney purple and nurse white, it promises cheery fun, not scary times. It's not cheap—$149!—but this is an investment in my future.

Stella is at the kitchen table, playing Words with Friends and sipping espresso, when I return. "Good for you!" she says. "Let's take a look."

I sigh and pull out my new toy.

Flipping it over in the palm of her hand, she says gently, "It's quite small, isn't it?" With a jolt I realize that it is indeed downright Lilliputian. Truth be told, if the handsome widower turns out to have an erect penis the size of this vibrator, I may want to reconsider my options.

Back to Babeland I go for a more practical practice penis. I find Boss Naked. It's a massively manly thing (8¾ inches long and 1½ inches thick), but it is smooth, almost velvety, with a pretty ridge, and I find I'm oddly moved by it, this disembodied erect joint looking for a home. It comes in two colors—a pink ("vanilla") and a gentle brown ("caramel"), which, I don't why, calls out to me—but I am on a mission to prepare for a pinkish person, so I opt for Mr. Vanilla (a more-affordable-than-last-time $69).

As I pay up, they award me a bonus gift for being such a good Babeland customer: a vibrator. It is turquoise and tacky, and for a while I snub it. But in the end, it turns out to be just the right size for me.

•  •  •  •

The handsome widower invites me to join him on a road trip. My spirit is willing, but my body still isn't ready. I stall for time.

I train and I study.

I once knew how to do things that men liked. But what were those things? Hand jobs: What makes for a good one, again? This, I do realize, is basic technique—like boiling an egg, or working with dough. But conquer the fundamentals, and it's cordon bleu time. I have become dependent on YouTube for cooking instruction, so I assume—correctly, it turns out—that I can find other instructional videos there. I will not tell you precisely what I search for or click on. But I will have you know that even in my amnesiac state I am more advanced than most self-videotaping teens molesting vegetables in their bedrooms.

Happily, there are also thoughtful, informational videos to be found, and they reawaken the part of my brain where sexual knowledge (and confidence) has been in deep storage. Praying my twentysomething daughter never borrows my computer and finds them, I download two well-executed videos narrated by a woman with a plummy English accent. I have to pay for them, but I don't begrudge a cent.

• • • •

In all training there comes a watershed moment when you know your efforts are producing results. A runner's high kicks in. A six-pack emerges from the waistband of your jeans. Your legs float up in a teaser. My moment comes on a cool September evening when the sun is getting low over Smith Street in Brooklyn, and I am walking home, and suddenly I begin—I swear—to actually *bounce*. From deep inside me comes a pulsing energy. On a Google map from outer space it would read as a hot spot.

We always talk about what's in men's pants, because it's so hard to ignore. From sixth grade on, there are these lumpy shapes that start shifting—in khakis! in denim!—at any given moment. At some point, a nice teacher or someone (certainly not my mother) explains erections. But there's a lot that goes on in women's pants too; you just can't see it. And here I am—a long way past adolescence—with this newly awakened nexus, fulcrum, pivot point, and it's making my hips swing, and I think, *Welcome back, body! Welcome back, self.*

• • • •

The handsome widower has a new proposal: meet him in a distant city to view a controversial art installation. At last, I am fully prepared.

In the weeks before I join him, I think about sex nonstop; my head is a naughty playground. In the morning, men on the subway rise to offer me their seats, and I offer them grateful middle-aged smiles, thinking, "Gentlemen, if you had *any* idea."

I recall being sixteen and in love for the first time with a sweet boy who would convince himself every time I got sick that I was dying, and then run away from boarding school and hitchhike to see me. What I knew of sex was mostly stumbled across in books ("Betty bled like a stuck pig") or somehow intuited. I remember a shack off a beach on a stupefyingly hot day, and swimming down sweat-soaked sheets to blow streams of cooling air on my beloved's penis, erect in that hilariously ebullient fashion that I'll never get to see again. I blew and I blew. Propped on his elbows, he looked down on me gently but quizzically.

"What are you doing?" he asked.

"Giving you a blow job."

I don't think he ever told me point-blank that my technique was off by a few key inches, but he repositioned me (what a surprise, that!), and trusting him, I learned well.

Now, preparing to be with a new man, I remind myself that

we're always having to learn, and if you've trusted once, you can trust again. I will soon find other things too that don't fundamentally change. Bodies, however wrecked and different they may be from their smooth-celled early selves, remain transporting and beautiful. When I am finally naked with the handsome widower and brave enough to open my eyes, I am staggered by the grace of two well-used bodies fused together. And I remain profoundly moved by, and grateful for, the sound of a man coming in my arms. The vulnerability and the ultimate intimacy of sex is even more profound when you've lost more than you ever thought you could lose, and at this age, we have all lost too much.

· · · ·

Our first New Year's Eve together, six months into the courtship, the handsome widower and I rendezvous in Denver, a city neither of us knows and both are curious to explore. Heading out to dinner in our black going-to-town outfits ("You look like a mobster and his moll," writes a friend when we text him a photo), we stand out—in part because we seem to be the only people in Denver who think you are supposed to dress up for New Year's Eve, even at the city's best restaurant. But it's also because we glow. We are in love, and we have spent the afternoon rolling around on a king-size hotel bed, during which time, in a moment of enthusiasm, he tucked his still very strong arm under my still very long legs and tossed them, emphatically, up over my head, and I became a human conch shell, swirled around myself. I was proud at that moment: *I am still bendy! Thank god for Pilates!* I also thought: *This is something he used to do, years ago.* And: *But is it right for now?*

I wake in the middle of the night on fire—not with lust, but with searing pain. My lower back, hips, legs . . . agony. I swallow four Advil and slide to the cold floor to try to stretch. Failing that, I roll over balls of socks to massage pressure points. Nothing works.

The handsome widower has bent me back too far, and my aging spine can't take it.

When my love finally wakes, he looks quietly alarmed. I think it's about me down here on the floor, but it's not. His heart is doing strange flips. From where I lie, I see him check his pulse; apparently I'm not the only one we have overexerted. We turn on Turner Classic Movies for distraction, and we wait for the dawn.

In the morning we ease ourselves into a taxi and get to the airport. He is flying to his city and his doctors, I to mine.

The next day, at the physiatrist, I am asked: Complaint? Acute back pain. Probable cause? Overly exciting sex. I wait for the doctor to smile, but he is too well trained to respond off script. Either that, or he sees this all the time. This is sciatica; my fifth lumbar vertebra is inflamed. He prescribes physical therapy and ice, maybe a cortisone shot. "You should be okay before long," he says.

Meanwhile, the handsome widower is at his cardiologist's. They review his various meds, put him through a stress test. I talk to him that night. "What did she say?"

"Good news," he says. "I'm good to go."

• • • •

And so he was, for another two years, until one evening on the phone he stunned me, saying, "I don't think I want this."

What *this*? A long-distance romance? Or someone like me?

A week before, in his town, in his bed, I had lovingly swum down his sheets and attended to his needs. Now, as he stammered out an end for us, I thought, *Are you nuts? You're on the cusp of seventy, and you want to give this up?* But I guess he was a better man than I, because he wasn't blinded by the sex. His feelings for me were beginning to wane, and he could no longer pretend this was the life he desired.

I will not lie: It hurt deeply. I had felt it a miracle to be swept away and returned to my sexual self: a miracle to lie in someone's arms and feel safe, an even greater miracle to lie in someone's arms and feel alive. I was loath to see that go. But I suppose miraculous moments are by nature transitory; what counts is the transformation that comes with them. The burning bush points the way, ultimately, to the land of milk and honey.

In the last years of my disappearing marriage to my disappearing husband, I felt lost in the desert. But I found myself again—through love, yes, but also through sex. Milk and honey. I can't know what comes next, but I do know this: I am sixty-one years old, and there is love in my future, and beauty, and sex—raw and caring and naked and alive, and age-appropriate. And when it comes, I will be prepared.

# Still in the Heart

## HAZEL MCCLAY

*Hazel McClay's piece in* The Bitch in the House, *called "A Man in the Heart," was about falling in love with a man with whom she did not have passionate sex. "This is about sex," she wrote in, and about, that essay. "It is also about love. I have never had the pleasure of confusing the two." Here's her update.*

First things first: Hazel McClay is not my real name. I am a private person, and my husband even more private, so in order to be honest, I won't reveal myself or him, just as I didn't fourteen years ago.

Back then, I wrote about my boyfriend, whom I called Charlie, and our lackluster sex life. I was thirty-six at the time. Two years later, I married Charlie. I got pregnant on our honeymoon, and the following year, I gave birth to our son. Charlie and I are still married, and our marriage is as comfortable and happy as any I know of. Our child is thriving. We travel when we can, work when we can't, watch TV when we're too exhausted to do anything else, and laugh—a lot. Like any family unit, ours has developed its own private and idiosyncratic language. Mornings find us all crammed in the bathroom, jabbering away together before we disperse for the day. When we come back together at day's end, that private and largely ridiculous dialogue resumes with more laughter, always laughter, which leavens every situation, no matter how annoying (tax time), mundane (teeth brushing, laundry), or lowly (toilet plunging). Who is to thank for the laughter? Nine times out of ten, it's Charlie, one of the funniest people I've ever known.

With Charlie, I felt, and still feel, like somebody in the world gets me; I feel, at the risk of sounding clichéd, loved for exactly who I am. This is something that was missing in every relationship I had before him, including the ones that were filled with sexual passion. For me, sexual passion, while not exactly ubiquitous, was easier to find than understanding. Until Charlie. Within weeks of meeting him, I loved him—his brain, his quirks, his humor, and the grounded way he made me feel. I still do.

What I didn't feel with Charlie was sexual passion. It wasn't that the sex we had was bad, but as I wrote it then: "This man has never wrapped me in his arms, never covered my mouth with his and kissed me until I gasped for breath. I have never forgotten where I was when we made love, or not cared. We do not tear off each other's clothes. We do not make love often, never have, and, I suspect, never will."

Fourteen years later, I'm here to tell you that my prediction was right, at least so far. We still have sex, but not often, and not passionately. "Charlie and I don't 'need' sex to connect," I wrote then, "and since sex was not what attracted me to him in the first place, I don't really crave it. This doesn't mean it doesn't feel nice to hug him, or to sleep next to him, or to feel his warm naked body against mine. It just means that I get enough from him without this, and often, if not usually, I'm just as happy to sleep in my pj's and go to bed with a book. Is this a problem? Depends how you look at it."

Staring down age fifty, I feel exactly the same as I did at thirty-six. Our relationship lacks sexual desire—something crucial for a good romance novel, but not for me. What's changed between then and now, besides our becoming parents, is what we've seen going on around us: one marriage after another washing up on the rocks. Divorce after divorce—couples falling like dominoes—while we, despite never tearing each other's clothes off, despite not having sex every week (or two), remain pretty darn happy.

I'm not saying that everyone should try a relationship like ours. I'm not saying that now and then, a dream or a movie scene doesn't make me miss what Charlie and I don't have. What I'm saying is that I'm willing to forgo that kind of passion if it means that I get to spend my life with Charlie.

. . . .

When our son was still a toddler, I joined a book group composed mostly of mothers of young children. Whoever hosted a session picked the book, and one month, the hostess picked *The Bitch in the House*. The book had been out for about five years at that point, and in all that time, I had never talked about it, or my essay in it, with anyone, including Charlie.

*This should be interesting*, I thought when I heard the selection. And it was.

We didn't have time to discuss all the essays, but we spent a good chunk of time on a piece about open marriage, which scandalized some of our members. Sex sells for a reason, of course. But although my essay was about sex as well, I was surprised when one of the mothers brought it up.

She said she'd loved the essay. She said she'd connected with it, that it reminded her of her own situation. I was gratified, even delighted—a kindred spirit!—but as she talked on, I realized that her situation was not the same as mine after all.

She had saved herself for marriage, she said, and at first they had struggled with the sex. Without giving specifics, she said that things had gotten better over time. They had grown more comfortable with each other physically, gained carnal knowledge, and as a result, worked it out.

I sat, hot-faced and silent, wondering how my essay had been so misunderstood. Her sex life sounded nothing like mine. For starters, I hadn't saved myself for marriage. Far from it. I'd had plenty of sex with plenty of guys, and some of it was excellent. Sex with Charlie was not excellent, but that wasn't because we needed to grow comfortable with each other. We were very comfortable with each other, almost from the start. Too comfortable, maybe. How do you work that out?

Meanwhile, this poor woman at the mommy book club had laid out her sex life only to be met with silence. No one (including me) came forth to back her up with a single "me too." I knew why I kept silent, but what about everyone else? Was it because nobody wanted to spill the beans? Or was it because everyone else in the room had a fantastic sex life and didn't want to brag?

I'll never know. When no one came to her rescue, she wound up by returning to my essay. "This sounds like a wonderful relationship," she said.

I smiled at her. I nodded. The woman seated beside me spoke under her breath. "Sounds like a boring relationship to me," she said.

Then she and the woman on her other side burst out laughing.

Now, instead of feeling misunderstood, I felt anxious. Could it be that she was right? *Was* my marriage boring? Maybe the fact that I wasn't bored by it simply proved that *I* was boring. I had thought I'd been around the block enough times to know true love when I saw it, but for the rest of that day, and a few to follow, I wondered if I was missing out on that magical package, profound fulfillment on every front. Is that what these women had?

Turns out they did not. A few months later, the woman who'd

laughed about my relationship started an affair—with the husband of the woman who'd laughed along with her.

When I learned this news, I was not pleased. Not quite. There
were young children in both families, and spouses who felt betrayed. Friends of both families were forced to take sides. Children
were routed to alternate schools. One marriage ended in divorce.

I did feel vindicated, though. I felt as if my thinking about sex
had been proven out yet again. Virtually everyone I know who
claims to have an exciting sex life—the ones who are married
with kids, anyway—also seems to have turmoil and unhappiness
in their marriage.

I'm sure there are exceptions to this formula. There must be. For
instance, the woman who spoke up at the meeting in the first place
seemed to suggest that the more time she spent with her husband,
the better their sex life became. I believe her, but this hasn't been
my experience or the experience of most of the women I know.

• • • •

About the same time my book group read *The Bitch in the House*, I
saw an ad in the local paper. Some company was looking for women
with low sex drives to try out a new drug that, the company hoped,
would increase their libido.

In the beginning, I'd attributed my lack of desire to my particular chemistry with Charlie. As time went by, though, and I didn't
find myself attracted to anyone else, I had begun to wonder if my
lack of interest in sex might be physiological—not psychological,
or however one categorizes desire. What if this drug threw a switch
in my body, and after years, I was suddenly horny again?

It wasn't that Charlie was asking for more sex; he wasn't, but
that seemed like my doing. He'd never asked for lots, but over time,
he'd stopped asking at all. "Whenever you're ready" was his motto,

and I couldn't help noticing that *whenever* I was ready, so was he. This worried me. How patient could one guy be? For how long?

So I signed on for the study and started the trial.

The drug—which I now know was likely flibanserin (or something similar), which has since been put on the market, surrounded by much controversy about both its effectiveness (low) and its side effects (substantial)—didn't work. It didn't make me feel more desire for Charlie, or, as far as I could tell, for anyone else. It did make my brain feel fuzzy and impaired, but in my experience, it is good sex that impairs the brain—and pleasantly—not the other way around. At any rate, I bailed on the study after a few months and stopped taking the drug.

I thought nothing more about drugs and sex drive for the next five years. Then, at a women's wellness exam, the nurse practitioner asked about my birth control and seemed surprised when I told her about our primitive methods—a simple blend of the rhythm method and withdrawal. I explained that my husband and I had sex infrequently, and because of this, our methods had it covered.

She asked why the sex was infrequent. I said I wasn't into sex. She seemed surprised again, and now *I* was surprised. I wanted to run my own set of questions past her.

*So, like, you're into sex? With your husband? Wow. Is that great?*

But I minded my own business. I played it cool. We were there to talk about me. Then she asked if I wanted to see someone about my "low libido."

*Libido!* I hadn't thought about that word since my drug trial, but once again, I liked the sound of it. It made my condition sound so medical, so not my fault. I wanted to want more sex, sure, but I also wanted to stop feeling like I was to blame for shortchanging my favorite man in the world. Drug trials and medical terms seemed to shift that blame away from me, or the essential being I thought of as me, and onto my body.

Meanwhile, the nurse practitioner had moved on to her next question: Did I want to see a specialist?

*A specialist? For women? Women and sex?* No one had ever told me such a thing existed.

"Sure," I said.

• • • •

A week or two later, the specialist summoned me into his office. It wasn't much different from a regular exam room, but this exam was psychological in nature—not what I'd expected. We talked about my low sex drive. Unlike the female nurse practitioner, the male doctor seemed unsurprised by what I had to say. He asked why I thought I'd lost interest in sex.

I explained a bit about my history. True, I had never been deeply attracted to Charlie, sexually speaking, but even with men to whom I was, the power of sex in the relationship, and the appeal of sex overall, had waned for me over time. Charlie was the only man I had ever known who I thought I could be with forever.

I told the doctor that my theory about sex is that some people—most people, I suspect—thrive on diversity. If they can't have diversity, then they settle for novelty toys or lingerie . . . or, as in my case, something other than sex entirely.

The specialist pointed to his head. "Ninety percent of sex," he said, "is up here."

I nodded. I think maybe I agreed, but it didn't matter. My brain's never been much for taking orders from my heart or vice versa. They have an uneasy truce.

That's when the specialist told me there was no FDA-approved drug for women. This was no revelation, of course. I thought back to the drug trial I'd taken part in five years before. Looked like I wasn't the only woman who hadn't seen great results from that drug.

However, he continued, there was a testosterone cream I could rub into my thighs each night before bed. A compounding pharmacy could make it for me, and the testosterone might boost my sex drive. He'd been prescribing it to women for years, he said, and some had seen positive results.

It seemed to me that if enough women had seen these positive results, the drug would probably be a household name by now. Still, I had come this far. Did I want to try this mysterious cream?

"Sure," I said.

An hour later, I walked into the compounding pharmacy, past the therapeutic shoes, and placed my order. I brought the cream home and showed it to Charlie, explaining how the testosterone might make me grow more hair on my upper lip and in certain other private places.

When I told him my voice might deepen, Charlie started laughing.

So did I. "What may happen," I said, "is that as I turn into a man, I want to have sex more, but you no longer want to have sex with *me*."

He laughed again. "Honey." He spoke in a gravelly voice like Marge's chain-smoking sisters on *The Simpsons*. "Let's get it on."

I started using the cream that very night. At first I was faithful in my inside-the-thighs applications, but as the weeks went by and nothing happened, I grew spotty. Sporadic. A little like my sex life. Perhaps I could've gone back to the doctor and had him ratchet up the testosterone ratio, but in the meantime I heard a news story about testosterone use in men and increased risk of cancer . . . and got a medical bill for $800. I had stupidly assumed that my visit to the specialist would be covered by the same insurance that covered the nurse practitioner who had referred me.

Cancer isn't sexy. Neither is negotiating medical bills. And of course, I'd never had much faith in the cream to begin with. Soon enough, I stopped using that drug too.

· · · ·

Meanwhile, everywhere I turned I was, and still am, bombarded with ads for Viagra or other male-equivalent drugs to boost sexual performance, and now we also have ads for flibanserin for women, which I suspect, from both my own experience and what I read about it, simply doesn't work. The fact is, lack of desire—one of women's main sexual complaints in long-term relationships—is simply harder to solve than men's failure to perform. I wish it weren't so. At the same time—and I say this even though I've tried drugs twice—I'd rather not have to take a drug in order to feel desire. It's a little too *Brave New World* for my taste.

I can see reading this to a roomful of people, and having some nice person—possibly a therapist—suggest that we try sex therapy. I guess to that I'd say, "Why?" Between the sheets, Charlie does a lot of things right. He goes down on me. He lets me be on top or bottom . . . whatever seems like it's going to work that time. In a way, our sex life is highly functional. I have more orgasms with him than with any man before him. But in my experience, orgasms and desire (or passion) do not go hand in hand. And in an ideal world, "functional" is not the first adjective most people would want to apply to their sex life.

I'm sure sex therapy can help fuel desire for some people—depending on their definition of desire. For me, desire, like passion, stems partly from mystery. And mystery and therapy seem to me like two horses trying to pull one body in opposite directions. Mystery and *power*—now, there's a combination that seems to me to work together. In my experience, there's a power dynamic that accompanies the most intoxicating sex that's got nothing to do with love or harmony; power never does, really. I'm not even sure love and the kind of desire I'm talking about can coexist—not a sustainable love, at least, the kind that keeps on working, rain or shine, year after year.

• • • •

Even though I've lost interest in sex, I have not lost respect for it. I understand why it's high on the totem pole of priorities for some people. For me, most days, I regard my sexuality in the same light that I imagine some priests or nuns might. I am sure there are plenty who, despite taking a vow of celibacy, nonetheless retain sexual desires year after year, but I also suspect that for others, after years of neglect, those desires might atrophy and die. This is not a tragedy, in my view, because I don't consider sexual desire or activity essential to being human. Sure, sex is by and large essential to maintaining the human race (seven billion and counting), but not to a meaningful life. Not mine, anyway.

I'm not a nun, though, so it's not that simple. Part of being human, for me, is loving Charlie. Who still likes sex. Who would miss it if we stopped having it. We have never had a brass-tacks, meat-and-potato conversation about exactly how much sex he wants. "Whenever you're ready," he says, so I try to be ready now and then, and to let him know when I am. Otherwise, he doesn't complain, ask, wheedle, or whine. He is dignified in this, as in many other matters. He gives me room to breathe. These are two more reasons I love him.

I do have one piece of information, though, that he doesn't know I have, and it concerns his sex life with his first wife (I'm his second). Apropos of nothing, one night an old friend of Charlie's told me that Charlie's first wife thought he might be gay, because she wanted more sex than he did.

I have never met Charlie's first wife, but I do know that back when they were married, they were young and poor, and he worked three jobs. I know they were trying to fix up a little starter home, so whenever he did have a day off, he was doing home improvements. I know (from his mother, not from him) that each time he mowed their lawn, his first wife made him mow it twice, in beautiful crisscrossing strips. I know he was tired all the time.

Maybe all this affected his sex drive, or maybe she pushed him for sex in a way that made him not want it. At any rate, this little bit of unasked-for gossip about my husband doesn't make me think he's gay. It makes me think that his sex drive—the amount he needs, likes, or wants—may be lower than a lot of men's. Tired or not, annoyed or not, many men still want sex on a regular basis. So if Charlie isn't one of those men, all I can say is, good. Something that sounds like it was a problem in his old marriage is a blessing in mine—one more of the many ways we're compatible. When we do have sex, I do my best to be an active participant, not just someone along for the ride. In fact, I enjoy the sex more that way, but I never crave sex, so if I never had it again, I don't think I'd miss it. If I never had another brownie, now, that would bum me out.

What I do miss, though, is how passion used to feel: that amplified sensation of being so lost in someone that you forget where you are, so turned on by someone that your bones seem to melt away underneath your skin. I haven't forgotten, and every so often—reading a particular passage in a book, maybe, or seeing a young man on a motorcycle who reminds me of one of my old flames—I suddenly find myself twenty-five years back in time. Then, for a moment, I'm sad. Then, for a brief moment, I feel I've lost something.

After all, passion is a powerful drug, and we all love to feel swept away. But like any sweet high, is it sustainable? Is it meant to be? The first taste is free (if you're lucky), but at some point, maintaining that high costs more and more, until it costs too much—at least for my budget.

. . . .

You can always ask more out of life. Sometimes you should. But of all the things you can know about yourself, one of the best is knowing when you've got enough—when "enough" is really everything; when to tell the proverbial dealer you're good, to cash in your chips and head home.

I'm good. I'm heading home. And when I get there, Charlie will be waiting.

# My Filthy Little Heart

## Love It? Or Lose It?

**CLAIRE JOHNSON**

grew up in Manhattan in the seventies and eighties, with my mother and two brothers—one older, one younger. My mother was a precocious farm girl from Vermont who started college at sixteen, got pregnant at eighteen, had a shotgun wedding, and moved to New York with her then husband, who she dumped before my older brother, William, was two. Besides being smart, my mother was beautiful, and some of her first work was as a model. I have a picture of her taken by a photographer at *Vogue* when she was six months pregnant with me, holding Will, who was four at the time. You can barely notice her baby bump, and her smile is both provocative and innocent: the original MILF. In fact, fucking was something she did often and with many different men in her life, and for decades I assumed this was because she wanted to. Only recently did she tell me she did it mostly because she felt that, in order to be a "gracious hostess," she had to. I smiled a little when she said that; it was yet another way we were, and are, opposites. In her forties, she fucked regularly yet rarely wanted to, while I want to regularly and rarely do. Then again, she spent many years unmarried, and I've been married for more than two decades. The question is how much longer I can stay that way without physical contact. I'm only now starting to figure out the answer.

· · · ·

By the time my mother married my father, she'd finished college—commuting to a prestigious school just outside the city—and had some success as a poet. She wanted to be a writer, not a wife, but the combination of early motherhood and the constraints of the 1960s led her quickly back to the altar, and soon she and my father—a handsome Republican stockbroker from Harvard—had a place on Park Avenue, and then me, and then my younger brother, James. Mom had several affairs during their union and left my dad after six years for a married man, keeping my brothers and me, though not necessarily by choice. (Back then, no divorce court gave the kids to the father.) I remember, toward the end, my father sitting alone in the dark watching Nixon on TV while my mother laughed with friends in the well-lit dining room as they assembled McGovern signs. Though I adored them both at that time, their conflicts and differences were painfully apparent to me, even as a kindergartner. I felt bereft for my dad, and I went to sit on his lap so he wouldn't be sad or the only Nixon fan in the house. But then he was gone, along with his loneliness, and by the time he disappeared into the elevator with his expensive leather bags, my mother had already moved on.

· · · ·

It was 1972 at that point. I was six. And predictably, the married man my mother left for stayed married, and she, in the soul-crushed aftermath, hit the party circuit hard. She was a regular at the hot clubs—the Factory, Studio 54, CBGB—and by the time I was twelve, she was taking me along with her. She had an endless line of boyfriends, and I had it on good authority that she gave the best blow jobs in town. I was never welcome in my mother's bedroom at night because there was always a guy in there with her—some of them the most well-known artists, critics, and writers of the time. By then she was working her dream job as a writer for a respected paper, and our house was like a salon for fascinating people. And so, even though I knew there was a lot wrong with what went on there, I also felt there was something cool and inspiring about it. Some of the men were kind: They threw James and me up in the air, brought us toys, and took us to the park. Others were less nice, including the cold and distant man who eventually became my stepfather.

By the time I entered the Upper East Side private girls high school I attended in the early eighties, there was not much I had not seen—including performance art by one of my mother's friends in which a cat licked cream out of her vagina—and pretty quickly, not much I had not done. My friends and I were beautiful and fast; half of us wanted to be models, the other half actresses. We made out with emerging rock musicians and thirty-year-old financial types in the same night just because they bought us drinks or drugs. I went to third base for the first time in a phone booth at 3 A.M. on Seventy-Seventh Street during a blizzard. It's hard in this day and age of helicopter parenting to accept that the parents I knew back then, including those of my friends, were either absent or as unleashed as we were. It was a different and wilder time.

By high school graduation, I looked hard at my scene (think New York City version of *Less Than Zero*) and made a beeline toward monogamy. I found it first with a college boyfriend and then, immediately afterward, with the man who would become my husband. I was twenty-two when I met Michael, a high-up in a creative department at the West Coast tech company where we both worked. He was thirty-two and dating someone else, but one day we kissed in his car, and soon that became a regular thing. We'd go to the movies and make out hotly; he'd push me up against the wall outside our office. I tell you this because it matters relative to how things went later on. My desire was stronger than his—I was younger, and I'd just come off a relationship where we sometimes had sex two or three times a day—but his was there too; perhaps we each pulled the other a little more into the middle. We married two years later. I was twenty-four. Michael was funny, alluringly awkward, charmingly aloof, and very, very handsome, all of which I liked. I was tired of being sought after, fucked for a certain period of time like a masturbatory prop, and then left feeling empty. Here was a man who I wanted to win, instead of vice versa. I wanted love, security, a stable family. And I found most of it with Michael, then and still.

• • • •

This month, we celebrate twenty-two years of marriage and two children who are almost grown themselves—no small feat, given the dismal statistics for couples who marry under age twenty-five (six out of ten don't last) and the amount of divorce and instability I lived with growing up. On the surface, Michael and I are an enviable couple: attractive, social, responsible, well-off, and kind. We both work and we both take care of our children. We don't fight, we don't yell, we don't throw things, and in all our years together I have only once or twice doubted his devotion, faithfulness, or love for our family. I chose Michael because, though I still wanted to have a healthy physical relationship, that desire paled in comparison to my desire to be protected and cared for—to have a family I could feel safe in. And I don't believe I made a mistake in that choice.

But before you accuse me of bragging, let me tell you this: Michael and I have not had sex, of any kind, in the past six years, and most likely never will again. Even our kisses have become the kind you reserve for your grandmother. And before that, for many, many years, when we had sex at all—maybe once or twice a year—it was fraught and difficult and often simply didn't work. For some couples, this absence in a relationship like mine might not be a problem, or at least not a deal breaker. For me, it was never okay, and it's gotten less okay over time.

And now, with one child heading into college and the other not far behind, I find I'm asking myself the questions that I pushed to the back burner in the years of young children and jobs and building and maintaining the safe and otherwise loving household in which we raised our kids. Are love and affection and shared history and parenthood enough without sex? Do I want to be like my mother, breaking up families just because she wasn't completely fulfilled or "happy"? What is happiness? When I have so much already, do I have a right to want more, to sacrifice other people's sense of well-being—the people I love the most—to have it?

I'm not sure. But what I need to do becomes clearer to me every day.

· · · ·

Loss of desire in a marriage doesn't usually happen overnight, and ours was no exception. As I said, even at the beginning I was the more ardent one—but back then, it didn't feel like a problem. Once Michael's and my car make-out sessions led into actual dating, we slept together, literally and otherwise, about three times a week. I usually initiated the sex—I would start the kissing—but that didn't bother me, and he always responded. In fact, at first I think he was turned on by how hot I was for him, and for sex. He told me then, and sometimes still does today, that I'm the sexiest woman he knows—which is great, but very confusing when it is not followed up by any indication of desire.

An inkling of what was to come revealed itself when we didn't experience much passion on the honeymoon—which at the time seemed fine; we were tired from planning the wedding ourselves and from finding a place to live, and he was loving and affectionate anyway. But pretty soon after the honeymoon, he stopped being able to get an erection with me. He was upset about it. One day when I came home he was in the stairwell waiting, and he tried to seduce me. It didn't work. He felt terrible, and he held me and told me he was sorry and didn't know what was happening. The same thing happened the next time, and the next. He eventually said he thought it was because, once we married, the idea of sleeping with the same person for the rest of his life freaked him out. But it's not like he wanted anyone else. It's not like he cheated. He just didn't want to have sex at all, it seemed.

At first I took it badly. I was young, and I had no experience with this sort of thing; I couldn't understand what was wrong with me, no matter how many times he assured me the problem wasn't about his physical attraction to me. I think now that if I had been older and less self-conscious, more vocal, I could have orchestrated things a little better. But I wanted him to take charge and teach me—he was so much older, and I was used to that dynamic—and he wasn't that type. He liked to be stroked, not do the stroking, so to speak. Not that he didn't offer to go down on me. He did, but after a few times, I didn't think he liked it, and I felt too guilty, so I just told him not to worry about it.

I don't want to play the blame game here anyway; we were both "guilty" and both "innocent," just by virtue of who we both were. He once told me, in a bittersweet way, that I was like a tiger to his bull, and it was exhausting for a bull to keep up with a tiger. I think, in hindsight, that my energy level was probably what attracted him to me in the first place, but after a while it left him fried. At the same time, I was attracted to his distance—his inhibition, even. In those days, I *wanted* to move lust to the back burner.

But I didn't want it gone altogether. *Forever.* I still wanted to feel desired, and I still wanted *some* sex. So I stopped sulking and getting angry and began working hard to get his attention—and erections. I gave him blow jobs in the car and pulled him into closets at parties. I talked dirty to him and tried to fantasy role-play. And eventually it got a little better. He always hated planning sex, and he liked getting oral sex, so once we figured out that combo—spontaneity and head—it worked, give or take. I rarely, if ever, had an orgasm, but I was happy to just get something moving. I figured once we remembered how fun and good sex could be, it would automatically feed on itself, and my pleasure in it would grow. At that point I was thinking way more than I was feeling.

So we slogged along, and then we were ready to get pregnant. When it didn't happen right away, we had to start timing encounters. That didn't work at all, and eventually we had to have some laboratory assistance. That turned out well: It was easier for him to come in a cup than to plan a sex session with me. Then, once I was pregnant, he didn't want it at all. And you know how it is after that. Sleepless nights, breastfeeding, nonstop physical contact with a baby. Two years later, I was pregnant again. I wasn't interested in sex, and he was happy without it. I think those years were the best we've had.

When I—and my libido—started to wake up from all that, the problems reemerged.

He worked on it then too. He went to a doctor and was declared in good physical health. He tried Viagra, which worked a little, but we both felt weird about it, and it involved planning, which he hated. Next step was marital counseling. We talked about his family, whether his lack of desire might stem from something in his childhood. Like mine, his mother had left his father for another man when Michael was young, though Michael and his siblings had lived with his father. But both of his parents loved him, and though his dad was a little distant, he remarried a nice woman, with kids Michael liked—all in all, it seemed, to me, a pretty normal childhood. At least compared to mine.

The therapists told us to give it time. (Yes. More time.) They said to accept that people have different appetites, and to spend one night a week just hanging out in bed together. But again, to Michael, that sort of thing is death: the pressure, the planning. It was okay a few times, but after that, it just felt like work. When we did have sex, I wanted more a few days later, and then he'd shut down and the whole cycle would start up again. After a while, he just gave up on the whole thing. "Do what you need to do," he told me. "But please, be discreet about it."

• • • •

It was a hall pass, but not one that did much for me. I've not had a lack of sexual invitations these past few years, but I also know that many of these invitations are less about me personally and more about the relative safeness of my unavailability. Or they are more about the people who ask. I also often find them pathetic or sad. The husband of one of my closest friends tried to seduce me at her fortieth birthday party. I rebuffed him, but for two weeks he persevered. They have since divorced—big surprise; he was a wild philanderer—and I have never told my friend. (It would only hurt her even more.) The point is, these kinds of men terrify me, and I am so grateful to my husband for not being one of them. To go out in the world and expose myself to this kind of behavior makes me quake. It feels too akin to my youth, and just as toxic. In contrast, I have had some emotional affairs over the years that I probably would not have had if I'd been more fulfilled with Michael, and one on-and-off, very physical relationship with an old lover—I'll call him B—that, whenever we decide to part (he has little kids, and I never want to leave mine anyway), leaves me grief-stricken and heartbroken. At worst, these things flatten and destroy me; at best, they take me only so far. And they don't make up for what I still feel is missing between me and my husband.

As for Michael, he has told me he's never cheated and he's not tempted to. I believe him most of the time. He does like to read erotica and look at porn sometimes—but no, not obsessively, and no, not gay porn, in case you're wondering; he has always denied that he's gay, and I have no reason to doubt him. (His relationships before me were all with women, and the sex was always fine, he says.) If you ask him why he's not attracted to me—as I have, repeatedly, in tears, in counseling, in anger, in surrender—he will tell you he just doesn't know and that he's hopeful it's temporary. He'll admit that warmth is more important to him than sex, and that he'd rather watch a good movie with me. And it's true. My husband is affectionate and sweet. He kisses his children and me and hugs us all with real emotion. We have never allowed our relationship issues to infect our time together as a family. I loved—and still love—the life we built.

But as a person, as a woman, I've grown more and more miserable inside over the years. As our romantic life dwindled and then disappeared, my self-esteem orbited the drain. I was working, parenting, and living this "coupled" lifestyle for all intents and purposes, but internally, I felt dead.

• • • •

I went into my own therapy about six years ago to try to figure out what to do, and to decide whether intimacy was that important to happiness when I already had so much. With a stable family, healthy kids, a thriving career, good friends . . . how could I complain? Couldn't I just "buy a vibrator," as a well-known sex expert once advised me?

What I came to understand, particularly in the last few years, is that it isn't the lack of sex that has crippled me (and my marriage), nor is it a lack of love. It is a lack of real partnership, the seeds of which are sown in the transparency and closeness that comes in the aftermath of intimacy; those moments of transcendence that occur when you share that total engagement and completeness. At its most essential level, intimacy is about letting down your barriers and allowing your partner access to your full and true self, including the parts that he or she—or simply your own ego—won't approve of: the limp penis, the curious predilections, the sad, sadistic, filthy little heart. It's about letting yourself be vulnerable, be seen in totality, for better and worse. And still finding a champion in your spouse. That's what I long for, and that's what scares the shit out of my husband—and there, in a nutshell, is the problem: The very thing I need to feel alive is the thing that shuts down his circuitry.

Without that shared-desire/body-rubbing/orgasm-induced sense of vulnerability and mutual openness that helps solidify an exclusive partnership, we are two separate people with a beautiful history together. And it is beautiful. The thought of breaking up my home, my babies' home, paralyzes me; the thought of leaving my husband—co-parent to my children, vessel of my memory, the man I have lived with almost every day of my entire adult life—is excruciatingly sad. It feels like severing a crucial artery. But for years I've been slowly starving, and what I've come to at last is this: I deserve more. Here in my later forties, poised on the brink of menopause, of an empty nest, of my parents dying, I want a full and dynamic partnership before it's too late. I know I have a great capacity for the full range of love. And I believe that I am worthy of it.

• • • •

Recently my mother, from whom I had become estranged a year before—I'd finally had enough of her ego, her craziness, and her abusive third husband—got cancer, and her illness immediately brought me back into constant contact with her. Ironically, part of the reason for that is my loyalty: I'm an absurdly devoted person, something that's both my blessing and my curse. I believe that *everyone* is damaged and sad and lonely on the inside, and the best we can do as humans is to forgive the few already in our tribe and hold on to them. Because of that, I have learned to see that my mother contains multitudes: Along with being self-absorbed, self-referential, and deeply insecure, she's also intellectual, vivacious, and a great connector—and after a lifetime I have finally come to have great compassion for her. And I'm glad.

And yet, I've also learned that we have to hold on to, and feed, *ourselves,* and sometimes that means letting go of a relationship that's continuing to starve us, even if it also means giving up something great—a lot of things great—in the process. So while my identity as a mother/wife/ neighbor/professional shrinks in fear at the thought of breaking up my marriage and family, my personhood says eat or die, evolve or die. It is time. It might even be now or never.

And so, though Michael and I still live under the same roof, we are in mediation now, discussing how to draft an official separation agreement. It is painful and difficult and sad, but we are as sympathetic and gentle and kind as we can be. I understand that this is not what he chooses, that he'd change if he could, and he understands the same about me. But while I'm heartbroken and terrified about the future, I'm also already the tiniest bit relieved to have made the decision, to be moving on to the next step. And I think Michael is too. Even our kids are getting used to the idea that something different is happening in our house that feels a little sad and wrong, but also interesting and true. As a grown woman, a wife, and a mother, I can say that my love for my family is rooted in my love for Michael. It has taken me a very long time (a lot longer than most) to come to terms with the idea that, though I cannot separate the two, the family doesn't have to dissolve if Michael's and my marriage ends, just as it won't dissolve when my eldest goes to college next year.

The divorce jury is still out for the moment, but I can almost hear it coming back in—and when it does, I'm ready to meet it at the door and accept its verdict. I am ready to proceed with the rest of my life, and for that to be a full life. For better and worse.

> **Postscript:** *Claire did end up separating from Michael, with the intention of exploring her feelings for B (who was already separated and getting a divorce). But B was going through some hard times, exacerbated by his divorce, and eventually suffered a semi-breakdown, and Claire spent the money she had planned to use to pay for her own apartment to help B get back on his feet. She stayed in the house with Michael during that time but was honest with him about B. To her surprise, Michael not only wasn't angry, but was generous and helpful (even offering to check on B once when Claire was out of town). B is better now, but for the moment Claire remains living with her family; she and Michael, though they still don't sleep together (and, she says, likely never will), have found a new kind of partnership, based on a sense of gratitude and mutual appreciation, that they are carrying into therapy and any conversations about their future. Claire still doesn't know what will happen after the children leave home, but for now, she's found a little island of togetherness, forgiveness, and peace.*

# Once a Week

## Take It or Take It

**GRACE O'MALLEY**

The drapes are pulled against the midday sun, the room clean and peaceful. Some days I'm naked between the white sheets, other days tarted up with a satin bra and thong I'd never wear otherwise. If he's in bed first, I might throw on high heels and saunter over to his side, like the cheap whore we both wish I could be. The thought is laughable when you know our history.

Right now, though, our history isn't the point. And the costumes might work in the screenplay I'm writing in my head, the one where it's all new and a little bit nasty, like when we first met almost four decades ago—me not long into college, he older, much more experienced. I counted on him to show me the ways of my body, and for a long time he did. But then something stopped working for me. And that's when our problems started.

But let me get back to the moment we're having in the room. Ignore the mole on his chest that suddenly looks irregular, the twitch in my elbow from too much tennis, and focus on the *good* sensations, the man in bed . . . and then flip it and pretend he's a stranger, and I am too, and rewrite the screenplay: sometimes familiar, sometimes new. Close my eyes and just make up the scene while my body acts it out. It's not automatic, but it's a skill I've learned, a meditative trance that allows me to relax and to ultimately connect . . . to make everybody happy.

Do I need to say it? Okay, I'll say it. Sex with my husband wasn't always this complicated.

. . . .

I grew up Irish Catholic in the 1960s and '70s, went to parochial schools, and somehow never got the sex talk from my parents—or anyone else. With no Internet back then, I gleaned what I could from the occasionally glimpsed *Playboy* or copy of *The Joy of Sex* at my friend's house. (They were Protestants; the mom was a *divorcée*. Enough said.) At eighteen—shy, naïve, still full of the warnings from nuns and priests about venereal pleasure and sacred procreation—I left for college. This was the seventies, the sexual revolution: think patchouli, waist-length hair, hordes of girls who suddenly, proudly, claimed to want sex as often and intensely as the boys. Intellectually, I did a complete 180. Of *course* I believed in open-mindedness, women's liberation, free love, and sex—constant sex! ecstatic sex!—for all. But shyness and inertia kept me a virgin until nineteen, and then, although my first time was with a sweet, tender boy, I was so busy holding in my stomach and trying to look transported that I don't remember much of it. Shortly thereafter, I met my husband. And this time, in the throes of love at first sight, I offered myself without a thought of my imperfections. I loved the way he smelled, loved his beautiful strong body, his wicked handsomeness. I wanted to *eat* him, in that ravenous way one loves one's children. From the first slow wink, the sex was exciting, un-predictable, and frequent.

But around our fifth year as a couple (not yet married, but long since monogamous and living together), I found myself losing my desire to touch and be touched by him. I thought it might be the painful urinary tract infections I kept getting, or the mild betray-als, fights, and disappointments causing anger to creep into my head and my bed. Or simply that, no longer new, sex wasn't as riveting. I didn't know. I still loved him. I still found him strikingly handsome. Nevertheless, I stopped wanting to have sex as often as he did (pretty much every night), and when we did, I wasn't having an orgasm as reliably as I had. This made me question my ability to perform, which made it harder for me to perform, which made him slow down and take more time with me—which was not at all what I wanted. (Despite the common belief that women want men to go on and on, that was never true for me. I wanted him to finish, so we could talk or read or just go to bed.)

Normally outspoken, I found myself not confessing my increasing lack of interest: I worried I would hurt him, or that telling him would mean we were in trouble. Instead, I said I was tired or stressed. While I never actually faked orgasm—a strange boundary for a woman hiding so much else—I did often fake willingness as I lay in bed, game face on, brain either neurotically going through all the things that could be wrong with me, my life, *our* lives . . . or off a million miles away, thinking about my deadlines or our upcoming vacation. Soon I began going to bed early or pretending to be asleep when I wasn't. It was as if the door to the wellspring of my sexuality had slammed shut.

This, I'm embarrassed to say, went on for many years. We got married anyway; we loved each other, after all, and we wanted to be together, wanted kids. And though I considered myself enlightened in many areas—I had a graduate degree, I was up on world news—I didn't talk about sex outside of my marriage, or much in it either. Meanwhile, by then the sexperts, from Dr. Ruth on down, all seemed to be pushing the same "truth": Sex is normal and natural, so do it as much as you like! *Glamour* and *Cosmo* offered different ways to keep your man interested, but no one seemed to be writing about the problem I had keeping *myself* interested. And while Dr. Ruth sometimes mentioned sexual problems, never, it seemed, were they about happily married women who didn't want sex. In movies, on TV, on the streets, couples seemed to radiate a heat I no longer felt with my husband.

*There must be an underlying pathology,* I would think. Had I been sexually molested and repressed it? Was I a lesbian and just didn't know? Or was it newly surfaced Catholic guilt coming back to haunt me, having been insufficiently dispatched during the sexual revolution? Whatever it was, I felt utterly guilty for not "loving" my husband as much as he did me.

Eventually I became desperate enough to confide in a few friends—educated, "liberated" women all. Although one friend had an enviable libido (which her husband couldn't quench), lo and behold, the rest of us had partners who wanted lots of sex, all the time, while we wanted it sometimes, rarely, or never—and almost invariably not as much as we had in the beginning. We whispered about how upset our partners would be at our airing what should have been so private, and—with great relief at having found each other—pledged ourselves to secrecy.

• • • •

Then the kids came along. Again, do I need to say it? I'll say it. We were new mothers, sleep-deprived, overwhelmed, angry about shouldering more of the child care burden than our spouses while also working part- or full-time (my own work varied between the two). Add to that the constantly suckling infants to whom we were human pacifiers, and, for me at least, any residual erotic impulse vanished. My formerly sexy boobs were now a cross between udders and a security blanket for this astonishing (and astonishingly needy) new member of the family. Weeks turned to months. My C-section scar still ached, my stomach sagged; I hadn't slept more than three hours straight or had a good shower in what seemed like a year. What's more, while I'd never been calm, in the period of early motherhood my brain became a teeming automat of fears and horror stories about raising a baby. There were choking hazards, SIDS, honey-induced botulism, suffocation, drownings galore. I became hypervigilant, hyperabsorbed. Sex with my husband? Let's just say it wasn't a priority.

He was a good sport at first, having been caught up in his own adoration of the infant. Eventually, however, he'd coax me into halfheartedly doing something. We limped along for a couple of years with him hoping this would get better, and me making excuses or faking sleep, unable to imagine ever feeling horny again.

Finally I got desperate enough to ask my obstetrician for testosterone. He said my blood work showed I had enough testosterone, and that for women and sex, it worked like wheels on a car: If you already have four, adding more isn't going to improve your ability to drive. Besides, he already had an opinion on the subject: "My patients come in begging for testosterone all the time," he said. "I'll ask them to describe their day. Invariably, they're up at six, making lunches, feeding babies. By nine P.M. they're exhausted." He added that while men often use sex to relax, women usually need to *be* relaxed, or unwound, in order to want to do it. "When a couple comes in here together," he said, "I tell the man, 'You want to get lucky? After dinner, hand your wife a glass of wine and tell her to sit while you clean up and put the kids to bed.'"

His advice, which I shared with my husband, produced only a curious nod. But even if he'd followed it, I doubted my gratitude for a glass of wine and reprieve from dishes would extend past falling asleep on the couch. (I was the primary caretaker and domestic doer, even though I was now back to work, albeit from home.)

By the time I turned forty, with two still-little kids, I was so starved for solitude and rest that even when my husband and I went away for a long weekend to celebrate my birthday, I shuddered at his expectations of a love fest. I wanted to read, take baths, and simply *think*. But I also couldn't demolish our last hopes for a rekindled sex life—plus, wasn't the whole point of a weekend away alone to make love? And in fact, once I finally relaxed, I actually enjoyed myself—not only the sex, complete with long-awaited orgasm, but also the relief at feeling so much better about what I had considered my "broken" sex equipment.

But the next night, my husband wanted to do it again. I almost couldn't believe it. I shook my head, climbed under the covers (in sweats), and told him I thought I was coming down with something.

Shortly afterward, I was out with friends who asked about the trip. My expression must have given things away, because one of them said, "So, happy birthday. He takes you away to a fancy hotel to fuck your brains out. Same gift I got!" Laughter erupted, followed by sighs.

We might joke about it, but despite our jobs, houses, kids, dogs, we felt pathetic, unloving . . . *selfish*. We were failures at the marriage contract, depriving our imperfect but nonetheless faithful and loving husbands of sex.

• • • •

It was around this time that I spotted a book in the library: *Not Tonight, Dear.* I plucked it off the shelf like contraband. Written by a psychiatrist and based on interviews with top sex therapists, the book proposed a new take on sexual desire, including case studies of couples with differences in how much sex they wanted, and tips on raising one's libido. Most happily, it repeated a new premise: *Desire is one thing, love another.* The authors called mismatched libidos "desire discrepancy," which, *if not discussed and dealt with,* could cause *enormous misunderstandings* between partners. Amazingly, this was the first time I had seen anyone with scientific credibility suggest an alternative to my theory of there being something incurably wrong with me—or my marriage.

Before then, talking to my husband about sex, I'd always framed the issue as more of a logistical problem—the kids were in our bed, someone needed me—or my own temporary state (exhaustion, stress, cramps). Now, carefully, I told him I'd read a book that enlightened me to the fact that I might just have "low desire."

He shook his head, looking hurt. "You used to love sex!" he said. "You can't just have 'low desire' now. Something else is up."

I dropped it for the moment. I had planted the seed, at least. And now I had the strategies from *Not Tonight, Dear* to try. Maybe those would do the trick.

In the meantime, life got in the way. The kids and jobs were a handful; money was tight. As usual, reprogramming my sexual self fell to the back burner. It soon became apparent that though desire discrepancy might describe our situation and though we were far from alone, knowing this wasn't going to solve our problem. Nothing countered my husband's reality of not getting laid nearly enough. Besides being frustrated, he also was hurt. I saw it in his eyes. He'd ask why I didn't initiate, why I never wanted to let myself go. Didn't I owe it to myself to experience pleasure?

"Of course!" I'd respond. "I just have low desire. Maybe you should marry someone else."

"I don't want someone else. I want you! But I want you to want *me*."

"I do!" I said. "But how can I know I do when you always want me first?"

We'd both leave these conversations unhappy, and soon I avoided them at all costs.

• • • •

One day, a decade or more into child-rearing and when sex had dwindled to once every three weeks or so, he took me aside. "I don't want to live this way," he said.

My immediate reaction was to assume this was a preface to leaving me. Tears rising, I gulped, "I understand," then added reluctantly, "I want better for you."

"Then . . . do you think we could have more sex?" he asked.

I looked at his eager, hopeful face, the face of a man who loved me and who I loved too. And I reached deep into my psyche and asked myself: *What do I want and what can I give?* I thought about living alone, or alone with my kids, and never being bothered for sex, and how nice that would be—until a kid got sick, or injured, or wanted to do something risky that terrified me but didn't bother my husband. I didn't want to lose him—as a father, a husband, my best friend, my financial and domestic partner. Put another way, in the battle between divorce and making love—*even when I didn't want to*—I chose the latter. Call me a doormat, an idiot, but don't leave me heartbroken, broke, and raising two kids by myself.

"Yes," I answered.

Back I went to the doctor, this time for anxiety medication—a long-overdue fix. I also went back to dutifully journaling and trying desire-rousing strategies. Most of all, I agreed to have sex on "a regular basis."

"Four times a week," my husband pitched.

"Two," I countered.

"But I'd *really* like *six*," he returned.

"And I'd really like once," I said (holding back from adding "a year"). "So I'm compromising."

I entered this new bargain with trepidation, if also high hopes. But I was the early-riser/early-bedtime person in our marriage, and we had to wait until the kids—no longer babies—were asleep. I was just too tired at night to want sex, and soon our goal of two nights a week faltered. At first I hoped he wouldn't notice. (Ha.) Then I apologized and tried harder. We still weren't back to twice a week, but we usually did manage once. The problem was, even when we did, he could see that I, well, just wasn't that into it.

Finally we saw a sex therapist. She suggested we both stop drinking (um—I don't think so), reduce stress (good luck with that), and maybe I should quit my anti-anxiety meds, which could be worsening my libido. I almost laughed out loud. It's not like my libido had been different before I'd gone on drugs (except, of course, for those heavenly few years after we'd met), and I didn't see how becoming even more anxious would help anything. Even my blue-balled husband wasn't buying that prescription.

On the way home, though—feeling desperate—I pitched an idea: What about having sex during the day, when the kids were at school and I wasn't tired yet? He would have to come home for lunch or go in to work late. Still, I pitched it hopefully.

He sighed. It was inconvenient, he said. He liked nights better. He—

"Well, I hate them," I replied, suddenly adamant. "Why should I be the one doing all the compromising?"

"I've compromised plenty," he said. "I've been one hundred percent faithful despite being basically starved of sex."

I laughed in spite of myself. But I held my ground, and so we tried my plan. And guess what? He didn't hate leaving work as much as he'd thought, and I didn't hate sex when I wasn't tired and the kids weren't home. I still had to psych myself up for it, but it seemed like the best answer yet. Indeed, by the time his crankiness disappeared (it's amazing how regular sex can calm a man's soul), he accepted the predictable devolution into once a week.

Scheduled sex had other advantages too. He didn't have to worry about being rejected, and I didn't have to brace myself for advances that I'd have to reject then feel guilty for rejecting: I could read a book at night without needing to decode (and deflect) the subtle signals of an incoming seduction. I'd long since stopped cuddling with him—since that might signal readiness for sex—and now I could once again indulge my affection toward him, something he liked too.

The weekly sex thing worked about 90 percent of the time. There were days when one of us had a meeting or was sick or traveling for work. And sometimes, scheduled or not, I still said no. Because in every woman's life (or at least in *this* woman's life), there are times when, even if she's not angry at her husband, or tired, or pregnant, or nursing, or dealing with a sick young child or a sixteen-year-old child who hates her or a mother who's dying or a house on the market, a yeast infection, crabs—or at least what *seems* like crabs—because her husband cheated on her—or at least she *thinks* he did (even though he swears he didn't) . . . she just *really doesn't want to have sex.*

Still, saying no wasn't easy. I continued to feel guilty. And I continued to worry, despite knowing better, that I was unfair, unloving . . . an aberration. At the same time, I started to wonder. Just how much of an aberration was I, really? I decided to do more research. *Real* research. I wanted answers, finally.

Over the next few weeks, and then well beyond—varying my searches from mainstream (think *Men's Health* magazine) to academic (think *Personality and Social Psychology Review,* volume 85, no. 1)—I learned a ton. For one, the bulk of evidence concluded that, notwithstanding the sexual revolution's misbegotten fruit, from slutty, come-hither magazine ads to porn teeming with hot girls who apparently love nothing more than a huge, throbbing cock down their throat, up their ass, or anywhere else on or inside their person, most men still have a higher sex drive than most women. (One study—by proponents of gender *similarities* theory, and seeking to *debunk* the idea that men are hornier than women—still found that men masturbated more, used more porn, and had more casual sex.) Then there was what happened in long-term monogamous relationships, particularly ones that included cohabitation: Many women—a much higher number than men—simply lost their desire for sex with their steady partners, typically after between one and four years. (One author later noted: "For many women, the cause of their sexual malaise appears to be monogamy itself.")

Research in one scholarly journal confirmed that, for the *majority* of sexually healthy women in long-term relationships, spontaneous sexual thinking is "infrequent." So not only was I far from alone in not wanting to constantly jump my husband's bones, but I was right there with most women. (In a more recent article in the *New York Times*, a well-known sexpert discusses the misconceptions around "normal desire" in women, particularly those in long-term relationships, saying, "I can't count the number of women I talked with who assume that because their desire is responsive ["emerging in response to, rather than in anticipation of, erotic stimulation"] rather than spontaneous, they have 'low desire' "—i.e., something "wrong" with them. In a subsequent interview on Alternet, she estimated that about a third of women experience responsive desire *primarily*.)

In the early infatuation stage, or "limerence," I read—the phase where most marriages begin, at least in this country—even low-desire partners will experience a surge in wanting to touch and be touched by their beloved. For an average of two years after falling in love, one study found, a couple's desires likely are as high as they'll ever be. In fact, during this time, the genders tend to be fairly equal—which "may lead couples to overestimate their sexual compatibility." But then passion dies down, and "men and women return to their baselines of sexual desire, which is on average much lower for women than for men." In one data set, 60 percent of men married for twenty years or longer wished they had more sex. But interestingly, in the same group, 32 percent of *women* wished the same thing. So while the majority of men wanted more sex from their wives, there also were plenty of couples where the reverse was true—like my libidinous friend whose husband couldn't give her enough.

Sometimes I shared what I'd learned with my husband; other times I spared him. But as the years went on, armed repeatedly with new knowledge, I finally was able to lose almost all my guilt and to simply tell him, whenever it was unequivocally the case, that I just really didn't feel like sex right then. The catch: I had to make a true good-faith effort at keeping the promise I'd made to him more than once before. And so I did that. Once a week, I gave it my all. And our relationship improved. We fought less, and even when we were mad at each other, going to bed connected us enough that we'd find ourselves much more likely to let the little things slide.

Our weekly sex dates have lasted for many years now. Once a week, we schedule sex like the clichéd couple we never thought we'd be, and when the time comes, we close the curtains and I strip down, or dress up, and try to make him happy. I still often feel resistant, at least at first, but as long as I'm not indisposed or incapacitated, I tell myself I'm doing it because he loves it, and I love *him*.

And once I've gotten over the hump of tearing myself out of ordinary life and into this oddly choreographed moment, I pretty much always come around, and usually even have a good time. In fact, and much to my surprise, I now believe that these scheduled appointments actually have improved my well-being. There's something about being skin to skin with my life's companion that makes me feel better. I find a certain pleasure in making myself vulnerable, and in seeing him vulnerable, and that carries us forward. Recently, I read that being capable of decent sex is as much about learning to *disregard* the things *overpowering* one's ability to be turned on—from the to-do list to not wanting to get pregnant—as it is about turning *on* the thoughts and sensations that make a woman want or be willing to have sex. Obvious, maybe, but still, always helpful to me. So I try to be mindful of the quiet and the sensations of physical intimacy. When I need to, I use fantasy: the costumes, the screenplay. It's all good. It's all right. For all of it, I am grateful. Relieved. I remember those years of not having much sex and feeling angry and distant. I'm not sure which was the chicken and which the egg, but having regular sex with him seems to bridge some sort of divide.

Sometimes I think about the future, when maybe we're too old to have sex at all. I try to appreciate that it's actually a privilege, a luxury, to be able to do it now. And while perhaps it *will* be a relief in some ways when he's too old to want it anymore—and we can sit together on the porch drinking tea and yelling into each other's hearing aids about the good old days—more often I wonder how it might feel to not be desired by this stalwart lover, this man of mine who's always there, always ready. Will I feel uncertain? Unattractive? Will I have the power to tell myself—as I hope he is able to now when I tell him it's not *him*, it's *me*—that it's not personal? And in that moment, will I know—as I do writing this—that there's ever so much more to it than that? That there's never just me and never just him, but always the two of us as well? I hope so. Because therein lies the problem, but also the beauty and solace, of marriage. Long-term, lovely, till death do us part.

# Fifty Shades of Free

### ROBIN RINALDI

When I was three years old, I stood on the back porch one summer afternoon ignoring my mother's repeated attempts to get me inside so we could go to the store. I could see and hear her through the door, which was part screen, part glass. Finally she picked up her purse from the kitchen table, turned, and said, "Okay, I'm leaving, see you later." My mouth opened in shock and rage. And as surely as if she had flipped a lever controlling my arm, I smashed my fist through the glass.

When I was four, my extended family lined up for a Christmas Day photo at my aunt's house. I was next to my cousin, just a year older; against my right shoulder, her fat arm stuck out of her velvet Christmas dress. Before I could stop myself—and to the gasps and horror of everyone—I turned and dug my teeth into it.

By the time I was five, though, the combination of kindergarten, Monday-afternoon catechism, and my father's temper had me on the inevitable and necessary track to socialization. Decades later, some people will backpack or scale mountains to remember who they really are. Some dive to the blackest ocean depths or don boxing gloves or parachute into thin air. I found a different way. But it took me a long time, and no little amount of soul-searching and heartbreak, to get there.

• • • •

In my mid-twenties, I lived on the ground floor of a gingerbread Victorian on a leafy street in Sacramento, California. I had broken up with a perfectly decent boyfriend for the simple fact that I felt too dependent on him and thought I "should" experience living alone. I was always doing things like that: checking myself from getting too content or lazy, watching my actions as if from above. I diligently put away part of each paycheck, took the boring lucrative job instead of the creative lower-paying one, obediently spilled my guts to a therapist each week about my father's violent outbursts and my mother's terrifying panic attacks amid the backdrop of my tiny Catholic hometown, scribbling her suggestions and homework into notebook upon notebook.

My neighbor in Sacramento was a woman about my age, but completely different: skinny, with long dark hair parted in the middle and an incessant rotation of The Cure blaring from her open bay windows down into my basement-level ones. (The Cure was not my thing. I had skipped straight over post-punk to the much tamer world-music forays of Paul Simon and Peter Gabriel.) Her boyfriend was skinny too, a drummer, and heavily tattooed long before ink was all the rage. They were always screaming or smashing things or screwing, and when they screwed, she made the most horrible sound: a swallowed, rhythmic bleat signaling either erotic pleasure or slow death by butcher knife. Often, each utterance was presaged by the hard thwack of what could only be the drummer's open hand. The summer heat was suffocating, and with no air-conditioning I was loath to shut my windows, but even when I did, I'd often still hear the dulled echoes of his palm landing, her vocal cords convulsing, all of it building to a crescendo of muffled moans and shrieks. Afterward, I'd stomp through the house slamming windows back open, feeling a strange mix of anger and fear.

My eventual next boyfriend was, of course, nothing like the

drummer. No tattoos, no screaming. He did have longish hair, and he did partake in the occasional dose of recreational drugs, but his job and bank account were as stable as mine. Raised in the Midwest in a happy family, he was quiet and generous both in life and in bed, where the love ran deep and the passion was sensed more than expressed. He offered the calm, stable presence I'd never known in childhood, a counterbalance to my own recurrent panic attacks and my general sense of the world as too big and threatening to ever feel safe.

The deal was, when we needed to suss out the status of our bond, I would break down and he would offer a silent, sturdy shoulder to cry on. As sweet as our sex life was, collapsing into him provided a connection that often ran even deeper than sex. Our energies mingled. I'd emerge from a good cry feeling I had taken him in, his clothes wet with my tears. The rest of the time, for us, it was work and leisure, home and abroad, all in moderation. It functioned so well that we married.

• • • •

But sometime around age thirty-nine, I started to feel much less afraid. My career was stable, and I had a chunk of money in the bank. I'd been through enough therapy to have dumped a good portion of childhood shame and more or less forgiven my parents. Lying awake in the middle of the night, I'd watch from my side of the bed the outline of my husband's broad shoulders rising and falling as he slept. We'd never, not once, had sex in the wee hours. When I'd asked him recently if he wanted to try watching porn together or maybe give anal sex a go, he'd said, "Not really." I bought a blindfold, but after five minutes, he took it off me. I had told him, in passing, how there were so many dirty things I wanted to say during sex. But when it actually came time to say them, I couldn't. Not a one.

He did try to accommodate. Once, while we were changing positions, he unexpectedly slapped my ass. My jaw dropped and I
almost laughed, but then I thought better of it. Laughing would
break the mood and bring us back into our safe harbor, and the
whole point of a safe harbor is to occasionally venture out onto the
high seas, no? But I couldn't help smiling, and then he smiled, and
our moment of dark erotic play dissolved.

If I grew too strong, what would glue us, since so much of our
love centered around my messy dependence on his cool strength?
At first I thought: *It's his turn to lean on me. Come on, I can take
it.* But that is not how my midwestern husband was built. He was
grain fed and skyward looking. He didn't need to lean. So then I
thought: *Okay, big guy, get bigger. Expand the container around me
to fit this larger self I'm growing into. Show me you can handle the
woman as well as the girl.* That's where the blindfold came in. But
it wasn't really working.

• • • •

Around the same time my urge to be blindfolded sprang up, I developed a latent and intense maternal longing. For me, it was more
than just the innocent dream of nurturing a child. I also wanted
a baby to—among other things—align the infinite potentialities
of each day into a path I didn't have to think about anymore. Forty
years of thinking were enough for me. I was ready for a mental
break consisting of breast milk and spit-up and shit, warm baths
and onesies and the smell of Johnson's Baby Lotion. I longed to go
on autopilot, if only for a year or two: exhaust the body, overload
the survival instinct, focus on someone else for a change. Not to
mention extinguish all the dirty words backing up in my throat,
threatening mutiny. My husband's progeny would weigh down my
belly, then my arms, and anchor me in place.

Apparently I wasn't the only one who felt this way. All I had to do was turn on HGTV or the Cooking Channel, or scan the food and shelter magazines lining the supermarket shelves. By then, the early years of the new millennium, the cult of motherhood had exploded, ensuring we didn't stray far from our biological obligation to the species—and with the explosion came an obsession with real estate, decorating, baby bumps, home cooking, attachment parenting. Everywhere I turned, it seemed, urban women were knitting, and soon they'd be canning and pickling as well. It didn't feel like a patriarchal conspiracy to me. It felt like we women were instigating it, even celebrating it. Something in us wanted to be tied down.

But my husband wasn't on board for fatherhood, and after a pregnancy scare—devastating to each of us for different reasons—he got a vasectomy and sure enough, the mutineers overturned the ship. I asked for—and received, if reluctantly—permission to open up our marriage for a year, and over the next twelve months, I went wild: moved out of our house for part of each week, placed an ad on Nerve.com for casual lovers, joined groups of sexual explorers whose mission was to better understand the female anatomy. All of that is a separate story. The germane bit here is that many of the men I took to bed turned out to be dirty talkers, ass slappers, firm hair pullers who liked giving orders. At the end of each encounter, my limbs vibrated with the aftershocks of human collision—both thrill and satiation.

The sex didn't always make me orgasm, but I didn't care about that; I could do that alone. What I couldn't do alone was order myself around, take such elegant control of myself—or when I did, it was always to do boring things like going to the gym or meeting constant deadlines. The rewards of daily submission to the elliptical machine or attending my Excel spreadsheet were so long-term as to seem invisible, whereas the rewards of submitting to a lover's faux discipline were immediate. It was playful, erotic, a great way to let down the hair after twelve hours at the office—but more substantially, it began to rearrange my outlook on power.

. . . .

Power is a funny thing. Spiritual people are apt to say that, as with money or love, the more power you give away, the more you have. In my experience, long-term love worked that way only occasionally, and money hardly ever. But in the bedroom with a new lover, the give-to-get equation functioned beautifully. The man realized what a rare gift I offered: a full forty years after Gloria Steinem and Dorothy Pitman Hughes raised their feminist fists in the air for *Esquire*, he was, if only for a few minutes, commanding a fully functioning adult woman at will. This, I found, inspired a kind of respect that could border on worship. I was letting him live something he'd only heard stories about, in a way that didn't make him feel guilty. It was, as Jon Lovitz used to say on *Saturday Night Live*, "Acting!" and as with any good theater, resulted in catharsis. For both of us.

I should say here that, like most women, I'd had my brushes with male violence over the years: my father hitting my mother and brothers and me, a teenage ex-boyfriend slapping my face when he saw me out with another guy, Peeping Toms outside the bedroom window of my twentysomething apartment, a flasher in the alley, frat boys grabbing women's crotches at a club, stories of friends being molested or raped. And of course an unending shitload of violence poured through the cable box and movie screen, where the female body makes a regular appearance in car trunks, on blood-soaked carpets, on riverbanks—gagged, bound, scantily clad or naked. My own memories mixed with the cultural tropes to form a hierarchy of fears regarding how a man might hurt a woman, starting with simple disapproval or name-calling and escalating to being groped, struck, beaten, raped, killed, dismembered. Luckily,

I rarely considered the latter horrors unless I found myself walking to my car in one of those multilevel parking structures at night. The more common and realistic fears centered around the lower rungs on the hierarchy.

An interesting thing happened, though, when my naked body was struck and called names by my *choice*. It wasn't scary. In fact, it went a long way toward eliminating some fear. A slap is just one sensation that quickly passes. But more than that, a slap woke me up, set me tingling. Sleeping beasts began to stir. Likewise, when a lover called me bad words—just a few letters strung together, really—it made me examine them from a different, more curious angle. *Slut, whore, bitch, cunt.* What's the big deal, after all? I *am* a cunt, among many other things. Look, there's my cunt right there, nothing wrong with it at all. I'm a bitch too; I'm angry about everything from bipartisan politics to subprime mortgages to global warming. Let's celebrate that. I embraced *slut* with particular affinity. I'd spent high school fearing that word above all others, watching the unlucky girls who'd dropped their guard long enough to get the moniker stuck to their backs for four years. Midlife gave me the strength to begin to claim all the taboos, gather them up in myself. When I did, I found them to be like those mythical monsters who shrivel to dust once you finally turn and embrace them.

Of course, what really made it okay was that I controlled the situation. My carefully chosen lovers—chefs, lawyers, musicians, taxpaying citizens all—were not psychopaths or even mean people, and I could stop them at any time with a word. For me, the bedroom theater was completely separate from the daily reality of patriarchy or real violence against women, except that by accepting a tiny, safe sample of male violence—a homeopathic dose, if you will—I slowly built in myself a level of immunity. I felt larger, stronger. While a few bedroom antics were never going to solve the problem of the dark, deserted parking structure, they did slightly alter my mental state as I walked to my car. They made room in my imagination for more than just fear. Now fear mingled with memories of strength, power, and eroticism.

Submission also freed up the aggressor in me, and I liked that too. Sometimes I'd respond to "bitch" with "bastard." If I was a cunt, he was a cock. Outside the confines of safe and quiet marriage, I found I could say anything in bed. It provided a kind of relief from the hours spent seething silently in traffic or scrolling inane social media until I wanted to scream. Sometimes I threw a man down and pinned his wrists. Sometimes I stridently ignored his commands, daring him to up the ante. Once, I turned a six-foot-four man over, grabbed his hair, and dry humped him until I climaxed.

At a dinner party I met a firecracker of a woman who, over several glasses of wine, shared with me her theory that the more of a ballbuster you are, the more you like to be slapped. "I call it the Club," she said. "We tough girls need to know the guy isn't afraid of us." And vice versa. I thought back to my neighbor in Sacramento. She let that drummer slam her around because she was a badass. She could take it. She liked it. This, by the way, is the *opposite* of the *Fifty Shades of Grey* story line, where the fragile innocent unhappily submits to please the control-freak man. When *Fifty Shades* came out soon after all this, I noticed it wasn't twenty-one-year-old virgins like Anastasia Steele eating it up so much as women my age, to enliven their own sex lives or for mere titillation. The author—a hefty, earthy forty-eight-year-old wife at the time—transcribed all that rowdy sex, and other middle-aged women used it to get off, while young, innocent Anastasia was nothing but a middlewoman, a docile little package into which all that ferocious desire had to be bundled. And not only because youth sells, but also so that none of us would freak out at the prospect of a strong woman taking command of her own taboos. It's a lot more comfortable for everyone involved if it's the man's idea, and the naïf tearfully submits.

. . . .

When I wanted to get pregnant, and then when I was searching out lovers and experimenting with submission and aggression, and then, finally, when I was leaving the calm, quiet marriage that no longer worked for me, I was, on the most basic level, seeking momentum. Approaching the midpoint, I longed to propel myself into the next phase of life, but without a baby I had no idea how. I was growing, but my marriage wasn't. Destruction was the first step to re-creation.

Certainly part of why change proved difficult for me came from my upbringing and inborn temperament. But there was also the more present-day issue of the increasing noise in my head. The to-do list, the nonstop e-mail and Twitter feed and texts, the screens of every size vomiting constant data—as the information dump accelerates, so does a sense of paralysis. We've lost touch with our creature selves, but some experiences remain to remind us: childbirth, pain, disease, disaster, food, sex, death. Submission and domination prevail in the wilderness. Friction equals attention. In missionary position with the lights off, fucking the same guy you've fucked for ten or twenty years, it's easy to spend several minutes mentally going over your grocery list. But facedown in the pillow with your hair pulled taut and your bottom high in the air, stinging from a slap or a smack . . . not so much. A man's firm grip around my neck constricted the airway just enough to make the breath audible, as in yoga. It rendered me present.

I left behind the hum of cubicle and freeway and supersize grocery store and became animal; I absconded from the sterile modern world back to the ancient one of temple prostitutes and warriors, back further to the caves and the savannah, all the way back to fur and all fours.

• • • •

It turns out that my desire to tussle with a lover peaked around the same time my biological clock hit midnight—age forty-five or so—as if in an attempt to toss atoms around in my very own particle accelerator, to perhaps create something new. In fact, it worked. New relationship, new city, new job. Six years later, I don't feel as much need to talk dirty or be spanked, though I can indulge when the mood strikes. The repertoire has grown. The boundaries that expanded each time I went toe-to-toe with a man have retained their girth.

And it takes a lot these days to make me cower. The first time I noticed this effect in the world at large was in the midst of all the spankings, at a tantra workshop run by one of the new-age gurus I'd been reading. He was said to be a master of masculine and feminine interaction and, as such, called participants up to the stage to assess how they carried themselves. Thirty seconds into my assessment, after he'd asked me to show him how I'd lure a man with my words and body, he delivered his prognosis.

"You see how stuck her energy is?" he said to the class. "She needs it moved. She needs to be slapped."

Yes. Exactly. "So slap me," I said.

He didn't. I'm sure his contract with the beachfront Miami resort where he held the workshop didn't allow for smacking women in conference rooms. But as I stood facing him, two hundred eyes on me, one hundred brains deeming me "stuck," I longed for nothing more than for his big hand to fly up and meet my cheek; for the sting, the jolt, the blood rising to the skin and with it, the she-animal who'd lived in me from before I could remember. From deep in the groin she would surface, growling a little, smiling wide to bare her teeth.

And maybe I'd just up and slap him back.

# My War with Sex

## LYNN DARLING

A strange thing happens when you are told you have breast cancer. Quite suddenly, there are two of you in the room. There is the middle-aged woman sitting calmly in a chair discussing what is to come (the scheduling of MRIs and PET scans, the appointments with oncologists and surgeons), taking notes in a new vocabulary, learning the upside of positive receptors, the downside of Taxotere, the odds of lymph node involvement. And then there is that other you, that patchwork quilt stitched out of all the many selves you have been throughout your life—daughter, mother, wife, widow, impostor, healer of sorrows large and small, stumbling explorer, quivering wreck, best friend, worst enemy . . . that ragtag collection of personality and character—and all that person can think is this:

*I am going to be a monster.*

That person hears nothing the doctor says—or hears it faintly, vaguely, as if the doctor is speaking in tongues—because she is standing on a vast empty plain, the place where she thinks she will live from now on, disfigured, set apart, forever the stranger. The woman shudders as she imagines looking into a mirror, looking into a man's eyes while he watches her undress, and she is holding her breath in horror when an oddly comforting thought strolls into view: *Well*, she thinks, *I guess that settles the whole sex thing.*

• • • •

Eventually, the nightmare images vanished. There would be no monsters, no exile, no lonely windy plain. But I was right about one thing: Breast cancer did, in fact, settle the whole sex thing, though not at all in the way I had imagined.

• • • •

I was fifty-seven when I was diagnosed. By then, I reckon, I had been waging war against desire for more than a decade.

Desire is a mirror: It can tell you who you are. When I was eleven, I wanted a boy named Skippy. He had blue eyes and blond hair and a mother just like the ones on TV. In my twenties, I wanted kisses that cracked me open like a tree struck by lightning. When I married, I thought the question of what I wanted was settled forever. But forever doesn't always last as long as you hope it will. I was forty-four when my husband died.

*Now what?* I wondered.

At first it looked like the question had been answered for me. My husband's death had triggered what was termed a traumatic menopause. I figured then that desire would simply go away, like a polite guest who looks up and realizes the party is over and the hostess would like to go to bed. I thought it might be for me like it was for a character in one of Isak Dinesen's stories: "What changed her was what changes all women at fifty: the transfer from the active service of life—with a pension or the honors of war as the case may be—to the mere passive state of a looker on. A weight fell away from her; she flew up to a higher perch and cackled a little . . . In her laughter of liberation there certainly was a little madness."

That sounded great to me. I remember walking through Washington Square Park in New York, around the time my status as a potential bearer of children had come to an irrevocable end. I felt a kind of lightness, a new connection to that girl I had been before the business of being a woman had begun. I felt a buoyancy I had not known in a very long time.

I looked at the young women sauntering down the avenues, their carefully made-up faces a studied mask of indifference to the comments flung at them; I looked at the couples entwined on the benches, at the mothers in the park hoisting children onto swings. *I've been to each of those places,* I thought, and now, for the first time in a long time, I was in a place I'd never been before, an émigré to an unknown land. *Who is this woman,* I thought, *who is no longer lashed so tightly to the world of men? What does it mean to be finally getting old, to live alone, to be invisible in a way that I have not been since I was a teenager?* I was nervous, I admit, but also strangely elated, as if I'd been handed the keys to a new, powerful, and very fast car.

I began to get excited about this new phase, in somewhat the same way I once had been about being pregnant. I wanted to think about my new condition. I liked thinking of this change as being as portentous as the one that made me fertile, as the one that ended my virginity, as the one that made me a mother. I liked the idea that menopause returned you to a sort of basic self, before the child-bearing years dictated a set of urges, a set of responses. It promised a kind of freedom, a lightness, a simplicity of being.

I looked for counsel, a *What to Expect When You Are No Longer Capable of Expecting* sort of guide. But there aren't a lot of road maps to getting older, and the ones available are fairly polarized when it comes to sex. On the one hand, there is the Wise Woman school of utter renunciation: Embrace your inner goddess, cultivate a garden, and wear large, unbecoming pieces of clothing. On the other, there are the Indefatigables, the ones promoting sex and plenty of it as the preternatural right of all women this side of the river Styx. The assumption here seems to be that all women want sex no matter how old they are, no matter how difficult it is to find and how uncomfortable it can be for those who do find it. Sex among the geriatric has become the new patent medicine, good for whatever ails you—a fountain of youth only an Internet dating site away. "Even a seasoned woman of 70 who is depressed and suffering from arthritis can revive her joie de vivre through the healing powers of sex," wrote Gail Sheehy in her book *The Seasoned Woman.* (Words like *seasoned* and *juicy* pop up a lot in books about aging women, as if an older woman's highest ambition is to resemble a bowl of well-dressed salad.)

*Nice work if you can get it,* I thought, but experience had taught me that it wasn't so easy for older women to find love or even companionship. Some of the most brilliant, charismatic, and beautiful women I knew found themselves mendicants in the marketplace of desire. That scared me. Instead, I wanted a graceful retirement: to quit before I was fired, to leave behind any expectation of love and sex before it became even less likely that it would come my way. I wanted to leave the world of desire the way Derek Jeter left baseball or Wayne Gretzky left hockey.

• • • •

Of course, it didn't work that way. Lust teased and beckoned, executing brief guerrilla forays across the borders of my self-containment. A sideways glance from a stranger, for example, could spark a sudden wave of longing, striking at the weakest point of my defenses: my love of the game of seduction, the sheer joy of flirtation, the glow in which a man's passion had once dressed me.

When I was young, the rules of attraction had been my theater of war, my coming of age, the weapon of choice in my own rebellion. In my twenties, that horrific decade of self-doubt and delusion, I found this the one arena where I didn't have to fake it: where I felt all the confidence and delight I utterly lacked in the adult world;

where I took the risks I was too inhibited to take when trying to forge a career, a life, a reality that didn't need drowning in a bottle of Jack Daniel's and a carton of ice cream.

I don't mean to say that love and sex had brought me nothing but joy—far from it. There were the usual crop of spectacular failures, bizarre (*what was I thinking?*) encounters, deep wounds, unrequited fancies . . . all the banana peels and pratfalls that come with the territory. But when I was young, those failures, as well as the occasional success, taught me something about myself. Taught me more, in fact, since catastrophe almost always teaches you more than victory ever will.

Sex had served, at various times, as a canvas, a discipline, a burning bridge, and finally, when I met my husband, a long-sought redemption. But what did I want from it now? What did it still have to teach? I was no longer at an age where I could or would bend myself like a pretzel to be the woman I thought would please the man I wanted; I no longer needed a man to tell me who I was. What, then, did I even want from love, assuming it should ever come my way again? The fact that rushes of intense physical desire still surged, that nostalgia for an intimate domesticity still surfaced, made me crazy. Not just because of how difficult it was to find someone in this youth-obsessed culture, but because I didn't want to cede the mental real estate that men demanded, because I wanted so dearly to need only myself. But the longing wouldn't leave, was in fact in open rebellion with my cooler head. "Heart, you bully, you punk, I'm wrecked, I'm shocked / stiff," the poet Marie Ponsot wrote. "You? You still try to rule the world."

I just wanted, I thought, to be done, left alone. But was even that much true? Desire brought chaos, and wreckage in its wake, but it also delivered exhilaration, intensity, a rush of blood and a thrum of nerves like no other. What would it be like to never again know that quickening that comes of turning a corner and seeing some lout in a baseball cap and sweatshirt who shines now in rags of light, all because of a single kiss? Or the giddy start of an affair that would end badly, of course, but would find you smiling years later? Desire heightened the senses, destroyed the routine, could make you alive in a way that nothing else did. What could possibly be its equal?

I wonder sometimes how long it would have continued, my war with wanting, how long I would have been marooned in that place where I was unable to escape the loneliness that desire can bring and yet unwilling to accept the idea that a woman's desirability was merely a season in a long life, best left alone as it departed.

Cancer made short work of all that wondering.

• • • •

Around the time my hair fell out, courtesy of chemotherapy, a male friend called. He wanted to know if I still felt "womanly." Of course, I answered. Never more so. And yet there was a strange contradiction at work. Breast cancer is a disease that goes to the very heart of being a woman at the same time it shreds your sense of what, on the surface at least, that means.

Simone de Beauvoir once remarked that in life, the members of her gender had two jobs—that of being a woman, with all its trappings and demands, its masquerades and its compromises . . . and that of being a person. I suppose breast cancer revealed to me the difference between the two. (Ironically, de Beauvoir herself never figured it out; in her later work, she argued that old age destroys a woman's reason for being.)

Breast cancer treatments, at least for veterans of the slash, poison, and burn school, are a crash course in what it's like to grow old, like those sped-up nature films that show a plant growing from blossom to compost in about five seconds. You lose your looks, you lose your energy, your memory is full of holes, and you are vulnerable to every virus that flies by. But at the same time, you also find yourself looking at the world in a broader, more expansive way.

I don't mean to make light of how awful treatment can be. There were days when I lay in bed staring out the window at a single birch tree, as if fixing on its sunlit beauty was like clinging to the only spar in a vast and very dark sea. But the birch tree reminded me of how large the world was and how unimportant was my place in it. It became a reminder: to let things be what they were, to live unsentimentally. To pare away the unnecessary neuroses, the compulsion to be at the center of every thought; to look at the world without the intervening lens of self.

One evening, when I was about midway through chemotherapy, I was sitting alone in my living room, staring at the night-darkened windows as the lamplight cast strange reflections in the glass. Suddenly I jumped; it seemed there was something or someone else in the room. Staring at me from the windowpane was a large pale oval, like a giant egg, but no—the shape was wearing thick brown spectacles. It was an old, bald, fat-faced man. I almost turned around to check, but then I finally understood: The old fat guy was me, hairless from chemo, puffy from steroids.

I was horror-stricken—and then I had to laugh. I thought of the endless hours I had spent in my life before cancer interrogating the mirror, noting the appearance of every new line, worrying about what sort of makeup and clothes an older woman should wear if she didn't want to look like "mutton dressed as lamb," as the Brits so splendidly put it.

Now, my bald head and pallid face, undefined by eyebrows or lashes, made such concerns almost comical, especially when defined against a landscape of recurrence rates and that ever-present word *incurable*. Men were no longer an issue; as my neighbor had said when he saw me a few weeks before, "Well, I guess you'll never have to worry about dating again." That stung for a while, but now, at least for the moment, it simply didn't matter what I looked like or how attractive I was. I just wanted to return to the other side of the wide river that separates the sick from the well. To once again have the luxury of taking my health for granted, to be annoyed in the middle of a traffic jam instead of panicking that the cancer had spread.

• • • •

Over time, I began to feel weirdly free. Breast cancer, it seemed, was allowing me to slip the leash of outward femininity.

I was so knocked out by this idea (and by the strange things a steady dose of chemicals can do to your brain) that I began to think I had found the solution I had been seeking for the problem of what to do—about not just sex but the whole doomed struggle to hold on to whatever looks I had possessed. Instead of worrying about how much of my old self I could hang on to, why not go the other way? The doctors had made it clear that if my chemotherapy regimen didn't shrink the tumor, a mastectomy was inevitable—they had already begun to talk about reconstructive surgery and the amazing realism of tattooed nipples. It was pretty creepy. Now I started trolling the Internet for images and blogs of women who had *not* had reconstruction. After all, what was the point of breasts at this stage of life anyway? Why not have done, go the whole way, escape once and for all the tyranny of appearance and what a woman is expected to look like? Then, I assumed, no man would ever want me and I would never have to worry about sex, or its absence, again.

It all seemed very logical at the time. But now I see how afraid I was of that part of me that still longed for an erotic life; so afraid that, in the spirit of a ruthless totalitarianism, I wanted the matter decided for me. I wanted to murder hope.

• • • •

No psychological strategy for combating cancer works better than any other in terms of survival rates, the research tells us: Straightforward denial, abject terror, and relentless positivity achieve the same results.

In other words, there is no correct way of having breast cancer, as there is no correct way of growing old. Some women thrive on the bouncy, bubblicious cheerleading of the pink-ribbon brigades who suffocate every legitimate fear in a blanket of pie-eyed optimism. Others are angry and feel patronized by the relentless sugarcoating, the denial of legitimate fear, the glossy distortion of panic and pain.

By the time I got to the end of treatment, I was amazed I didn't burst into flames when I saw the color pink or heard myself and other breast cancer patients described as "survivors." In the first place, not all of us would be. And besides, aren't we all survivors of whatever life, in its infinite wisdom, chooses to hand us?

• • • •

As you can see, anger worked pretty well for me. Anger was power and energy and wildness, a cleansing fire fueled in part by the humiliation of a breast bared, pierced by biopsy needles, tattooed for the benefit of radiation beams, burned, exposed to anyone who asked. There was fury as well at the entrenched inequality of it all: Study after study has shown that women with less education and money have fewer options, more mastectomies, botched lumpectomies, and miserly insurance companies.

But the heart of the anger lay deeper. Breast cancer patients are encouraged not to look at the thing for what it is—a bleak, lonely slog through a terrain that will form the background of the life you live for the rest of the time you have. And yet looking, really looking, at what was happening to me gave me the answers I needed to understand: not just desire, but the blueprint for my life, in this time, at this age.

To stare down a life-threatening disease, to look mortality in the face and not flinch, to find freedom in the idea that there is nothing left to lose . . . these are cancer's great gifts. They brought me, in a slow and winding spiral, face-to-face with someone I hadn't seen for a long time—my *self.* Not the wife or the mother, the flirt or the bitch or the wretched failure I sometimes imagined myself, but someone underneath the many accreted layers that shape us as we grow up and grow old, forging a personality that can cope with the demands of the world. Under the onslaught of treatment, aided by the exhaustion that set in at the end, I finally saw that the self I was trying to save was none of the roles I had attached to it, but a raw, pulsing, trembling thing, so elemental it didn't even have a gender. It was simply the I who wanted to live. And I could do anything it wanted.

• • • •

Five years later, I am no longer the bald, bespectacled egg in the window. And slowly, like the silt accumulating at the bottom of a lake, the old desires, hesitations, and self-doubts have quietly let themselves back in. And yes, desire came back too, in all its teasing frustration. But something had changed: I had laid down my arms. I was no longer at war.

I still carry around with me the memory of that small raw being, and I want to do right by that essential self I glimpsed so fleetingly. I want, finally, to stare down illusion, to see life as it is when it isn't about me, to look at the world without the blinders of vanity and need. But at the same time I have gained some respect for the heart's complexities and contradictions. I know now that I will never be rid of erotic longing, of loneliness, of the hope for romantic love, and in the end, that is a very good thing. Cancer has given me a larger perspective than I ever allowed myself before, and I welcome it.

Not that a larger perspective necessarily saves you from making an ass out of yourself. I'm beginning to think that as I age, I grow more stupid about love. The last time was a lulu: I fell for a man who decided, about five minutes after the first kiss, that he preferred the twenty-five-year-old who had left him. Or any twenty-five-year-old, for that matter.

It took a long while to recover—*really, how bad a kiss could it have been?*—but it wasn't as bad as I expected. I knew a few things by then that I hadn't before, and despite the ritual self-pity and self-loathing, I had begun to see desire for what it was—and what it was sometimes, I suspected, was laziness. Perhaps that yearning—to be loved, or simply to be made love to, by a man who knows what he's doing—was sometimes just a fallback position, a lack of imagination, when it came to finding other ways of adding adventure and depth and drama to my life. A narrowing of options instead of an opening up.

. . . .

Freud once said that when you love, you pawn your heart. You have given someone the key to your peace of mind. I don't want to pawn my heart. I want to give it away, in great and boundless measure, to those I love, to the life I live. And I want to grow old with clarity, with fierceness, to see what is there, not what I wish or hope to see. To meet the road before me head-on, without illusion.

And desire, no matter how you slice it, is about illusion—we make each other up, we blind ourselves, we see what we want to see. Love is a sleight of hand, and when the trick goes wrong, when the rabbit won't come out of the hat and the cards slip and fall in chaos to the floor, the disappointment is keener than it used to be when there was always someone else around the corner.

St. Valentine's Day arrived this year while I was still picking the thorns out of my paw from my tentative lunge at romance. Given the pain I felt, I dreaded a long evening of self-pity and loneliness and way too much Leonard Cohen. But in the end, it wasn't that way at all.

As I walked along the street that evening, I watched the young men hurrying by, holding roses in that awkward way young men always hold flowers, and I smiled. At home, I toasted love with a glass of Perrier and looked back for a moment over my own long, eventful life of the heart, lingering on the lottery I had won when I married the man I did. And in that thronged company of past and present memory, there was not a regret to be found. Outside my window, a full fat moon hung low, tangled in a net of bare branches—a happiness that no one could take away. What else did I need?

Nothing, at least for now. I think it is time to live not as I "ought"—doing what's appropriate, adhering to convention—but as I must, open to everything, wishing for nothing, walking in the high grass, with nowhere to go, with everything to experience. Surely that would be a good life. And if somewhere, unseen in that high grass, love lurks, like a snakebite, like a fallen star, if one day it trips me up and I fall, or even if it takes me in its talons and sends me skyward one more time, then I will learn what happens next. And for now, that is enough.

# 3
# To Hell and to Hold

*What I most enjoy about meeting Cusk is her*
*uncompromising intelligence. But for her, the*
*lack of compromise has been a mixed blessing.*
*It is something she is belatedly recognising*
*about herself. She talks about looking obsessively*
*at married couples after her divorce, silently*
*congratulating them on their staying power.*
*And then it came to her—it would be obvious to*
*another sort of woman—that it was not all about*
*luck, that will came into it and compromise. "It*
*was more conscious than I'd realised, this creating*
*of bonds." She started looking at women and*
*thinking, "You knew. You knew . . . you knew you*
*had to live by this system that involves a lot of*

*compromise but it means you are safe and you*
*have bothered to make yourself safe and I never,*
*never, never have. And why haven't I? Am I stupid?*
*Clearly, yes."*

*—Kate Kellaway, writing about*
*the novelist Rachel Cusk in*
The Guardian, *August 24, 2014*

*"Did you think marriage would be like this?" I ask.*
*"I thought there'd be more fucking," he replies.*
*"I thought there'd be more money," I say.*

*—Annabelle Gurwitch,*
I See You Made an Effort

# Her Life.
# My Life.

## Two Women, Two Worlds

**ERIN WHITE**

When I was twenty-five years old, I went to Paris with the woman who would eventually be my wife, although at the time—this was 1998—a legally binding marriage between two women was not a possibility. We flew to Paris the day after Christmas. Our plane landed just before dawn, and we went straight to the hotel. "My god, I'm exhausted," Chris said as she walked into the hotel room. She dropped her bag and started to undress. She pulled the duvet back from the bed. "Let's sleep."

"We can't sleep," I said. "We have to get ourselves onto Paris time." I walked over to the double window, which I realized was actually the doors to a small balcony. I turned back to look at Chris, who was now in bed, and at the room, which was green and gold and smelled like wealth. It smelled like nowhere I had ever been before. "We should walk," I insisted. "Or eat some breakfast."

Chris beat the pillow to fluff it, then flipped it over and lay her head down. She lifted the covers in invitation. "We're here for a week," she said. "There's no harm in a nap."

Chris did everything her own way, which was the most exciting thing about her. By the time we were in Paris, she had been my girlfriend for more than a year. We had met at a dinner party, to which I had been invited to meet a man. But I went home with Chris instead. Later the party's host would say that if she had known about me, she wouldn't have bothered with the man. I told her not to worry. How could she have known when I barely knew myself? For years I had felt flickers of wanting for women, but they faded quickly. But when I saw Chris, when she reached out to shake my hand with her strong hand, a red string tied around her wrist, when she said, "I'm Chris," and smiled, and I saw her eyes brighten into small suns, I thought that I would like to look at that face, and to hear that voice, for a very long time. And when she kissed me I did not feel what I usually felt during a first kiss, which was a sensation of leaving my body, of hovering above. When she kissed me, I felt myself stay.

• • • •

So that morning in Paris I crawled into bed with Chris, and we slept until afternoon. We went out into the falling dusk and stopped at a café for omelets and wine, and when we had finished, the time on the clock no longer mattered. We weren't tired and there was plenty to do. And when we did tire we just pulled the heavy silk drapes over the balcony doors and slept. It was winter, so the sun rose late and set in midafternoon, and for the brief time it was in the sky, it barely shone. For a week we did all the things that people do in Paris: We walked until our legs ached; we sat for hours in the hotel bar where Chris drank cognac and I drank champagne and smoked.

Before I met Chris, my life was a quiet one. I was a cautious and serious person. I worked long hours for a community organizing project and spent my weekends reading and seeing foreign films. When Chris started sleeping over, we went to dinners at restaurants I had only read about in magazines. We made out in the library of her law firm and went to Final Four basketball games.

On nights when she came to my apartment late, I cooked for her, simple meals of pasta and eggs, food she loved. She also told me she loved my worn slippers, my short nightgowns that I wore with wool socks, the way I slid around my apartment in them when she turned on the jazz station. Before I met Chris, it had never occurred to me that someone might love all the things I was and I did, without trying.

Chris introduced me to myself. This is who you are, she seemed to say to me every time she touched me. At first I was startled; at first I demurred. Oh, no, I wanted to say. I think you are mistaken. But she wasn't. By the time we were in Paris, I had stopped asking myself how she knew. By the time we were in Paris, I had learned how to just enjoy myself. Which was exactly what I did. On our last night, when we were walking back to the hotel slightly drunk and slightly lost, she stopped, took me by the arm, pushed me against a wall, and kissed me, hard. And when someone honked at us, called out his car window, I pulled away only to laugh, and then I kissed her back.

• • • •

Five years later, Chris and I were one of the first same-sex couples in the country to be legally married. Our wedding was more humble than historic: A minister friend of ours came over one evening after work and, after leading us through vows and reading a few psalms, pronounced us wife and wife. I was barefoot; I was eight months pregnant with our first child.

In the months before our daughter was born, Chris and I decided that I would stay home with the baby and Chris would continue to work full-time. I was compelled by the idea of full-time motherhood; my maternal ambition was as strong as my professional one. I had studied child development in college and later worked as a preschool teacher, and I'd long been fascinated by philosophies of human development, the brilliant work of Winnicott and Erikson, Piaget and Montessori. For years I had longed for a child of my own, for the chance to nurture a life from its beginning, to observe and shape a child's development. I saw motherhood as an elementally human experience, one that was separate from all the other professional and material strivings of adulthood. And while Chris didn't share my drive (or even necessarily understand it), she was happy to have me stay home with our baby, even though it meant the end of my salary for the indefinite future. Because she had recently taken an in-house counsel position, which meant both fewer hours and less pay than her law firm job, we decided to move to a tiny town in the country where we could buy a less expensive house and afford to live without any income from me. We decided, in other words, to enter into a division of labor and responsibilities that had once started a revolution.

• • • •

"I really can't wait until a Tuesday is just a Tuesday," I said to Chris one morning as I tried to shove a pile of student papers, my lunch, and my exercise clothes into my work bag before the beginning of my hour-long commute and long day of teaching and grading and meetings. A straight colleague had recently told me she was jealous of my impending lesbian-mom status. "The great thing about your life is that no matter what, you'll never be mainstream," she said. "You'll always be a radical." I loved her for saying that. Here I was, a pregnant woman who wanted to stop working and stay at home with my baby, fully supported by my spouse . . . and I still got to be a radical.

And yet, just a few months later, as Chris leaned over to kiss me good-bye while I nursed our daughter in bed, my heart sank—as it did every morning when she left. That morning she smelled like an unreachable heaven: shampoo and face cream and coffee. She wore a neatly pressed button-down shirt and small gold earrings, a diver's watch. All the things she had been wearing forever, all the things that used to make me crazy with desire for her. But now I was just crazy with envy. No one had told me how lonely your world becomes when a Tuesday is just a Tuesday.

The tedium and isolation of stay-at-home motherhood is a story as old as water, but in every generation we are caught off guard by its oddities, its strains. We can't imagine anyone ever being as stunned by love and boredom as we are, can't translate the peculiarities of our days. I didn't want to be away from the baby, but I was so tired of being with the baby. She was fascinating, but her demands were endless. And I was meeting those demands all on my own, all day long. As I spent hours in the bathroom because the baby was soothed by the sound of the exhaust fan, the brilliant developmental theorists I'd once loved began to seem detached and academic. Grandfatherly. They couldn't tell me how to get this baby to stop crying, to go to sleep. And so I devised my own practices. I read the same book page dozens of times because the sound of a turning page would wake her. I drove snowy back roads for hours just so she would sleep, biting the inside of my cheek to stay awake.

My life had become very small. And despite the words of my straight colleague a few months before, I knew, now, that there was nothing radical about it. Chris and I were supposed to be different because we were two women. The prevailing wisdom, created in part by the increasing visibility of same-sex marriages in the media and popular culture, told us that we were inherently well positioned to create an equitable arrangement, a feminist household. After all, who understands a woman's burdens better than another woman? The problem was, we had entirely different burdens. Chris was supposed to know what went in the diaper bag and to do the night feedings with a bottle of pumped breast milk, but she didn't. And I didn't earn a paycheck. I depended on her to fill our checking account and she left her coffee cup in the sink for me to wash. In the evenings Chris was tired and distracted by work; I was exhausted and overwhelmed by the baby. We wanted each other's attention: She wanted to talk about her cases; I wanted to talk about our daughter. Should we delay her immunizations? Wait until her first birthday to feed her eggs? We feigned interest in each other's disparate concerns, unable to comprehend their importance.

We were lesbians, but we were the very opposite of radical.

• • • •

When our first daughter was four and our second a year old, I told Chris, "I'm going to put the baby in child care. I want to start working a few hours a day."

"I think you should," she said. "I think it's a great idea." And I could tell she meant it. I knew Chris was happy to have me at home with our girls, but I also knew she was tired of hearing me complain about the drudgery and loneliness of stay-at-home motherhood. "I just want you to be happy," she had said on more than one occasion. The confusing thing was, much of the time I *was* happy. All in all, I liked being home with my children. What I didn't like were the attending domestic responsibilities: the dishes, the endless straightening up, the snack making, the towel folding. These jobs were mine because I was home to do them, but they were tedious and unrelenting. I needed a life outside our house, apart from both my children and the domestic chaos they created.

During the months and years that followed, we made some changes that were good for both of us, not to mention for the kids. On days when I had late meetings, Chris left work early to pick up the girls. When I had a deadline, Chris took the girls away for the weekend so I could work. She took on the invisible tasks that are so hard to explain: wash the beloved red leggings every night because the six-year-old won't wear anything else; pack a snack for the three-year-old because she can't survive the five ravenous minutes between school and home. Although Chris still worked full-time (and was the primary breadwinner) and I was still the primary parent, we became more like partners in our domestic endeavor.

But the dynamic between us, improved as it may have been, was distant. I hadn't married Chris because I wanted to be her partner in domestic endeavor; I had married her because when she kissed me, my body said *stay.* But now that we had become so focused on our responsibilities, I wasn't as interested in kissing Chris as I once had been. I was more interested in telling her what she owed me, comparing my chores and my obligations to hers, and always, always wanting to prove my deficits of autonomy and rest. *Stay,* my body once said. But not anymore. It is hard for your body to speak when your mind is so very busy keeping score.

I told myself not to worry about the distance between us, about my lack of desire. *The kids are young, and so demanding,* I thought. *Think of how you met! Think of all the things you did with her! That's still you!*

But it wasn't still me. Motherhood had changed me. I had *wanted* it to change me. I had intentionally fixed my gaze on my children; I had entered into a relationship with them that was complex and mutual and interesting. But that relationship was also consuming in a way that I had not expected but also did not resist. I devoted myself to my children and I relegated my marriage to the realm of domestic management and scorekeeping. I was making a mistake by continually telling myself not to worry about the distance between Chris and me. And I might have kept making it if we hadn't decided to go back to Paris.

• • • •

For years Chris had been telling me she wanted to take me there for my birthday. "When you're forty," she started saying when I turned thirty-five and was still nursing our second baby, "we'll go back." At the time, I just laughed. I couldn't imagine an ocean separating me from my babies; I could, at that time, barely imagine missing bedtime. Our second baby had made me more efficient, more unflappable, but I still was bowled over by the constancy of my children's physical and emotional needs. When I closed my eyes each night, I saw their faces, felt the weight of their bodies. I woke often, thinking I heard them cry out for me, only to find them quietly sleeping in their beds. Paris might as well have been the moon.

But when I was almost forty and that second baby went to kindergarten, Chris booked plane tickets and rented an apartment. "You should think about what you want to do there," she said again and again in the weeks before we left. "Oh, I will," I told her. But in truth I hardly thought about the trip, other than the details of our girls' care while we were away. I couldn't begin to think about the realities of Paris itself. "I just want to sleep," I said flippantly. "I just want to get through dinner without someone spilling her milk."

. . . .

From the moment we arrived, Paris was lovely, and I was sad—sad in a way I had not felt at home. The beauty stunned me; the vaulted churches, the dark and narrow Seine, the marble café tables, the chocolates in the shapes of seashells and jewels . . . I loved it all, and yet I could not shake an unexpected grief. I couldn't stop thinking about the girl I had been when we were here before: the girl who would rather go to a bar than to a museum; who bought sexy bras at Aubade, not little-girl tights at Monoprix. I had returned to Paris with the hope—the delusion, really—that I would be her again, that I would just slip into her skin. But that transformation wasn't happening. When I saw my reflection in a store window, when I looked at my freckled hands wrapped around a coffee cup, the sight of my forty-year-old self disappointed me.

So the second afternoon, when Chris stopped outside our old hotel—the hotel we had stayed in during our first trip to Paris—and asked if I wanted to go in, I hesitated. "Come on!" she said excitedly. "Let's have a drink and take a picture." She smiled at me. She was thinking about a picture we had in our bedroom, one taken in that very bar fifteen years before.

"Really?" I said. "Why don't we go somewhere new?"

As soon as the words left my mouth—as soon as I saw the look on Chris's face—I knew I'd made a mistake. "Oh, okay, let's go," I said, trying to match her earlier excitement and lighten the moment, which suddenly felt alarmingly heavy.

But it was too late. Chris just shook her head, and we walked the rest of the way back to our apartment in silence. When we got to the door, I reached for her arm. "Let's not go upstairs quite yet," I said. "Let's get a drink."

Chris still didn't answer, but she put the key away and we walked to a bar just around the corner. Chris ordered a beer. I asked for water.

"Look," I said quietly, leaning across the table. "I'm sorry. It's just that—"

I paused, not knowing how to explain. "Since we got here, I haven't been able to stop thinking about last time. And that girl in the bar with the champagne and the cigarettes, that girl who was never worried, never tired? That's not me anymore. And I just couldn't, I couldn't face—"

Chris interrupted me. "Why is it you can only think about yourself?" she said. "Did it occur to you how important it might be to *me*, going in there with you again?"

*No*, I thought but didn't say. *You did not occur to me at all.*

We sat in silence for a long time. Finally I tried again. "I thought that eventually, when our kids were older," I said, "when everything settled down, I thought I'd be able to pick up where I left off and become that passionate girl again." I laughed a little, shaking my head. "But now I realize I can't. That person is gone."

"Not to me," Chris said, her voice wavering with hurt.

I didn't know what to say. But this was what I was beginning to understand: Chris and I had lived the last decade in entirely different ways. I had lived mine in a land outside of ordinary time, where I believed (if I had even stopped to consider what I believed) that our children, and my all-consuming endeavor of caring for them, gave me some sort of temporal dispensation, as though everything I treasured—about both myself and Chris—would return to me, intact, when I came up for air. As though, when I came up for air, I would still be that twenty-five-year-old girl in the Paris bar. But Chris knew better. She too had raised our children during this decade, but she also had worked and traveled, dedicated herself to new interests and ideas, spent days and even weeks away from me and the girls. And over the years she'd made peace with what had passed, with who we no longer were: women guided only by desire. She knew that now we were wives. And she knew she loved me still. So when she said, "Let's go to the bar, let's go have a drink," she simply wanted to visit the graces of our past and raise a glass to them. To wish them, to wish us, well. I didn't know how to do that yet, but I knew that it was time to try. It was time to catch up with my wife.

I looked at Chris and I thought, as I had not in so many years, of that late-August evening when she first put her hand out to me. Her eyes were still like small suns, but there were creases at the edges now. I looked at her and knew there was a reason that Chris loved the memory of the girl I had been, and the reason was simple: She loved me.

"I am so sorry," I said finally. "And—you're very beautiful." I meant it. She was.

She looked away, but I saw her eyes soften. "That won't get you anywhere," she said, and then she smiled.

We ordered a bottle of wine. There was nowhere we had to be, no one who was waiting for us to come home. I was struck by the magnitude—the magnificence—of what we had done, of what Chris had insisted we do: We had left our children on the other side of the Atlantic. We were alone together in Paris.

We stayed in the café for hours, eating delicately arranged plates of food, drinking wine that had nothing in common with the wine we drank at home. I was careful, and I could feel Chris being careful too. But it was not awkward. It was the opposite of awkward, really. We were separate but not distant. We were generous. It was an extraordinary feeling; it had been such a terribly long time since I had felt it.

After that, our days in Paris passed quickly—but slowly, luxuriously, too. I dragged Chris across three arrondissements in search of a bakery I had read about in the *New Yorker*; I stood patiently next to her while she studied a display case of hand-forged knives, and I told her yes, absolutely she should buy one, every woman should own a good knife. We went to the Musée d'Orsay, and I wept looking at Caillebotte's *Planers*, that sublime rendering of sunlight on wood and bare skin, just as I had when I first saw the painting all those years before. We walked and we slept and we drank. We made a new mark on the city. And as we did, I began to feel a fondness for the girl I had been. I remembered what I loved about her, and what I missed, and what I wanted to get back. I began to feel small and treasured parts of myself returning, like starlings to a spire.

On our last day in Paris we took the train to Versailles, and we walked in the gardens where the mist of the water made it seem as though we were walking near the sea. Later we sat on a stone bench to eat a chocolate bar and a few apricots I had in my bag.

"I'm ready to go home," Chris said. "I miss the girls."

"I don't," I said, laughing. "I could stay another week." And it was true. I didn't, and I could.

It was a pleasant reversal. I appreciated her for missing them, so I didn't have to.

# Jason, Me, and Jesus

## The Other Guy in Our Relationship

**VERONICA CHAMBERS**

*In a piece titled "Getting the Milk for Free" in* The
Bitch in the House, *Veronica Chambers wrote about
being done with dating men who relied on her, as a
successful, hardworking woman in her twenties, to pay
for things—from necessities to luxuries—for both of
them. At the end, she met Jason, who seemed different:
Not just wry, warm, and intelligent, he also had a
career and his own apartment. The relationship felt
equal in a way her past ones hadn't, and she decided
to give it a try, despite their living in different cities.*

*Fourteen years later, Veronica has been married
to Jason for thirteen of those years, and they have
an eight-year-old daughter. She was right that he'd
pull his weight in the marriage. What she didn't
anticipate was that, as two Christians (she a black
Latina, he white and raised Southern Baptist), they
would find faith to be something that divided them
deeply—though it also would prove invaluable to her
when the going got rough. Read on for her story.*

The year before I turned thirty, my friend Lise set me up—
three times—with Jason. Jason and Lise lived in Philadelphia,
and I lived in New York. The first time, Jason thought we were
meeting professionally, a networking thing. He ran a travel website and I was just back from a three-month stint in Japan.

I liked him. He was funny and sarcastic, but not unkind. But
after that meeting, Lise told me Jason didn't seem interested. So
the second time, when we all met up in Philly at a Belgian mussels
and fries place—this time we would just hang out as friends—I
thought, *If he isn't interested, I'm not going to be nice.* So I got drunk.
Now, Drunk Veronica isn't at all like Sober Veronica. Drunk Veronica talks a lot of trash, like she's a professional athlete about to wipe
the court with you. She's overconfident and underskilled, so when
she says she can do some cool party trick like stacking wineglasses
in a pyramid, she can't. Oh yeah, and she thinks she's hilarious.

Turns out Jason *loved* Drunk Veronica. But we were both in other
relationships—him with a girl who lived with six cats, me with a
guy who, to this day, is known as That Cheating Bastard. After
both of those relationships (thankfully) ended, Lise suggested that
Jason gave me a call. About damn time.

Six months after our first date, Jason proposed and I said yes. It
was a leap. But as the child of an ugly divorce, I believed deeply that
every marriage was a leap, a step into the unknown of faith and
blind trust. What I trusted was that Jason was a good and honorable
man—not just appealing on the surface, but also the kind of man
who kept his promises and took his responsibilities seriously. I knew
he would work hard at the marriage, and that hard work, combined
with how much fun we had together, would give us a shot.

• • • •

A few months into our engagement, we went out to dinner. We
were talking about God, and I said, in response to something, that

my God was not a jealous God. Jason looked at me. He took a sip
of wine. "I don't know what you are," he said, sounding friendly
enough, "but you're not a Christian."

I stopped chewing and looked at him. "Excuse me?"

"You misquote scripture," he said. "A lot."

I put down my fork. I felt my anger form a little ball at the pit
of my stomach.

"Like—just then," he offered. "When you said, 'My God is not
a jealous God.' "

"Right," I said. "My point being, I think all religions are valid.
Not just mine. Or, you know. *Yours.*" I glared at him, feeling the
anger ball begin to grow.

"I don't disagree with the *thought*," he explained—a bit patron-
izingly, I decided. "But the Bible verse is about how my God *is* a
jealous God. ' . . . for I the Lord thy God *am* a jealous God.' You
can't just re-create the Bible to say whatever you want and pretend
that's Christianity."

The ball in my stomach was now the size of a grapefruit, and
rising up toward my heart. In fact, I had to hold back from turning
over the table, like a ticked-off rapper in a music video.

I stood up, holding on to the table so as not to smash him or anything else within reach. "I think this dinner is over," I said.

• • • •

Growing up, Jason was raised by conservative Southern Baptists.
He went to Christian private schools, which he hated. He went to
church five nights a week. Which he hated. His parents mellowed
with age and eventually found a nice multi-culti Presbyterian
church. But for Jason, church was a mélange of hypocrisy and in-
adequacy, and he declared himself "interested in the mystery and
literature and history of world religion, but with no interest in organized religion." That struck me as okay.

In contrast, I had grown up being shuffled from household to household. I'd been hungry. I'd been homeless. I'd been abused. When I was very young, my mother taught me prayers, and every New Year's Eve, we did a traditional Latina ritual of bathing in a tub full of flower petals and essential oils to cleanse the spirit. For me, religion was a comfort during hard times, and because my childhood was so skittish, I mostly made it up as I went along. I went to Lutheran church for a little while. I sometimes attended a big traditional black Baptist church with my crazy Bible-thumping aunt. I went to Buddhist temple with my serene favorite aunt. And in truth, I loved it all. When, at sixteen, I went to Bard College at Simon's Rock and found there girls in macramé vests and boys in tie-dye T-shirts playing Frisbee on the lawn (this even though it was the late eighties, not 1968), I felt very much at home. I am the definition of a New Age hippie when it comes to religion. I take a little bit of everything I've been exposed to, and if I like it and it feels good, I call it God. In my life, this works.

And in my life, when I pray to God, I pray to Jesus, and that makes me a Christian. I prayed to Jesus when our family had no food or money. I prayed to Jesus when I walked the streets at night because back at home, the adults beat me up. I felt the *presence* of Jesus as I walked, praying no one would attack or accost me when I lay down on the side of the road to grab a few minutes of sleep because I had to get up for school and keep an A average because college was my only hope of escape.

I had prayed and felt guidance, insight, and wisdom, and it saved me when I was in the 'hood and out with the wrong people and two guys took out their guns and I figured out how to get out of the room before it all went to hell.

I had prayed my way through school every semester when it turned out that the mix of scholarships and loans didn't quite cover the balance due and I had to come up with $5,000 by making $3.25

an hour working six jobs at once on campus (I was a resident advisor, a Spanish tutor, a Quaker meeting babysitter, a desk clerk at the library, a switchboard operator, and a cafeteria dishwasher). Still, I had no idea how I was going to find that money, let alone keep finding it for a whole four years so I could graduate. I prayed to Jesus to help me figure it out.

After college, my brother went to jail—three times—and my parents refused to go see him or come to his aid. Jesus helped me roll into the prison visiting rooms, put money on my brother's books, deal with shady lawyers, and try to get my brother on a path where maybe he might live to see thirty years old.

It was Jesus who helped me not lose my mind when I had to navigate a path as a young black woman in predominantly white workplaces. It was Jesus—as in, "Jesus, help me not slap this b\*\*ch"—when a white woman colleague told me that even in that Donna Karan suit, I had a "butt like a stripper."

• • • •

So there was no way this man—engaged to me or not—was gonna sit at my dinner table and tell me I wasn't a Christian. Because while it may be true that I'm not a *typical* Christian and I don't know the Bible back and forth, I do know that Jesus—or the symbol of Jesus and all the things I've thrown into the mix with him: meditation and prayer, Sunday church services and gospel music—was, and is, my own internal guiding force on how to be good. I believe that my relationship with Jesus has made me more compassionate, less needy, more driven to service, more patient . . . just an overall better, kinder person.

Which, ironically, is part of what kept me from punching Jason or smashing things that night at dinner, not to mention banishing him from my apartment, in Brooklyn, when I went home afterward—though, admittedly, it also helped that he lived a hundred miles away, in Philly; there was nowhere to banish him to. So I prayed to Jesus, my Jesus, to give me strength to get through the night with him by my side. And He did. And in the morning, Jason said, "I don't get why you're furious, but I love you and I don't want you to be mad, so tell me what to do." Which was very winning, and made me forgive him.

· · · ·

We went to premarital counseling with my minister, and our wedding was officiated by two ministers: my cool older black guy from Brooklyn (think a tennis-playing, Lacoste-wearing Denzel Washington), and Jason's parents' minister, John, a cool older white guy from Pennsylvania (think Kevin Costner when he plays a cool older white guy minister from the suburbs of Philadelphia). The ministers had jokes for days up on that pulpit—and it was a great way to start our life together, those two guys having such a good time, hamming it up like it was an HBO comedy special.

· · · ·

After the fight that almost ended everything, Jason declared that since religion was so important to me, he would come to church with me—even though he hated going to church and believed he had attended enough service to last him a lifetime. He also felt that since I was so New Age in some of my religious ("religious," he would say, miming the quotes) leanings, he wanted to know who and what I was praying to, so that he could declare "bullshit" when he felt I was being sold a bill of (holy) crap.

I was happy about this; I felt strongly that we raise our eventual offspring with some sort of religion, and I wanted to find one, or some combination of several, that worked for both of us. Our first and probably best church was the chapel at Princeton University. I loved how intimate it was, with its small, diverse congregation: It mirrored the community feeling I had loved in my Presbyterian church in Brooklyn. Jason liked the fact that so many of the people who preached were visiting academics, so their sermons were more intellectual and thoughtful than what he'd grown up with. I love myself some charismatic preaching, but Jason would rather hear a thoughtful meditation on ancient Egypt and the class system and how it affects class and society today. Princeton was not a "Let the choir say Amen!" type of church, but I was happy that Jason was happy.

• • • •

Two years later, when we moved to Los Angeles, we switched gears and went to a big black megachurch. At first Jason wasn't excited. Every service was as dramatic as a Tyler Perry movie—you could count on at least one person fainting, two people screaming out "Lord, have mercy!" and one well-dressed man in a flawless suit dancing so fervently that he needed to pat his forehead with a handkerchief like James Brown. For Jason, this was a little too close to the Southern Baptist style that he'd found so theatrical and fake. But I convinced him to go with the promise of great music and—yes—fried chicken afterward. (One of the great ironies of my interracial marriage: I am not a chicken fan, while my white husband *loves* fried chicken and other southern food—which I actually know little about, because I'm black Latina, not black southern.) He ended up liking the church fine, though the chicken didn't hurt the cause, and I still think that those Sundays were an important building block in the early days of our marriage. Getting up early and putting on our Sunday clothes: him a shirt and sports jacket, me a dress and heels. We played gospel in the car, and one of my favorite and oft-played songs—"I Believe in You and Me," from *The Preacher's Wife* soundtrack—was a song about not just faith but love, loyalty, and marriage.

Which was a good thing, because soon after that, our relationship hit another rough patch, this one long and dangerous. Jason hated his job, and he became, increasingly, sarcastic and hypercritical. He lit into anybody who dared ask him a stupid question or present a lazy idea at work, regularly sneered on conference calls with his superiors . . . and then came home and continued his ranting at me. He never raised his hand to me, but the yelling and the anger were palpable. He seemed like a complete stranger, and I went to bed every night crying.

I had steeled myself against all the things that I had seen go wrong in my parents' marriage and the marriages of my older friends. I was prepared to face infidelity and to draw the line at the first sign of physical violence. But I didn't know—still don't, exactly—how to put into words the feeling I got when he yelled at me; the closest I can come is to say that I felt like I'd been slapped. I didn't know how to categorize the way I began to shiver every time I heard his key in the door and how unprepared I was to have a knockdown screaming match about whatever random topic he might land on that night.

It would be wrong to say that I prayed on it. I didn't get on my knees and ask for help. Instead, I did a kind of nonstop muttering to God, using one of my favorite gospel music expressions: "Jesus, take the wheel. Jesus, take the wheel." In my car, on the way to work: "Jesus, take the wheel." At night, when I took long showers because I was so sad and angry that I didn't want to crawl into bed with him: "Jesus, take the wheel." When he called and I saw his number pop up on my cell phone and I wanted to dash back in time, take off the white dress and reverse to the moment when he handed me that ring and say, *"Hell* no!" . . . in those moments, I just muttered to myself nonstop, the way my aunt, the Buddhist, chanted for peace and clarity. "Jesus, take the wheel. Jesus, take the wheel."

My biggest fear was that I'd married the wrong person. That I had somehow failed to see his dark side. Yes, he was easy on the eyes and he made me laugh, and we wanted the same kind of life: small house, big travels, small family, big love, and someday, a nice big dog. But this anger was new, and I couldn't live with the yelling, the glaring, the insults, the stomping. I couldn't spend an indefinite amount of time curled up on my side of the bed, listening to Sarah McLachlan and crying myself to sleep. I wanted to leave. Cut my losses, go back to Brooklyn, and start stalking ex-boyfriends on Facebook.

Instead, I kept praying. And a few weeks into it, I had a very clear thought: *He's unhappy. He's more than unhappy; he's miserable. He needs help.* That level of compassion wasn't me, people. That was Jesus.

So I told him I was kicking him out. I said he had one week to get a therapist or he was going to have to find someplace else to live.

He started sobbing. "Are you divorcing me?" he asked.

I said—or rather, Jesus inspired me to say—"I'm not threatening you with divorce, but you need help. You've got seven days to show me you want help and will get it, and then we can continue the conversation."

The next day he found a therapist, covered by his health plan. Two days later, he had his first appointment. Right away, the therapist checked him on being insulting and aggressive. (Apparently, within the first ten minutes of the appointment he had insulted her outfit, her scrawny ficus tree, and the shitty parking situation in her office complex.) I felt reassured that within one session, she'd so clearly seen what I had been seeing for weeks. By day seven, his temper and his ire had dampened. He needed help and he was getting it, and something in him began to calm down.

• • • •

This June, Jason and I will have been married thirteen years. Lest you think that the therapy that year in California cured everything for us, let me assure you that all hell has broken loose in a similar fashion probably every other year since our wedding day. Just a year after the first meltdown, Jason lost his job. Which seemed like a blessing in disguise until a year later, when he was reading six newspapers a day and slow-roasting his own coffee yet still didn't have—nor was he looking for—actual paid work.

Then I developed a trifecta of pregnancy complications, including one so rare that most women in the United States never get it anymore. I almost died in childbirth, and after I survived and our baby survived, Jason, who had been holding it together like he was part Dalai Lama and part George Clooney on *ER*, went *nuts:* screaming, angry, raging. The therapist he found then explained how he had caretaker fatigue and that, on some level, he was disappointed and angry that the birth hadn't turned out the way he was hoping. I thought, "Yeah, you and me both, pal." But this is the simple truth: My faith is my rock. My faith saves me again and again, while for Jason, when the going gets rough, he often feels like he has nothing. This makes him scared, and when he's scared, he gets angry. And that's when our troubles start.

• • • •

Each time he goes off the rails, there are weeks of misery, with him losing his shit and me muttering for Jesus to step in and give me patience and compassion. And it's not that I'm some hand-wringing martyr; I get angry too. I yell. I occasionally break things. But my faith calms me down and leads me to believe that there is something underneath our anger and arguments that's worth working toward—that our hope and love and joy are not merely illusions, but experiences and feelings meant to outweigh all the heartbreak and sadness that creeps into every life. I have never threatened

Jason with divorce. I have never left him. When things blow up, I pray and I mutter and I keep my distance until I can feel some clarity and my instinct is to help, not just to hold my ground and give him hell back. And again I say: For me, that's religion. That's Jesus.

•  •  •  •

My husband still does not believe in God. I believe, deeply, that I would not be married today without Him. That Jason comes with me to church, that he's accompanied me on a few yoga and spiritual retreats, and that he joins me in grace at mealtimes . . . all this feels like some small acknowledgment that spirituality, if not Jesus per se, has played a role in our marriage—a role I think Jason is grateful for. And I am grateful to him for coming around, for meeting me halfway—or more, really—on this.

Of course, it helps that I let him do things in his own fashion. Just a few months ago, I scored us some very hard-to-get tickets to a weekend away with the great Buddhist teacher Ani Pema Chödrön. Jason liked the pretty cabin we stayed in and he was A-okay with our daughter going off to make mandalas and do yoga at the children's center. But he decided that he didn't want to spend the afternoon in meditation and hearing a lecture by Ani Pema, even though she's like a goddess to me.

Jason had been doing some Googling and, go figure, he realized that the Brewery Ommegang was just a short drive from the retreat center. He asked if it would be okay, since it was such a beautiful day, if he drove through the mountains in our MINI Cooper, blasting Dylan, then proceeded to the brewery to do *his* worshipping at the temple of beer. I rolled my eyes, but the truth is, I was fine with it. For one, I was grateful he'd asked—and that, if I'd said no, he would have stayed there, uncomplaining (or mostly uncomplaining, anyway), for me. But fancy beer makes Jason happy, just like my religion makes me happy, and who am I to tell Jason how to worship, as long as he doesn't tell *me* how to? Sometimes we can do it together, which I love. And sometimes we can't, or just really don't want to—and that's okay too. After more than a decade of marriage, I've learned the value of parallel play and differing belief systems.

James Baldwin once wrote: "Love does not begin and end the way we seem to think it does. Love is a battle. Love is a war. Love is a growing up." For me, prayer is a time out in the middle of that battle. It's reaching for peace in the heart of that war, even when my fight-or-flight instinct says to lash back or run. It's choosing Jason, flaws and all, and being grateful that he has chosen me. Because while I love myself some Jesus, I do admit, in the end, that my Bible-quoting skills could use a little work.

# Trading Places

## We both wanted to stay home.
## He won. But so did I.

**JULIANNA BAGGOTT**

When Dave and I got married, we were both jockeying for housewife. We met in graduate school for creative writing. This was post–*The World According to Garp*, both the book and the film, and despite his adultery, perversion, and violent death, we both thought Garp had it pretty good as the stay-at-home writerly parent.

But to clarify the terms, we made a few pacts, or rules, early on:

1. We would never let money dictate how many children we would have. This was smart only in that it dovetailed with our situation: We had no money and wanted a big family.

2. One of us always would stay at home with the kids. So, on top of our unmarketable creative writing degrees, we basically committed to a largely (if not fully) single-income household, halving any potential earnings. In our defense, our earnings were so overwhelmingly low at that point that halving them didn't seem like much of a sacrifice.

And 3. The person who made more money would be the one who worked outside the home. It was like a game each of us wanted to lose.

At first, due to simple biology, I got to be the stay-at-home person; pregnant not long into our marriage, nursing after that, and then quickly knocked up again, I simply had a better case. Dave's first job, as editor of a small weekly newspaper, paid $17,000 a year. Because we couldn't live on that income, we rented out two of the bedrooms in our three-bedroom condo to foreign students at the University of Delaware. As our end of the deal included room and board, I found myself presenting fish sticks and chicken nuggets to Koreans and Brazilians as Typical American Cuisine, as if this were an important part of their cultural experience. (Maybe it was.)

Soon Dave moved from one job to another, and in a few short years, his salary nearly doubled. By this point, I'd had a third kid: three in five years. I was in deep—enjoying the complexities of motherhood and my cozy community of other young mothers—but I also couldn't help noticing that sometimes being a stay-at-home mom felt like a defeat: I was seen as either a Good Mother, sacrificing for the noble cause, or as a loser who'd abandoned her dreams for the drudgery of parenting—neither of which was right. For one, I was there because I wanted to be (see rule #3). For another, I was still writing. Amid the chaos of three kids and running a boardinghouse (eventually out of a four-bedroom home), I jotted notes on receipts in the grocery store line and scribbled sentences on the backs of my kids' refrigerator art while heating Tater Tots in the toaster oven.

This felt necessary and important: As much as I loved motherhood, I had been a writer for as long as I could remember, and it's not like that part of me vanished just because I'd had kids. I kept at it, and soon I started publishing—poems and short stories, a few essays. Eventually an agent came calling, so I turned an eleven-page short story into a novel, and the agent sold the novel in an auction. And in this one fell swoop, I outearned Dave. We dismissed it as a fluke. But the following year, after I wrote a second novel and sold it just as I headed off on a tour for the newly published first (Dave wrangled time off work to watch the kids, and my parents were on call), it didn't feel like a fluke. It felt like a career.

And so, rule #3 went into effect: The person who makes more money makes the money, and the other stays home. Thrilled, Dave quit his job and became the stay-at-home parent. Our oldest daughter, then around six, stitched his now-useless neckties together to make an apron. And we were happier. A former Gap employee, short-order cook, camp counselor, and semi-pro soccer player, Dave was better suited than I for the at-home job at this point in many ways. The clothes were crisply folded, the food tasted better, the household games were louder and sportier. As for me, I no longer had to squeeze the novel writing into what I could scribble in ninety seconds on a gum wrapper in the pediatrician's waiting room. I had all the time I needed.

The shifts were minute—still mostly working at home, I could do a fair amount of domestic stuff at first—and yet profound. We seemed to change even on a biological level. When Dave was working, I had been the one who woke up in the middle of the night when a kid cried out, while Dave "didn't hear it" and slept. Now, within seconds, he was bolt upright at any cry. At first I still was too. But eventually there were times when, exhausted from being on the road or on deadline, or with a big meeting the next day, I was the one to sleep through a call, knowing subconsciously that it wasn't meant for me.

It was right, it was liberating, it was cost-efficient; our income rose, our quality of life followed suit, we reclaimed our house and lost the fish sticks. But it was also tricky, and sometimes sad. To honor Dave's work, the sacrifice of his career to give me the time I needed, I felt I should work long, hard hours, which I did— and mostly loved. But I will never forget the day I came home after some author event and didn't know if our youngest had been changed, couldn't find the diaper stash . . . and burst into tears. I'd signed away things I hadn't expected—the shorthand language of a toddler, the inside jokes. The kicker: When my youngest skinned his knee or woke up in the middle of the night, his instinct became to cry out, "Daddy!" Even writing this now, more than a dozen years later, I feel my eyes flood with tears.

Still, because a livelihood based solely on a novelist's salary seemed hard to sustain, I took a post as a professor of creative writing. The idea was that I would be under less pressure financially and could slow down to a more manageable writing rate, but instead, the opposite happened. I worked harder than ever—for my family, yes, but also because I hit some sort of creative, generative stride, further fueled by the competitive atmosphere at the university where I taught. I was now writing novels under two pen names as well as my own, and had started publishing essays in newspapers and magazines as well as on NPR. I was visiting schools to give author talks, touring for my books, and mentoring graduate students.

Meanwhile, Dave had taken over virtually everything domestic—from the taxes and the dentist visits to volunteering at the kids' schools and organizing and hosting playdates. It required some rerouting. Mothers would seek me out to set up activities and I'd have to tell them that Dave was the keeper of the calendar. To be honest, I didn't mind getting out of a lot of these duties. I wasn't really designed to excel here. My own mother had sat me down at a young age and told me that the teacher, at some point, was going to ask for parents to volunteer for some kind of classroom party, and when she did, I was to raise my hand immediately and say, "My mother will bring the cups and napkins." I had learned from her. I was never going to be the mom who brought in prizewinning cookies, and that was just fine with me.

(Interestingly, when we lived in the South, which we did until a few years ago, our arrangement seemed easier for people to accept. Because—where we lived, anyway—more households were traditionally labor-divided, meaning more stay-at-home moms and sole-breadwinning dads, our flip on this was actually accepted pretty easily. In contrast, in the progressive enclave of our current New England town, where more families divide labor between two working parents, relationship equality often is measured task by task, so the notion that I'm not picking up my share of the child-rearing and homemaking doesn't win either of us any points.)

. . . .

Through it all, Dave also was—as always—my creative partner: talking through scenes with me, revamping my website, negotiating my speaking engagements, even writing some of my radio shows. It satisfied his leftover urge to write and teach and edit, maybe, and it met *my* need for organizational help and collaboration. By now I was publishing two or three books a year (under three different names) as well as teaching full-time, a tenured professor in a graduate writing program.

Meanwhile, Dave was having mixed though mostly positive results as a stay-at-home dad. On the downside, especially in the earlier years, he found there was no real community of people for him. Most stay-at-home fathers he met were forced into it by job loss; others wanted the position, but after giving it a brief if valiant go, usually slunk back to their day jobs. Without the peers I'd had when staying home purely because I'm a woman, Dave found it a much more solitary—and therefore sometimes lonely—endeavor.

On the other hand, among the many mothers with whom he became friends, Dave was sainted—lauded as a Man in the Role— and he walked around seemingly freshly confettied. This was due at least partly to our living in, despite its mostly traditionally labor-divided homes, a relatively progressive southern town where the idea that a man could be not just at peace with emasculation by his overachieving wife, but *proud* of it . . . well, this was still a little shiny and new, and therefore seemed to inspire commentary. Dave rose gorgeously to the cause. He liked to tell people that he was a "homemaker," and soon he was writing it in on forms when asked his profession.

It was around this point that I realized Dave and I really had set up a 1950s division of labor, albeit with the roles reversed. We'd started out in a retro marriage in many ways: I was twenty-three when we married—an average marrying age for a generation ahead of me—and started having children at twenty-five, a decade earlier than most of my friends. But now, based on our parenting philosophy, not to mention our particular desires and talents, we'd swapped everything. And so far, mostly so good.

And then our fourth kid arrived, seven years after the third. I, of course, still bore the biological burdens of pregnancy, birthing, and nursing, now while also working full-time plus to support a family of six. My career was intense and public—I had a novel trilogy contract, a film deal, the teaching, touring, events—and though the baby was planned and wanted (see rule #1), I was overwhelmed. I was under so much pressure that I asked, very sincerely, for an EKG for Christmas. (I have a slight murmur, but otherwise I'm fine.)

To compensate, Dave took on even more. He drove me to campus because I didn't like to drive. He packed my lunches when he knew I was running late. Here's some damning information: When people stopped by to see me at home, he'd greet them, set them up with a drink, call me down from my office, and then, after a certain amount of time, remind me of some appointment—real or not—so I could get back to work. It reached an extreme the time I was packing for a trip and he rushed in to remind me to add tampons and pads because my period was coming. (But honestly? If he hadn't said it, I'd have forgotten.)

I didn't scrub dishes, hadn't done laundry in over a decade. And I didn't even do the traditional manly stuff—barbecue or mow the lawn. One night I confessed to my mother, "I feel like a Bad Husband."

She said, "That's funny, because that's what we all call you behind your back."

"What?" I said, shocked. "Who is *we*?"

"Me and your sister and that nice couple next door . . ."

It hit me that she was right. I was one of *those guys*. I showed up and smiled and pretended to know people I couldn't place. I couldn't keep track of the names of the parents in my kids' classes or the other kids on my kids' soccer teams. I was blurry on teachers. Dave picked up the slack.

At a family reunion, I called for Dave from the noisy kitchen. I used my nickname for him, Davi, which my sister—a stay-at-home mom at the time—misheard as Dobby. She thought I'd nicknamed Dave after the house-elf in *Harry Potter.* She lit into me. "That is so awful! I can't believe you call him Dobby! What are you going to do—throw him a sock one day and grant him his freedom?" I had to clarify what I'd said, but not before the damage was done; I saw how she viewed me, and it wasn't pretty.

But that was years ago now. And while Dave still does the lion's share of the child care and all things domestic, I like to think, now that our fourth, our baby, is almost eight, that I'm missing out a bit less, and that we're a little less bifurcated.

The other day, for example, while Dave drove the soccer carpool for our fourteen-year-old, that "baby" called up to me in my office, where I was preparing my syllabus for the upcoming semester. She called because she was sewing, and as Dave wasn't there to fix the machine when it jammed, she turned to me, Parent B.

At first I went down, both a little annoyed and a little happy to be summoned. But the second time she yelled, I lugged the machine to my office so I wouldn't have to trek downstairs for every jam. And there, my baby—no longer a baby—sewed quietly next to me while I worked. In the meantime, the phone rang—my oldest, calling from college (art school) to tell me to watch her video essay for an upcoming project and give her feedback. No sooner had I hung up than my secondborn called from New York, where he's studying acting, for advice about how to graciously withdraw from a class. Had Dave been home, he would have fielded those calls; had I been on the road or off teaching, the kids would have called Dave's cell phone. But I was here and he wasn't, so I got to be the primary parent. And I don't mind saying, it felt like a privilege.

Which brings me to another pact. Within our first year of marriage, Dave and I made a promise never to fight about who's working harder. (This was tricky at first because the argument takes on so many disguises. For example, overreacting to pee on the toilet seat, someone might yell, "Would it kill somebody to wipe a toilet seat around here?" the implication being that this person, the yeller, is slaving away 24/7 to take care of the household—i.e., working harder—while others blithely and literally piss on it.) At times we have had to acknowledge that one of us is going through a really hard crunch—but that's different from arguing. The truth is that we're both working our asses off all the time, so why bicker over some martyr-inspired point system?

This simple rule has huge implications, however, with regard to a couple's definitions both of work and of their own value. By viewing *as entirely even* the enormous effort that goes into running the household and the heavy responsibilities of being the sole breadwinner, we created a philosophy early on that, though it seemed retro/sexist at some points and progressive and antipatriarchal at others, ultimately has been based, intimately and personally, on a sense of equality. Both of our roles were equally valued when Dave was the breadwinner and I was the stay-at-home mom. And they are equally valued now, in reverse.

I credit this in part to my father, from whom—ironically—I learned the value of motherhood and homemaking. Raised himself by two women (his mother and his aunt, after his father's death when he was five) and smack between his own two feminist sisters, he had a deep love and respect for women, which made him unusually progressive for his era. He often said that my mother, home with four children while also teaching afternoon piano lessons in our living room, had the more important role in raising children and making our house a home, while his job was just bringing in money.

Dave's parents, in contrast, divorced when he was eleven. This was difficult and painful for him, and especially as we started having children, he took issue with his mother's choice to seek liberation from her marriage and her homemaking role when he was a young adolescent, often leaving him in charge of the household. Perhaps for this reason, he finds satisfaction in taking on the devoted homemaker role; not only can he make sure his children don't feel abandoned, as he did, but also his devotion can feel almost like a defiant way of correcting his own childhood.

Still, we are very aware of the major flaws in our way of dividing labor: for one, complete and utter codependency. Without Dave's holding up the household, my work isn't possible. Without my work, we'd have no income and there'd be no household to hold up. And if something happened to me and Dave needed to rejoin the workforce, his enormous gap in employment would hurt his earning potential terribly. There's also the fact that, like everyone, Dave has days where he doesn't love his job—not so much the one where he runs the household, but the one where he's my creative partner. Turns out that—go figure!—I'm not always easy to get along with, and dealing with me is just not super fun all the time. While my job offers me the renewal of teaching emerging writers, the elemental joy of creating, and the satisfaction of working with brilliant editors, day after day Dave has one main colleague: me. (*My* challenge here is that I have to let him complain about this colleague, but not take it too personally.)

But if codependency is the flaw in our design, it's also our strength. Last year my twenty-first and twenty-second books were published, and I credit a large part of my productivity to Dave, not just because he contributes so much to my psyche, my inner life, my soul and how it's been mined, but also because this gift he gives me—time—is still holy, still something I refuse to squander. Because it's really a gift of love. The real story of me as a successful writer and provider is the story of a strong marriage.

Strong . . . and romantic. In fact, Dave would say that one of his primary jobs is to protect me so that I can have the creative space to work—something he likes to do at least partly because, despite the pouring of tea and seltzer for my at-home callers (recall how he "sets them up with a drink"), it can be a very masculine role; one that helps compensate for his perhaps occasionally being seen, by the more unenlightened in our midst, as less than macho purely for the nature of his daily toil. Sometimes, in protecting me, he responds *for me* to some ugly barb or criticism of my work. Here and there he has offered to punch a critic and nemesis on my behalf, and though he knows I'd never take him up on it, I appreciate the gesture.

So you see, in the end, he's not too worried about what anyone might think—even those who, given that Dave and I both started out as writers, ask the impolite question: Is he jealous of my success? He's got a stock answer by now. "If you knew how hard she works, you'd know I don't really have a right to be jealous."

But his longer answer is this: Besides truly enjoying his work in our home, at least most of the time, he simply didn't need or want writing as much as I did. He knows that I'm better off trying to control a known world of my own making than the brutal world we endure, the brutal world our children walk off into. He knows what keeps me breathing, what makes me steady. And he gives me that, with love; he feels good about it, and it works for our family. Besides, he's not jealous of my need. Who would be?

This is not to say that being the stay-at-home person never makes him feel anonymous and inconsequential—or that being the sole supporter of six doesn't sometimes make me feel overworked or slightly panicked. It does, and it does. And someday—just like every full-time parent—Dave will have to figure out his post-kids-at-home life, not to mention how to help me with the earning, with three and a half more college tuitions looming. I'd be lying if I said that our choices and our life didn't sometimes cause a twinge of stress for both of us. And there are still adjustments and readjustments and a lot of conversations about this work we do together and how to continue to make it work. It's an ongoing experiment, but so far, despite the typical challenges and frustrations, it's mostly successful and rewarding for both of us.

I think what helps a lot is that we both *get* it; we both sympathize, from those long-ago days when we were reversed, with what the other is feeling. Dave remembers lying awake at night, restless and worrying, when he was the sole breadwinner. I remember, as a mother of small kids who also had boarders to feed (and a writerly mind), how very much there was to keep going, how many balls in the air at once—sometimes with no acknowledgment whatsoever from society at large. And we both remember that through twenty years and four children—with I hope many more years to come—we've been in this together: this intricate architecture of motherhood, fatherhood, homemaking, breadwinning, labor, work, and love.

# Beyond the Myth of Co-Parenting

## What We Lost—and Gained— by Abandoning Equality

**HOPE EDELMAN**

*Like so many in her generation, Hope Edelman
entered marriage, in 1997, expecting that she and her
husband would work, earn, and parent all roughly
equally—only to find that things didn't play out quite
that way. Hope wrote about this conflict in* The Bitch
in the House *in her piece "The Myth of Co-Parenting."
She described the disappointment and anger she felt
when the high-tech company her husband started shortly
after their first child was born led Hope to ultimately
have to parent two young daughters by herself much of
the time, sacrificing her own work in the process. Hope's
life—and marriage—evolved accordingly after that.
Fifteen years later, that first child now in college, here's
what it's become—and what she's come to think about it.*

Our house is in start-up mode again. I know this from the
piles of paper strewn across the living room. From the weekend meetings starting at 7 A.M. From the way my husband

wanders through the house at all hours, laptop pressed against his chest as he Skypes with colleagues in India and Germany and Brazil. São Paulo, Bombay, Berlin: It's always 10 A.M. somewhere.

This is our second time at the start-up rodeo. The first was in the late 1990s, when our older daughter was one, then two, then three years old. By the time she turned four and her sister was born, that start-up had evolved into a dynamic small business. For the next fifteen years, my husband put in a solid sixty to seventy hours per week as its CEO. Often more. Our family life shaped itself around the needs of the company and its employees. His long hours in the office and nights at home on the computer became our norm.

I had friends in Los Angeles married to film-industry guys whose jobs took them out of town for months in a row, and others whose husbands worked backbreaking hours to make partner in law and consulting firms. When these friends talked about the challenges of solo parenting for lengthy stretches, they often added, with a rueful shrug, "Well, I knew what I was getting into when we married." Does it sound naïve, then, to say I didn't? My husband and I hadn't lived together before marriage; ours had been a bicoastal relationship. When I moved from New York to L.A., I was already four months pregnant, and our pre-parenthood plan, if you can call it that, had been to share child care and home responsibilities in a sort of semi-equitable fashion after our daughter was born.

That "a sort of semi-equitable fashion" was as specific as it got reveals a lot about what we did and didn't understand at the start. In our prenatal classes, so much emphasis was placed on unpredictable first-time labors and deliveries that anything afterward looked manageable by comparison. I figured I'd work on the computer while our infant napped. (Ha!) That I'd breastfeed while doing phone interviews. That the worst of sleep deprivation would last a week or two. (Double ha! there.) Then our colicky infant arrived, screaming eighteen hours a day, and any plans became irrelevant.

I'd wanted to co-parent with my husband. I'd wanted it badly. I'd grown up in a suburban two-parent household with a stay-at-home mother and a wage-earning father until my mother's early death, after which my younger siblings and I were raised by a father who, though well meaning, was impaired by alcohol and debt. Having left child care entirely up to his wife, he had no idea how to take over or where to begin. So as a newly minted parent, I felt it imperative—in the way that adults compulsively try to right their childhood wrongs—that our daughter have two consistent, reliable parents raising her, just in case something tragic or unexpected befell one.

But in those first months of parenthood, a wide gulf emerged between the dual-income, co-parenting family I'd hoped we'd create and the de facto one-parent household we became. I know it didn't happen this quickly, but it seemed that only weeks after my husband and his partner drafted a business plan—about the time our daughter started to sit up—we were discussing how lucky it was that my work hours were so "flexible." How fortunate that my job was so "adaptable." When we married, we'd been earning about equally; I'd published a bestselling book three years earlier and was, in many ways, at the pinnacle of my career. Yet knowing that this start-up would be the fruition of my husband's entrepreneurial and leadership skills, I wanted him to succeed. I knew the exhilaration of watching an idea slowly grow into something 3-D and real, and I hoped he could experience it too. Also, I'll be honest: If ever there was a time to make a killing in high tech, it was the 1990s. Securing a family's future was by no means a given, but it was possible, though only for those who tried. And I mean *really* tried.

So I was willing to cut back on my work hours—temporarily—to be the point person at home. I just didn't realize *how much time* a start-up actually required—that it would be measured in years, not months. I didn't know the toll it could take on a new marriage, that so much of the domestic side would fall to me that contractors and new acquaintances would assume I had no partner. Or that those years would create patterns in our family that would become systemic and very difficult to change.

Did I mind the way my work hours became more expendable than my husband's? Well, yes. At first, a lot. I hadn't spent a decade carefully constructing a career so I could start disassembling it upon the one-two punch of marriage and motherhood. And yet growing a family, I soon discovered, is much like running a mini corporation. Before any major decision, a cost-benefit analysis must be run. Given that we had no family nearby to help with child care; the exorbitant cost of full-time babysitters in L.A.; the disparity in earning power between a writer and a high-tech CEO; the versatility of my one-person workplace versus the complexity, for him, of dozens of employees on four continents; and the indisputable fact that I was the one with the equipment to bear and breastfeed children, simple economics and elemental physiology both pointed toward me being the principal caregiver at home.

Yet emotionally, my decision to scale back on work was much more complex. I'd been fully self-supporting for a decade before our marriage and had emerged as a trusted voice in my field. I loved holing up in an office or library and immersing myself so deeply in a project that I'd look up and discover the sun had long since set and I'd forgotten to eat lunch—and then collecting a paycheck for those efforts while feeling I was contributing to a greater good.

Even more complicated was the contradictory but undeniable sense of relief I felt from not *having* to fully support myself for the first time in my adult life. That part took me by surprise. I'd been an uncompromising advocate for independence in all my prior relationships, and in addition to sharing child care after marriage,

I'd been prepared to earn half the family's income. I was the one who insisted on keeping separate checking accounts and pooling our money only for shared expenses. This puzzled my husband but made sense to me, the daughter of a woman who'd never had resources of her own. So to deliberately cut my income by half and become financially dependent on a man—*everything* about that felt wrong to me. Yet at the same time, I was immeasurably grateful to have that option. My early attempt to work full-time while basically single parenting had resulted in frustration and exhaustion beyond anything I'd ever encountered. I didn't know how working single mothers raised infants on their own. My respect for them bordered on awe, and still does.

Dropping down to half-time work meant I could accept small, short-term projects but not anything that involved travel, tight deadlines, or long hours at a computer screen. At first I painfully missed the satisfaction and productivity a full-time career had offered. Some days, as I packed up to vacate my office at 2 P.M., I would fantasize about what might happen if I didn't show up at home. Would the babysitter call my husband? Would he fly back from New York or San Jose? Would that be a bad thing? Then I would think of my daughter clutching her stuffed orange kitty as she waited for me, of her absolute trust in my return, and I would get into my car and drive home to spend the hours until her bedtime giving her dinner, running her bath, and putting her to sleep.

These are activities many women consider a luxury, I know. That was never lost on me. It was a privilege to spend undivided time with my daughter, and to have a child at all, when so many women my age were looking for life partners, desperately trying to get pregnant, or accepting that they'd never have kids. But it still was hard not to resent the domestic tasks that took me away from other work I wanted to be doing, had expected and been conditioned to be doing, on a Wednesday afternoon. Then I'd try to reprogram myself. *A scaled-down career is still a career,* I would tell that inner voice of resentment. *Your husband's working hard to support the family. What's your problem with that, really?*

This ambivalence went on for years. Seven, to be exact. That's how many passed between the publication of my third book in 1999 and my fourth in 2006.

Note that latter date, because it's important. My younger daughter was in preschool by then, so I had more time to work. But the stock market plunge of 2007 had had a profound ripple effect on book publishing, and authors were now being paid considerably less for their efforts, while having to do much more of their own publicity and marketing. "Half the pay for twice the work" was the catchphrase tossed around. I couldn't imagine where I'd get those extra hours from.

Despite my new book, my income dove from a career high in 1996 to a career low by 2010. Justifiably or not, with so little earning power I felt I merited less decision-making power at home—and had no right to complain, when my care and feeding was mostly bankrolled by someone else. I want to point out that my husband never treated me as a lesser partner. He frequently told me how much he appreciated my efforts for the kids, the family, the house. But the narrative spinning in my head was that the one who earns more is the one with the real power at home. It was a lesson carried over from childhood, and a hard one to unlearn.

For most of my daughters' younger years I was home at night with them, in an isolated house atop a canyon, helping with homework, packing lunch boxes, corralling them into bed, while my husband worked late or attended industry events. I became strangely obsessed in those years with reruns of the TV series *Felicity,* about college students starting out in New York. The characters had a sense of wonder and possibility about whatever lay ahead. Like them, I'd once believed that anything—anything at all!—could happen next. And now here I was, a mother in my thirties, sitting alone in front of a television at 10 P.M. waiting for a husband to walk through the door. All that was missing was the fresh martini waiting in my hand. What had happened to romance? To partnership? To basic companionship? I was angry I hadn't foreseen this, hadn't advocated better for myself from the start, hadn't made a hundred little different choices about work and child care and choosing a house in a "real neighborhood," where I might have neighbors to visit with after 6 P.M.

When he was home, my husband was a devoted, get-down-and-roll-around-on-the-floor kind of father who adored his daughters, the kind of father I'd known he would be. It's just that, for the better part of a decade, he was hardly ever home. At times it plunged me into near despair to acknowledge that our daughters had only one parent consistently available to raise them. Because what if something were to happen to me? Who would take care of them then?

"*I* would," my husband would say, kissing the top of my head. "Of course." Then he'd take off on half a day's notice for Silicon Valley, and I'd wish I could believe him.

• • • •

Imbalance, inequity, loneliness: We all encounter these states at some point in a marriage, but the way each of us reacts is what distinguishes one union from the next. Some spouses withdraw emotionally; others sink into depression. Still others grab the car keys while sprinting for the door. Some, or so I've been told, blithely shrug off their dissatisfaction and accept that we don't always get what we want. And some, like me and so many other women I know, let marital disappointment fester into outrage and smoldering resentment.

I saw a T-shirt the other day that read, *If I hadn't gotten married, I'd have no one to blame.* I might have laughed had it not rung so true. Energizing and powerful, anger and blame became my strongest allies during those early years. Without them, I felt needy and dependent and risked plunging into sadness and despair. So the more our marriage departed from my fantasy version, the angrier I became, and the angrier I became, the more I tried to get my husband to change. Predictably, the more I tried to make him change, the more he backed away. And the more he backed away, the less our marriage resembled my ideal. You can see where this was heading. We cycled in place like this for years. More than once, I considered leaving. I'm sure he did too.

But I never left. I loved the man. I still do. The qualities I'd married him for—kindness and loyalty, patience and good humor, a quiet, steady beauty both inside and out—didn't disappear because of his work hours. They just became less accessible. Eventually a therapist told me, *You have a choice here, you know. You can continue complaining or you can make a change.* If I wanted this union to work, and she knew I did, then I had to let go of my fantasy marriage and discover whether I could find happiness in the marriage I actually had.

*I can do that,* I thought. It didn't sound impossible.

My husband had to work late on weeknights? All right. I'd find friends with children who could meet for an occasional dinner. When he had a conference to attend during the kids' spring break, I planned a trip with my sister and her partner instead of staying home every day with the kids. I joined a writing group that met every other Tuesday morning so I didn't have to find child care at night. Every July I taught in Iowa City and the girls came with me and attended summer camp there, while my husband stayed back in California to work.

Over time, I created a rich, fulfilling, parallel world of my own that combined part-time work, good friends, and evenings and weekends with the girls. When my husband's work hours finally settled into a predictable pattern and he was able to help more at home, he did, though by then, it was often more efficient for both of us to keep doing what we'd already been doing for so long—for me, the majority of shopping and cooking, orthodontist and pediatrician appointments (in other words, the everyday "mommy stuff"), and for him, fixing computers and cars as needed and doing monthly Home Depot runs. I grew to both cherish the time we had as a family and value the separate, independent life I'd cultivated. Working three-quarters time, with both girls in school, was a compromise that finally felt like it worked.

And for a solid while, it did. As the girls moved into middle and high school, I took on more teaching and speaking and traveling and wrote two more books. My husband successfully steered his company through some choppy years and started positioning it for a sale. In those first fifteen years, I convinced myself that happiness in a marriage could be achieved through adding new activities and interests on my own, and multiplying the ones that worked. This wasn't entirely wrong. But a better method, I realize now, might have been for two people to honestly assess what did and didn't make them happy in their marriage and then work to create deep, substantive, lasting change together.

I tell you all this so you can understand what happened next.

When the second start-up came around, I braced myself for the fallout: The insistence (his) that the hundred-hour workweeks were necessary. The impassioned speeches (mine) about the importance of family time. The way I'd begin to toss around labels like "unavailable" and "absent," which would cause him to use adjectives like "demanding" and "inflexible." The many nights I'd spend without him, even when he worked out of our guest room.

I thought I was prepared.

And to a large extent, I was. While my husband got on the phone and essentially stayed on it for the next year, the kids still made it to school in the morning and home in the afternoons. Soccer games were lost and won, college essays written and sent. The new start-up required several long trips overseas, but I was traveling more for work too, sometimes as much as or even more than he did, and we planned our trips around each other's. We lived by a shared Google Calendar. In fact, my husband was the one who struggled more this time around—the late nights and early mornings harder to sustain in his fifties than in his thirties—and it pained me so deeply to see this that I was willing to take on even more at home, this time with support and concern instead of resentment and rage. For my part, the frustration, the anger, the loneliness that had infected the first two years of our marriage—with this second start-up, they just weren't there.

It's tempting to say this was because our kids were older and more self-sufficient—sixteen and twelve, well past the years of labor-intensive child care. Or that achieving rigid, quantifiable equality in a marriage, which had been such an urgent quest in my thirties, became less important by fifty, when good health and saving for retirement mattered more. Or that the stunned outrage of early marriage (*What? This is how it's going to be?!*) had slowly transformed into a subdued acceptance (*Oh. So this is how it is*), and anger began feeling like a waste of precious time and energy. Or that this time I understood, with a damning self-awareness I didn't have at thirty-three, that the dot-com widows (as the media once called us) who wanted the perks of a high-tech salary had as much hubris as their spouses if they didn't want the kind of marriage it took to produce them.

And while all these explanations may be true, I suspect there's another, more sobering reason too: that after eighteen years of marriage, I've become accustomed to spending time alone. I don't expect adult companionship the way I once did. I've become content with having less of it than I ever thought I'd need.

Not long ago I spoke with a friend I'd lost touch with nearly twenty years ago. He was going through a terrible divorce, uncovering lies, betrayal, infidelity, all of it. "What do you think makes a marriage work?" he asked, partly of me, partly of himself.

I was, I told him, probably the wrong person to ask. "Mine has survived, I think"—my words tumbled out quickly, before I had a chance to censor them—"because we spend so much time apart."

I could tell how odd this sounded to someone who hadn't seen me in two decades, who'd known me as a chronic people person. How to explain that what once felt like loneliness now feels like a blessed independence? That too much togetherness might feel claustrophobic to me now?

I held my hands parallel, palms touching. "We began like this," I said, and as I moved my hands forward, I separated them. "And then we went like this for a while and then like this," and I brought my palms back together and moved them apart, together, apart. In these motions I saw the nights my husband and I had both lain awake with a squalling infant; the separate vacations we've taken; all the birthdays and Thanksgivings celebrated as a family at the house; the past twelve summers I've spent in Iowa with the girls; the occasional mornings we both work from home instead of from our offices just to share the same space for a while; and the evenings and weekends when I see him, if at all, only in profile as he stares at his laptop screen. As much time apart as together. Never would I have expected to have this kind of marriage. Never would I have expected it could come to fit me so well.

Without a doubt, my husband's steady work ethic has provided for our family for nearly two decades. I've been a beneficiary of his success—hardly a victim. But unlike other couples I know, we haven't watched all of *Breaking Bad* or *House of Cards* together, and we don't have a favorite bar we frequent or a vacation destination we escape to together every year. I have my favorite activities and places that feed my soul, and he has his. Sometimes I wonder whether we're missing out, whether true companionship might have been, or might still be, attainable with another person. Yet on other days I love that we still make each other laugh every morning, truly *every morning,* despite our differences, when so many couples around us haven't survived nearly this long. And on these days, I wonder if a partnership that becomes less about two spouses' ideas about equality and romance and even companionship, and more about raising two content, productive, well-adjusted citizens of the world together is, despite occasional frustration and loneliness, a mostly ideal arrangement when children are involved—or as ideal as many couples can hope to get. Maybe that's what it means to grow up and surrender to parenthood: to accept that my immediate happiness and fulfillment is not always what matters most. And maybe what has made our marriage endure for eighteen years—learning how to show up every day with a good attitude; supporting and parenting children if not equitably, at least always with commitment and love; treating each other with true kindness and loyalty and respect—will be exactly what makes a marriage fulfilling after the child-raising is done.

One of our daughters started college this year, and the other is just a few years behind. When I peer into the marital future, I can't see what it holds. Will the patterns that evolved out of necessity once we had children still work for my husband and me after the heavy lifting of parenting ends, or will we discover we're two people with completely different interests who happen to live in the same house? And if so, is that situation as terrible as it sounds? As my friend Kitty, who's ten years further along on this path, says, "There are so many ways to have a marriage. Why do we think there's only one?"

I don't have any better answers now about what makes a marriage work than I did when we said our vows. I only know that, against some pretty steep odds, mine has survived for this long. And that I'm asking—I hope—better questions. I no longer ask, "Why doesn't my marriage match my fantasy version and how can I get it to change?" but instead, "What does our marriage offer, and is it enough for me right now? And if it isn't, what's possible to change as a team?"

It took me almost two decades, but I've come to realize I wasn't a casualty of circumstance in our family. I was making a hundred little decisions all along. Of course I was. To work and to parent in equal measure, even if my co-parent couldn't do the same, and even when I wanted to work more. To stay married, even when my husband couldn't or didn't give me what I wanted at the time. To keep waking up every morning with a man who's always happy, motivated, and ready to go, even when it means going without me. When I was thirty-three, this felt like a grievous compromise. But now, at fifty-one, I see it as an extraordinary achievement.

# Now There Were Two

**JILL BIALOSKY**

*In her essay "How We Became Strangers" in* The Bitch
in the House, *Jill Bialosky described how the passion
changed in her marriage after their baby arrived. Fifteen
years later, their son now grown, Jill and her husband
are still faithfully married, each having worked hard
to both make a living and be a firm yet adoring parent.
She returns here with a slice of what happened after that
baby left the nest and it was just the two of them again.*

Here's the thing no one tells you when you drop your Beloved child at college for the first time, wave a tearful good-bye, and find yourself face-to-face with the man you married twenty-five years ago: You do not know each other anymore. Now free of the "Dad" and "Mom" disguises you've worn for eighteen years, you look at this man—handsome, with just a little salt-and-pepper in his still-full head of hair—and you see that, though he belongs to you, though he is your Husband and you are his Wife, you have no idea who he is. You would like to find out; you would like to know him.

Who you do know, of course, is the man you watched tenderly for almost two decades become a father. That man was appealing too.

Since both of you have demanding day jobs, that man was as involved in raising your Beloved as you were. A twenty-first-century couple, you split the shopping, cleaning, cooking, homework help, weekend chaperoning. A typical day went like this: alarm off, Dad in the shower, out of the shower, waking Beloved, while Mom takes her turn in the shower and Dad rushes out to pick up coffee, bagels, orange juice, and the car (this is the city, after all) before swinging back to get everyone. Meanwhile, along with getting dressed, Mom has dragged Beloved out of bed, nagged him into the shower, and is now pushing him out the door just as Dad texts, asking, *Where the #$%# is Beloved? He is going to be late!* In this morning scenario, as in others, there is no room for the man and the woman to linger over each other, as they once did.

Beloved is finally in the car, half-asleep in the backseat; Mom and Dad are in front, heading for work. Do you have baseball practice today? asks Dad. Did you get your essay finished? asks Mom. A few grunts come from Beloved, who, dressed in his very cute prep-school uniform—tie, blazer with school logo—is now consuming a bagel and juice. At the school, he reaches for his backpack and rushes out, looking back to give Mom and Dad a killer grin that will last them all day. Now in the car without him, pushing through rush-hour traffic, they review and divide the day's agenda. Who will arrange Beloved's tutor, turn in his school forms, sign him up for batting practice, get new strings for his violin? Who will get home first? Pick up dinner? At the next stop, the office where she works as an editor, if she doesn't have to scoot out too quickly to avoid oncoming traffic, she gives him a quick peck on the cheek. He responds with a nod or a pat on the hand before rushing off to his job.

Much later, everyone back home again, Mom and Dad enjoy seeing Beloved for an hour or two before he goes into his boy cave to video chat or watch movies on his computer that he is not supposed to see. Both adults have brought home work they need to do tonight, and as soon as Beloved disappears, out it comes. For this reason, they are perhaps not as diligent as they might be in attending to duties as Husband and Wife. Those duties involve *time*, after all—time they just don't seem to have.

Before Beloved was born, they had time. Before, Husband and Wife were kind of sexy. Once, they had sex in the alley of a restaurant; another time, fun was had in the car on the way to a skiing weekend. They had sex in the morning and afternoon; sometimes on weekends they barely got out of bed. They went antiquing up the eastern seaboard and traveled to the Caribbean, where Wife could still wear a bikini without being afraid to take off her cover-up. They were free and uninhibited and had their whole futures before them.

Once Beloved joined them, though, he took up most of the room in their bed. And they were not complaining! It had taken them a long time to have Beloved, and when he finally arrived, a tiny miracle in a blue blanket, all they wanted was to be parents. "Date night" never quite won out over staying home with Beloved on weeknights, or taking him to see *The Lion King* on a Saturday night, or ice-skating on a winter Sunday, or playing hide-and-seek with him at the Temple of Dendur in the Metropolitan Museum of Art. And though they often were tired, sometimes their eyes met across the table at Barney Greengrass, where the three of them were having brunch, and they both smiled at Beloved gleefully eating his blintzes, and the look they exchanged was better than anything; in it, they acknowledged how lucky they were that instead of two, there were three. And Wife and Husband still had their time alone together, only it was different—quieter, so as not to wake Beloved, and fast, because they were tired and had to get up early, even on weekends, because there was so much to be done, and so many places to take Beloved.

• • • •

But now Beloved is eighteen (how did that happen?), and Husband
and Wife are "empty nesters"—though the term, once she can
walk past Beloved's room or come upon one of his baseball socks
intermingled with hers in her drawer without breaking down,
feels wrong to the Wife; in fact, she feels filled to the brim with
love for Beloved. But she also feels at a loss for who she is at home
without him if she is not picking up his T-shirts and folding his
laundry and filling the refrigerator with Gatorade, yogurts, and
the deli turkey he likes to eat. Not only does she not quite know
who she is anymore, but she wonders who the man next to her
in bed will be, now that he is not getting up at 6 A.M. on a Saturday to pack the car with Beloved's baseball equipment and drive
him to a tournament. Because over the years of being a father as
well as an accomplished professional, he has deepened and taken
on edges, grown in numerous ways. There's a touch of sadness that
comes with the passing of time and the realization that there is no
longer room for much reinvention. But mostly there is this interesting, edgy, slightly ironic, intense person for the Wife to get to
know all over again. For instance, sometimes she hears him on the
phone—pounding out a deal or going over some of the fine points
of a contract or law, merging companies, working out employment
agreements that affect hundreds of lives—and he is self-assured
and confident, exact and literal. This is fascinating to the Wife,
who rarely sees this side of him at home.

She remembers, now, that this is one of the things that first attracted her to him; somehow this memory had been buried under
family dinners and emergency runs to the pediatrician and ski
trips, field trips, baseball games. *This man truly knows a lot*, she
remembers now. *This man is powerful.*

In fact, now that Beloved is gone, Wife has the mental space to
imagine Husband in the office with the younger associates looking up to him. He is their mentor. He has learned a lot being a

father, lessons he has taken to work and beyond. He has watched his Beloved son fail and excel, watched him play violin and act the lead in a play and accumulate a roomful of sports trophies . . . and also do what teenagers do: break curfew, come home from a party trashed, have his first girlfriend, tell his parents he is doing one thing while doing something else entirely. This man, as the Dad, has witnessed broken bones and high fevers, has been called into the headmaster's office when Beloved and his friends got into trouble. He has beamed and angered, worried and defended, loved and mourned and rejoiced watching Beloved grow up. And the experience has changed *him:* deepened and matured him in ways that suddenly seem incredibly sexy and new to the Wife. (Of course, it doesn't hurt that now he also has more time to exercise, as he no longer needs to rush home after work to be with Beloved.) And Wife knows that she too has matured and deepened. She knows that, free from their Mother/Father outfits and masks, they are potentially interesting, exciting, and substantial people, to themselves and to each other.

• • • •

And soon she finds that it's fun to become acquainted with Husband again. After twenty-five years, it is a little, just a little, like falling in love for the first time. She remembers when, just after she first met Husband, he accompanied her when she tried on a new dress in a store—how he sat in the chair near the dressing room, and when she came out, he looked at her, looked and looked. Things are not quite as novel or exciting now, but suddenly there are just the two of them again, going to the movies on a Friday night and eating Dots and sometimes holding hands. Suddenly there they are after a long day of work meeting at a bar and having a cocktail like young lovers. Now, instead of talking about the Beloved, they discuss not only politics, current events, books and movies they've read or watched, but their own lives, what went on at work, and what trips they'll take away together: their own future, not just Beloved's.

• • • •

For their twenty-fifth anniversary, they book a hotel room at a resort in Montauk, and if pressed, Wife admits to herself that she is a little bit anxious. What will they have to talk about with all this time alone together? At home they can distract themselves with work and fixing things in their apartment and planning and throwing dinner parties with friends, but alone for forty-eight hours, what if they discover they have nothing in common anymore? What if they can't quite get their rhythm back? She actually has butterflies in her stomach, the way she did when, two weeks after they first met at her ten-year high school reunion in Cleveland, he flew on People Express ($29!) to visit her in her New York apartment, where, once she opened the pullout sofa bed she slept on, there was no walking space at all.

• • • •

They plan the trip carefully. They splurge on a hotel, and they make a dinner reservation at a place called Dave's, which has the best lobster rolls on the island. It's October, chilly, and by the time they arrive the sun is going down; there's no time for a beach walk holding hands, so they decide they will first hit the gym. Checking in, the Wife is a little disappointed—the lobby is a bit musty, a bit worn, and she so wants everything to be perfect!—but upstairs, their room is gorgeous: sparse and modern and opening out onto a deck twenty feet from the desolate beach. They can hear the crash of the waves from the room. They are pleased, but they're also so used to Beloved sharing the room when they go on vacation, they almost don't know what to do without him. And they had *liked* being with Beloved! He'd made them laugh, and after dinner they all would come back to the room and watch a movie and eat M&M's until they fell asleep. Now there's no excuse for M&M's, and it is suddenly oddly quiet without the sound of Beloved's video games pinging.

Husband and Wife have dressed and undressed hundreds of times in their bedroom together, but suddenly Wife feels a little timid changing in front of Husband. So she takes her gym clothes and bathing suit with her to the spa. She wishes she and Husband had decided to forget their workouts and begin the long-awaited moment, since the waiting now is making her tense. It's not that she and Husband haven't slept together a million times since Beloved arrived, but suddenly, here in the quiet hotel, it feels almost as if she will make love to a stranger tonight. She remembers before she was married the anticipation and fear (what if somehow there is no spark or magic?) of sleeping with someone new for the first time, and suddenly she is filled with that same feeling of both desire and dread. But when Husband returns from the gym, she notices that he is extremely fit, and when he takes off his baseball cap, he looks at least ten years younger than he had an hour ago. Wife hopes she does too. She has gotten a mani-pedi before the weekend, has starved herself to lose a few pounds.

After showering and dressing, they decide to have a drink at the hotel, outside by the heat lamps, before dinner. There is another couple there, wearing matching sweat suits, also drinking. They are twenty years younger, and it's obvious to Husband and Wife that they are having a weekend away from the kids—or the kids are in the hotel room with the babysitter—because every few minutes they check their cell phones, and they talk nonstop about their children and compare photos and laugh. Wife finds the couple dull; she remembers when she and Husband, in their rare times away, had Beloved at home to check on, but they don't anymore, and now it feels boring, to be like this couple, and when she looks at Husband she can tell he registers the same thing. So they finish their drinks, and get in the car and drive to Dave's.

The night doesn't go as planned. Their reservation somehow is not in the book, and their only option is to eat at the bar. And guess what? There's only one stool, so Husband has to eat his dinner standing. Sitting next to them is another couple, this one cool, in their late thirties or early forties. The guy, a shadow of beard on his face, is dressed in a leather jacket, black T-shirt, jeans. The woman is Madonna-ish: platinum blond, buxom, mole on her cheek. (Wife can't decide if the mole is real or not.) She wears black gloves without fingers and a tight leopard sweater, has a sort of slutty, glamorous look about her. The couple is splitting a bottle of red wine, and each of them has an iPad and looks at it often, occasionally pointing out things to the other. Wife is starting to wonder if this is a new language, a new way that couples interact—talk a little, look at something on a screen—but somehow, unlike the hotel couple, this couple seems sexy. Their steak and lobster arrive, and they take bites off each other's plates. Looking at this couple, Wife thinks that they will be a hard act to follow.

And perhaps Husband feels some of the same anxiety, because right then and there, Wife and Husband begin to fight. Later they won't even remember what the fight was about—most of their fights are silly and in retrospect just ways to let off steam—but regardless, that night, they fight and then eat and then fight again, and during the car ride back to the hotel both are silent, steaming in their individual disappointments. Wife is not the sexy young woman wearing gloves without fingers, and Husband is not the dude drinking red wine and showing his girlfriend interesting things on his iPad, and they are never going to be that couple again. And when they get back to their room, Husband turns on the television to check out the game, and suddenly Wife can't look at him. She goes out on the deck to listen to the waves, and stays there awhile. And when she goes back in, Husband is asleep, with the Giants game blaring.

The next morning, they both get up. They are in Montauk, for Christ's sake. Why are they fighting? It's a beautiful day, a little cold, but the sun is enough to send them onto the deck for their coffee. And when they look through the ornamental potted trees that divide their deck from the deck of the room next door, they see, sprawled out on the double chaise longue, the couple from the night before. In broad daylight, the couple looks different from how they did in the dark bar at Dave's. She is wearing the white hotel robe, drinking coffee, and he is dressed in running gear. They are talking loudly, and as Husband and Wife sit in their own double chaise, they realize the couple is fighting. Simultaneously, it occurs to both Husband and Wife that this man and woman are having an affair. The man has a wife and child at home, and the Madonna-like woman is fed up with their situation.

Suddenly the air deflates, and this formerly glamorous, mysterious couple is no longer interesting or attractive; they are *stupid*. Maybe even a little pathetic.

I turn and look at my cute husband—yes, he's mine—and he looks at me, and we begin to laugh. And my husband reaches for me, and we kiss, and we glance out at the ocean, the furious waves crashing against the shore, and my husband takes out his phone and snaps a picture of the beach and texts the image to our Beloved boy. And Beloved texts us right back, which is unusual now that he is at college, and we smile at each other the same way we did when we watched him eat his blintzes or get on base in a game or do well on a school paper, and we are suddenly no longer strangers. We are us. And it is perfect.

# Living Alone: A Fantasy

**SANDRA TSING LOH**

S andra, before you rush to move in with Charlie?" warned my therapist, Ruth, shaking her cloud of silver-gray hair, her geometric earrings. "To find out who you really are? You should spend at least six months living alone."

Ruth had been my husband's and my couples therapist for over a decade. For ten years before that, she was our friend and neighbor. She'd been around for our wedding, the purchase of two homes (the second one, next door to our first, was hers), and the births of our daughters, now six and eight. Ruth was as close to a tribal elder as I might ever hope to have.

And yet, I felt—I *knew*—in that moment that my sensible, Jewish sixtysomething maiden aunt therapist was dead wrong. Or perhaps she was just giving lip service to a nice idea, like how dentists say to floss or doctors to drink eight glasses of water a day. I should live alone for six months—right! I'd rise early, meditate, drink green tea, journal! Surely after six months of calm reflection, as with a waiting period to buy an automatic weapon, I would come to my senses and go back to my marriage with Ben—or at least, that was her poorly hidden implication.

But that wasn't going to happen. My love for this other man, Charlie, was a runaway train. At forty-six, I had found my soul mate—something I'd not thought was even possible. True, the details didn't look that great on paper, just yet. Charlie and I were both still married to other people, both of us with school-age children. We had started an affair four months earlier at, okay, Burning Man (but it wasn't how you think!). We had continued it in hotel rooms with liberal amounts of vodka, pot, and cigarettes while I was on book tour promoting a memoir about, um, parenting. Over the weekend before the aforementioned therapy session, our spouses had found out and they'd kicked us to the curb, our shoes, socks, and wrinkled clothing thrown into the proverbial twist-tied garbage bags.

So yes, it wasn't the cleanest start. But we were trying to fix things, beginning, in my case, with this emergency shrink appointment on this wintry January afternoon. Charlie and I had discussed bringing in a therapist anyway, possibly a team of them, to help our families manage this . . . this "domestic transition." But sitting now in Ruth's familiar den, sunlight slanting across Balinese masks on faded tangerine walls, I realized she wasn't going to help. Clearly, she thought I had lost my mind. Clearly, she thought I was destroying my family. To her, Charlie was an interloper, a louche cheating husband sent from central casting whom she barely gave a second glance.

Six months of my living alone would solve this crisis? How little she knew. Because however messy our beginning, this was no passing Facebook fling. Charlie and I had been business partners—he managed my theater productions (I perform comedic monologues, both onstage and on radio)—for ten years. Over this same decade, when our spouses were traveling for work (often), we had been each other's social escorts. We had gone on the road together. We split small plates of hummus and calamari in restaurants. We were best friends. After confessing that our outwardly successful marriages were inwardly emotionally barren, we had realized that *we* were the couple who made sense. Our finally living together now, then, would be a party—but not in hotel rooms. Because I had enough money, it would be in our own wonderful shared new home. And, organically, all the other details would fall into place.

• • • •

And how did that all work out for you? one might ask.

• • • •

Well, not in any way you could predict. Or perhaps you could, depending on what romantic novels you read (and from which era— the eighteenth, nineteenth, or twentieth century).

To begin with, what I could not have guessed (but what you might have) on that wintry Monday? Four months later my soul mate would break up with me and move back home to his family.

To say I was devastated would be like saying all Sylvia Plath needed to bounce back was a power nap and a little hydration.

Now I was getting divorced (my husband moved quickly), I was single, and my garbage bags of clothes were piled in a rusty tub in the cramped rental unit in which Charlie and I had been cohabitating while we looked for our dream house for me to buy for us to live in.

Quickly and immediately, I needed to find a more presentable home, one that my daughters would live in 50 percent of the time. Thanks to some slender thread of cosmic grace, I stumbled across a house on the market so adorable I thought that, if I could get it, I just might survive my personal holocaust. It was a charming 1,500-square-foot Craftsman bungalow, big enough for my daughters but small enough so that when they left, it could, like a cozy houseboat, shrink to fit. It had flowering plants, a wooden deck, a sleek converted-garage office, nooks, alcoves, a sun-warmed window seat.

I put in an offer. Then, while I waited, and because I was such a wreck, I took the unusual (for me) step of hiring a personal assistant. Tom was a younger male friend who was trying to transition from engineering to writing. The plan was that I would advise him, and he would help me out by picking up milk from the store and stamps from the post office. And for a few weeks, it worked. Tom was cheerful and witty and had a clingy girlfriend, so sometimes, since my rental unit was clearly a safe house from any kind of emotional commitments, he'd come over and cook dinner on my tiny crappy stove so he could dodge her calls. We'd drink beer and make plans for our productive writing lives once I got my magical cottage. Tom would bring coffee and bagels on weekdays, and we'd type on laptops facing each other, like Dorothy Parker and Robert Benchley. I know that looks strange on the page, but I was out of my mind, and sometimes, to certain people, that sort of overly close (literally) arrangement can be weirdly compelling.

Tragically, through a technicality I can't explain even today, my magical bungalow got scooped up by another buyer. I was devastated yet again. To keep me in the game, my Realtor had me toss in a Hail Mary offer $150,000 below the short-sale asking price of a nearby three-story Victorian home. And because the L.A. real estate market had hit bottom, a couple of months later, it was mine. This to-me giant home, a vast 2,600 square feet. We will return to this shortly.

Fast-forward seven years, which is approximately the present. In between shows and travel, I work from home on various writing assignments, and one day I am asked to write something about Living Alone After Fifty. Specifically, the bright, thoughtful guy assigning this means (perhaps not so flatteringly) "the anxieties of living alone in middle age, of becoming forgetful, losing your mind." This person is thirty. I am just over fifty at the time. Still, he seems a smart fellow and I can use the money, so I rack my brain trying to think of depressed middle-aged singletons.

I myself am not single, because just about the time I bought my 2,600-square-foot house, Charlie's wife kicked him out again, and he moved in with me. So now my soul mate and I have been living together for six years. In this giant home. We will return to this shortly too.

I begin working on my article, calling and e-mailing all my middle-aged girlfriends who are living alone, because that's the lazy way I tend to start. And horribly for me, to the last woman—it is true they are mostly all divorced, not never married—they are thrilled, thrilled, *thrilled* to be living alone! Flashback to therapist Ruth's geometric earrings, shaking their tiny gleaming heads at me.

I head over to one of their places for dinner to complain about how difficult this assignment will be—my friend Nadine, the proud owner of a brand-new townhouse she wants me to see. I arrive at six. She opens the door—"Aw, honey!"—and pulls me into her tasteful living room with colorful accent pillows and fresh-cut flowers and wonderful air-conditioning and, on her Bose sound system, I want to say . . . Sade? "Honey, honey," she murmurs, leading me to her spotless all-white kitchen, which features a Paris-style bistro table and two black metal chairs. She opens her gleaming refrigerator and pulls out a chilled bottle of Grey Goose and two martini glasses. I notice some herbs in tiny colorful pots in her jewel-box garden window. None of them are dead, dying, or brown.

"I love your new place!" I exclaim, sincerely. I'm really surprised at how much I love it. Shocked, in fact. It hits me in the chest. It's like a boutique hotel I want to check into immediately.

"It took a lot of work to get it to here," she says. "We had to practically gut the place to get the flow I wanted." "We" includes her and her dream contractor/sometimes actor, John Kennedy. "Isn't that funny?" she says, pouring the vodka daintily. "My handyman's name is literally John Kennedy."

Nadine picks up her iPad to Yelp Thai delivery. "This place is excellent," she says, checking off larb, pad Thai, spring rolls, lemongrass soup; a couple of swipes and it's done. Then she begins our tour by swinging open the red door to her home office.

It's like an IKEA catalogue page sprung to life. "Oh my God!" I exclaim, because it's a veritable creative sanctuary of glowing track lighting, blond wood desk, custom-fit bookshelves which—I can see, looking closer—have only classics on them. Unlike me, Nadine has culled her books. Just perusing her quality personal library (and it's *alphabetized*—Cheever! Didion! Eggers!), I feel my mind start to clear and brighten, as sometimes happens when you step into quiet deep woods. My own boxy house is defined by large square public rooms, ideal for Quaker meetings or Lutheran potlucks. Which is to say, for all its square footage, I do not have an office. I type from my unmade bed. Collapsing bookshelves on my right are choked with not just the occasional classic but also food magazines, computer manuals, *Online Investing for Dummies* . . . none of it mine, I might add. (Have I said yet that Charlie has a hard time weeding and throwing away?) Along the wall on my left is a ragged skyline of old *New York Times* and half-read *New Yorkers*. Yes, also Charlie's.

"Can I move in?" I am "joking," by the time we get to her spa-like master bathroom (fluffy white towels, eucalyptus soaps, flickering aromatherapy candle).

Nadine looks at me, surprised. "But I thought you were living the perfect life with your dream man!"

"Oh, I am," I assure her. "It's just . . ." As we begin to eat our delicious food (which arrives in thirty quick minutes) with our wooden chopsticks, I tell her about Charlie's and my latest fight. This one was about, well . . . hardwood floors. It sounds so small, but in a way it isn't.

"I'm a person who has never thought twice about hardwood

floors," I yap, slurping some lemongrass soup. "In my youth, I was the sort of free spirit who would rush in from the pool in a dripping swimsuit to type a poem. However, in midlife, even I recently started noticing that, after six years of wear? Our downstairs floors are so scratched and worn there are parts that are black.

"I am realistic enough by now," I go on, sipping right out of my bowl, "to expect that my soul mate will not even notice, let alone gather a handy group of guy friends some weekend to sling off their shirts and refinish the floors. Although in some far-flung portal of my imagination, that fantasy still exists. Anyway, nor do I expect my soul mate to consult Angie's List, compare prices, and hire a refinisher. My plan is to do that myself, and hope that afterward he will at least say, 'Babe, the floors look nice!' But no. What happens is that I research and book the refinisher—"

"Which you also are paying for," Nadine adds, picking through the larb.

"Of course. But when I tell Charlie they're coming, he complains that now he has to get his many piles of magazines, tchotchkes, and guitars off the floor and he doesn't feel like doing that this weekend. To which I say, 'Either this stuff goes or you do. The refinishers are coming Monday. Move your shit.'"

"Ohhhhhh, Sean had a terrible clutter problem too," Nadine moans sympathetically. "Baseball cards. I didn't let them in here. Made him get a storage unit." She explains that Sean is—*was*—this guy she met on match.com. "He came to spend a weekend here and never left. He was nice enough—funny, cute, smart, initially said he was a 'producer,' but as I've learned, if you're over the age of forty in Los Angeles, TV or film 'producer' is a synonym for homeless." She rolls her eyes. "Anyway, he was depressed and would spend much of the day watching old sitcoms on Hulu—which was fine with me, but he wanted me to watch them with him! We went to therapy about it." She went on for a few more minutes. "Anyway," she concluded, "so now I'm doing the math. I'm calculating the price, literal and metaphorical, of a man."

Nadine ticks it off on her fingers. "His income? I don't need it, I make my own living. The sex? It was okay, but you can date and get that—I've been seeing this guy I recently met on OkCupid and arguably it's better. The ability to fix things is a plus, but Sean was completely inept and I have John Kennedy for that anyway. I do like to watch TV at night with someone, but Sean would talk all through *Downton Abbey.* Can you fathom?" She shakes her head. "He wasn't a bad cook, I guess, but who needs that when you can Yelp anything you want?"

"Exactly!" I say, pulling out the pad Thai. "Charlie loves to cook, but he makes it such a project. First comes an hour of Talmudic study of the *New York Times* food section. Next is a trip to the farmers' market to buy exotic vegetables, some of which he may cook for dinner, possibly grilling them, in some fussy experimental manner. In the process, the kitchen sink will start to fill with pots, pans, a colander, a mandoline, both a large and a small food processor, dinosaur-sized tongs. Still on the counters is the farmers' market produce that wasn't used. Mystery leftovers will start to sprout in the fridge, in leaky Ziploc bags.

"I am a horrible housekeeper," I continue, dipping a spring roll into sauce, "but every six months it is I who goes through the fridge and throws out all the rotting food. Do you know raw carrots eventually suppurate? Have you ever seen bacon that's blue? And now come the insects. Fruit flies cloud over the produce. Pipe flies mist from the drain. Last summer Charlie bought brown rice and quinoa from a health food store. Turns out, they were full of pantry moths. Have you heard of these? Their worm-like larvae breed in your grains. Then they flutter around your kitchen, hang in your cupboards, and *lay their eggs in the stud holes in shelving units.*" Here I pause and actually put down my chopsticks, remembering. "It got so bad one week I spent three days—I am not kidding—twirling toothpicks into *every single stud hole in the kitchen* in order to dig out the black fuzzy pantry moth corpses within! At fifty-three, do I HAVE A RIGHT TO AN INSECT-FREE KITCHEN?"

I don't mean to shriek, but Nadine doesn't seem to mind. "Oh my god," she says, refreshing our martinis, as Sade or someone like Sade croons gently on.

I take another slug. It calms me—a tad. And I realize . . .

This—what I'm telling her—is like some kind of terrible fable! The clutter, the dishes, the fact that Charlie simply doesn't "see" insects. ("Here they are!" I'll shrill, pointing accusingly from a stepladder . . . but of course at that moment we'll have only one set of reading glasses, and I'm wearing them.) "For our exes," I say wonderingly, "it's really the perfect revenge, served cold. The jilted spouses of the world should pray that all their philandering mates end up moving in with each other and setting up households. It is a most fitting punishment."

• • • •

Driving home, I find myself wondering who—or *what*—I would have found if I had followed my therapist Ruth's advice those many years ago.

What if I had calmed myself and wisely chosen to live alone for six months—or even more? Even if I hadn't been able to buy that magical cottage, maybe I'd have had the wherewithal to wait for the right place to come along, instead of carrying unsorted garbage bags of my clothes into a giant house with too many closets. What if, like Nadine, I had lovingly curated the Houseboat of Me, becoming, in the process, a better person?

Instead of trying to make sense of having a middle-aged, live-in "boyfriend," what if I had let in a *few* good men—but mindfully partitioned them into more realistic and clearer roles? Take Tom, the paid personal assistant, beer buddy, and platonic writing friend. Truth be told, Tom disappeared from my life when Charlie came back, and I'm now wondering what personal growth and happiness potential I may have lost when he fled. Living alone and unencumbered, I too could have had a dream contractor named John Kennedy, a no-strings-attached Saturday-night hookup on OkCupid or Tinder, or even, if I felt like staying in . . . —what? The Twitter feed of, say, George Clooney. (Does George Clooney tweet?)

In fact, what if instead of a boyfriend at all, I had a *dog*—a cheerful golden retriever that would bound onto my bed at dawn to pull us both out for a cool and refreshing walk? With that magical dog, I sense I would wake early, exercise daily, feel terrific.

Instead, I have Charlie, with whom I also have the bad habits we've always had. Many nights when my girls are away we drink, smoke pot, and fall asleep in front of the TV. I wake up in the morning in a sea of Kettle chip crumbs—"Oh, honey, no, did we eat that whole bag?" Opening my e-mail, I see the iTunes store is claiming someone named "Sandra Loh" bought the entire *Lord of the Rings* trilogy at midnight for $19.95, a trilogy I already own. Sure, it was fun at the time, but . . . does it really need to be this way?

And yet . . . And yet . . .

To be entirely honest, being a divorced mom living with Charlie has in some ways also been a huge blessing, a gift sent from the cosmos.

When I was married to Ben, who's a musician, he traveled almost half the year, so I was essentially a solo parent. Instead of quality time, as we have now, my daughters and I had *quantity* time. I would type on my laptop at the dining table and throw stale Halloween candy at them while begging them to watch television. But no, my girls wanted us to do *projects* together! To bake cookies, or squeeze lemons for lemonade! I could barely keep the cooking and laundry and driving together, barely keep us in milk and underwear. The thought of the exploding flour and sticky lemons and a seventeen-piece juicer? It was too much to contemplate.

But now, because I see my girls just 50 percent of the time, I have gazelle intensity and can bring on the Mom they never had before. I help with homework, draw baths, rub backs. We've gone places once unimaginable—bowling, miniature golfing, county fairs. We've painted watercolors, knitted scarves, built missions out of Styrofoam and toothpicks. One year we carved a jack-o'-lantern out of a pineapple, just to see what would happen. When back at their dad's—where they also have quality time (he is used to packing in a lot, as he must around his frequent travel)—they message and text me and I respond instantly, resulting in a kind of immediate and perhaps even more intimate (because it feels a bit secretive?) teen-girl intimacy. Best of all, when he's doing his thing with them, I don't have to be involved; there is no "family time." (Think Dad's annual "family camping trip," where Mom can be found in the Porta-Potty miserably guzzling from a small twist-top bottle of wine she's smuggled in in her sock bag.) Meanwhile, messy or not, Charlie does put a healthy meal on the table almost every night and insist we sit down together to eat it—something I rarely, if ever, managed when I was a de facto single parent.

As for my ex, when I arrive at his house—my old house—to pick up the girls, Ben's pleasure that I no longer live there is visceral. In relationship's seesaw, while I've become more anal in certain ways to balance Charlie, when I was living with methodical Ben it was I who made the messes. Ben has always been a master declutterer, and in the end I think I became a kind of clutter for him; even today, seven years from my departure, he will hand me a sack of my mail, old CDs, or errant photos that have turned up in some far corner of the house, in what feels like a subtle way of saying "Yet again, good riddance." And I've noticed how he continues to make pleasing improvements to the house, how there is always an update to admire. The driveway is newly asphalted, the living room is repainted in soothing coral, there are vases of fresh flowers. (Fresh flowers! This I do not remember!) In the kitchen, there is newly baked bread, hand-squeezed juice; ceramic bowls cradle perfect fruit—without a single fruit fly! Yet again, a small thing—but I now see this as an utter marvel.

Held forever now at arm's length, a permanent visitor to his home, I appreciate my former husband in a way I never could before. I'm touched by the framed photographs he displays of our girls, their stacks of clean laundry I know he has folded, and his regular, concerned e-mails about their orthodontia, misplaced cell phone chargers, shifting school schedules. He still goes on the road a lot—and I happily get the girls at those times—but I see how he's always trying to eke out every spare minute with his daughters, sometimes driving six hundred miles round-trip so he can see them for twenty-four hours. While married, I bemoaned his absence; divorced, I see his abiding love, devotion, and presence, the glass half-full.

(When thinking back, our problem was not that we didn't love our children, it was that we held ten different notions of what roles we were supposed to be playing. At the very least, a husband and wife in a Norman Rockwell portrait of a family. But I also had a full-time career. So, yeah, that wasn't working.)

The only thing I don't love about Ben's home now is the cat box and the occasional hallway floor smear of cat vomit. But I know the girls love their cats. And I love that they can have cats and I don't have to clean up after them.

• • • •

Now home from Nadine's, entering once again my Huge House of Clutter, I remind myself that for all her Zen calm and gorgeous white counters and couches, Nadine *had* admitted that, very occasionally, she wishes she had a real love in her life—someone to tell about her day, to complain to about the battling guests at the dinner party on the way home. And that's enough for me. No one gets everything, right? Plus, let's face it, there probably is no nobler self inside me. If a dog put his paws on my chest at 6 A.M., I'd likely just kick him to the door to take a walk on his own.

So in the end, I've come back to thinking that Ruth really *was* wrong. Single or partnered, I will always be one to roundly blame my circumstances. There's a little bit of me in all of these disparate people.

Meanwhile—for the moment, at least—I am a person who dwells in a home with nicely refinished wooden floors (they *are* down there somewhere, underneath . . . ), the occasional pantry moth (but most of them gone! For which I give myself full credit), and my *New Yorker*–tower-building but lovable, getting-on-in-years "boyfriend" waiting to greet me. We don T-shirts and underwear, pour cocktails, take a few hits of pot, and settle down to watch *Game of Thrones*, the cannabis perfectly setting up the midnight munchies for later: chocolate ice cream, eaten with a shared spoon (the only clean one in the house), right out of the container.

# 4 Starting Over

*it will take all your heart, it will take all your breath*
*it will be short, it will not be simple*
                    *—Adrienne Rich, "Final Notations"*

*Live your life, live your life, live your life.*
                    *—Maurice Sendak*

# Second Time Around

## Letting Go of Convention
## (and Listening to My Mother)

**KATE CHRISTENSEN**

*Kate Christensen's essay in* The Bitch in the House, *"Killing the Puritan Within," described her attempts to come to terms with a marriage that was problematic in ways she hadn't anticipated. By the end of the essay, she had met her husband halfway in many of their conflicts, and had decided and accepted that their problems had to do at least partly with her unrealistic expectation that marriage should or would be perfect. For the moment, she had learned to live with its flaws and challenges and was committed to staying in it.*

*But by a few years later, still craving a union that felt truly right for her, Kate was less willing to blame her perfectionism for her lack of contentment, and more inclined to move on. Her new thoughts and wisdom follow.*

One recent chilly, rainy afternoon, Brendan, my boyfriend of almost seven years, and I drove down to a memorial service in Boston for an old friend of his family, a man who had lived a full life and died at eighty-nine, leaving behind a wife, grown kids, and many other people to mourn him. He was a brilliant, generous, complicated iconoclast, and he was deeply loved.

As memorials will sometimes do, this one made me thoughtful. At the reception after the service, sipping wine, I found myself looking at one of the speakers, a man I guessed was in his early fifties—my age. He was a filmmaker who taught at Harvard. He had an English accent and a hipster ponytail, and he was slovenly and interesting-looking.

"You think he's hot," Brendan said suddenly, into my ear.

I turned to him and laughed. "No!"

He stared me down.

On our drive home to Maine after the service, I said, continuing out loud the unspoken conversation we had been having, "I wonder what I look like these days. I mean this entirely without ego. My mother always told me aging happens in plateaus and landslides. Since we met, I've been on a plateau, looking pretty much the same age, and suddenly now I look older in a landslide. I see it in the mirror."

Brendan—tall, blond, sixteenth-century-French-viscount-meets-wild-Irish-poet handsome, and all of thirty-three at the time—said, "What makes you say this?"

"It was that guy," I said. "It's not that I was attracted to him, or anyway, that's not the point. It's that he's exactly the sort of man I pictured myself married to when I was younger: a liberal arts university professor. We'd live in Cambridge or Berkeley, in a Victorian house full of books and musical instruments, and we'd have two or three kids."

We both laughed. Our house is properly old and stately, but otherwise, my life is quite different from the one I had thought I'd be living. For one thing, I don't have children. For another, I left my husband almost seven years ago, after twelve years of marriage. But also, Brendan—who for all intents and purposes is my second husband; we've lived together for more than six years and are rarely apart—is a full two decades younger than I am. In other words, I'm old enough to be his mother.

Though I fell in love with him on our first date, seven months after the night we met, and never fell out, it took me years to accept that a relationship this uneven agewise—with me the older partner, no less—could work. Part of this was because of the way a small and naïve but (at that time) important handful of people in our lives treated us. But more of it, I admit, stemmed from my own prejudiced, unimaginative, society-fueled ideas about what constituted an acceptable marriage, or even an acceptable couple. Only over time and with much persistence by Brendan did I finally give myself over to this "unconventional" union, which for the past six years has made me happier than any other relationship I've ever had.

Ironically, part of the reason I came around had to do with my mother, someone who—with her serial divorces, her life of frequent upheaval and periods of solitude and financial hardship—I once vowed never to emulate. Now I thank her for giving me the strength and example to ultimately follow my gut instead of convention. I learned beautifully from her mistakes and her wisdom, but not until I let myself pursue my own true desires instead of some external idea of what I should do or how I should be.

• • • •

My mother married and divorced three different men—four if you include the man she lived with for seven years in her sixties and early seventies but never legally married only because neither of them saw the point. All four of her husbands were highly accomplished and intelligent—a lawyer, an architect, a professor, and a psychologist—though they also each had serious emotional and psychological problems: Two were alcoholics, the other two controlling and abusive. My father, a charismatic charmer, regularly beat our mother in front of my two sisters and me. At ten and the oldest, I was the one to finally call the police; he was taken away in handcuffs, and we didn't see him again for years.

I won't go into the reasons my mother chose these men, other than to say that her entire childhood was marked by both neglect and abuse at the hands of otherwise intelligent, interesting people, so her husbands must have felt deeply familiar to her on many levels. From what I observed, my mother was an excellent partner. She gave her husbands sex, companionship, and affection, even as she was strong, ambitious, and financially contributing. She did, though, have occasional bouts of depression; once every few years, for a couple of days, she couldn't get out of bed. And sometimes, especially when she was working a lot, she was anxious and tense. But she was monogamous and rarely flirted and cooked delicious dinners and was generous and devoted to her husbands. And I never had any idea she suffered so much, because she always kept going. She's told me that her work saved her sanity, and she was glad she had to work so hard.

• • • •

I later found out that the reason for her tenseness was at least partly that my mother felt she had to diminish part of herself with all of her husbands in order to make the relationship work. She believed that she had to protect them from the unadulterated force of her strength and power, from her true feelings and needs and desires. She stayed silent, suppressing her anger when she realized that venting it would get her nowhere. She stopped asking for what she needed and wanted when she realized her husband couldn't give it to her. But that anger, and those wants and needs, didn't go away. Being married, for my mother, was a forced but voluntary bifurcation of her psyche and soul. It was worth it, at least at first, for the perks even a troubled marriage afforded: social and economic and emotional stability, the comfort of having someone to gossip with in the car on the way home from parties and to fall asleep next to, the relief of giving her daughters a male parental figure. But she always eventually imploded or exploded, realized that she couldn't do it anymore, and left—all four of them.

It was a pattern, over and over: I watched her go from being a conventional, good, diminished, and repressed wife to being an autonomous, courageous, and wholly present but also struggling and sometimes lonely divorcée. Her divorces happened when I was six, then fourteen, then twenty-seven, and the upheavals made a deep impression on me. When she was single again, we always had to move, and financially, at least, we lived less well. When she left her fourth "husband," I was in my forties and struggling simultaneously to leave and to stay in my own failing marriage.

• • • •

In 1996, when I was thirty-four, I got married. My new husband was thirty-two—and that's only one of many ways in which, on paper at least, we were well matched. I went to Reed, he to Bennington; we graduated the same year. He comes from a cultured, highly educated, successful Jewish family, and my family, although atheistic and fractured, is also artistic and highly educated. We both had parents who divorced, and all of them remarried. He was— and still is—a photographer, painter, and musician; I'm a musician and a writer. He also was generous, attentive, and loving—as am I—and I fell in love with him in part because I knew he'd be an excellent father, the kind who would give his kids boundless love and security and would never, as my father had, abandon them.

After our wedding, I moved into his Brooklyn loft, and eventually we bought and renovated, together, an old nineteenth-century row house. In our dozen years of marriage, we shared both a love of eating, drinking, cooking, and traveling and a large group of interesting, artistic friends who worked in their studios or work-rooms by day, and by night went to art shows and readings, bars and parties—more than a few thrown by us. People knew us as a unit as much as individually. And I loved that; I loved the ramifica-tions of being married, loved the social approbation that went along with being part of a long-established couple, financially secure and rooted in our neighborhood.

But much was missing in my marriage, and the longer we stayed together, the more problematic this became for me. I had always wanted children, but when I was ready to get pregnant, two years after we married—I was thirty-six—he wasn't willing. At first I was patient, and then persistent, and then I resorted to crying and pleading. After a long time of this and not seeing him budge, I gave up in despair.

Over that period, I began to see our marriage more clearly. Yes, we were two committed artists who shared friends and good times and a house. But we weren't truly connected in the way of people who are aligned and fundamentally compatible. We didn't, in the end, want the same things. He wanted to live a life that was focused on his work, unburdened by dependents, in a glamorously ram-shackle house jam-packed with art and cigarette smoke and music and friends. I eventually wanted to move on to our next phase, something more conventional: kids, routine, shared worries and re-sponsibilities, abundant love, a bright, comfortable, "grown-up" (as I thought of it) house.

Most of all, I wanted a strong, instinctive bond with my husband that was fed and nourished by our shared experience as parents, a shared vision for our life together. But—and this is something I didn't realize, or didn't *let* myself realize, when I married him, so focused was I on how much fun we had together and what a great father he could be—no matter how much time we spent as a couple or how much we went through together, he always seemed somehow just out of my reach. I didn't know why, I couldn't figure it out, but on the deepest level, I was lonely with him. No matter how hard I tried, and I tried everything I could think of, I never could figure out how to feel I'd reached him or made myself known to him, this person I lived with and was legally bound to.

On top of all that, my husband, though sweet-natured and easy-going much of the time, had an explosive, unpredictable temper—something that, somehow, I also had failed to take note of before we wed, though, in my own defense, he truly didn't act that way until we got married. In fact, our honeymoon was the first time I saw that side of him, and I was justifiably shocked. And every time he blew up—when he yelled about the broken printer, or exploded at the slow driver in front of us—even though his temper was rarely directed at me, and I knew he would never hit or physically hurt me, I recoiled into myself, traumatized by the echo of my father's violence toward my mother.

At first I blamed myself for my feelings, and I told myself his anger was not a big deal and everything was okay. A good wife weathered her husband's mood swings, right? I tried to understand his outbursts for what they were, to soothe him, roll with it, stay connected to him in spite of them. But it wasn't okay—at least not for me. His rages freaked me out. They turned me right back into that ten-year-old girl watching her father punch her mother. I hyperventilated, my heart raced, and my panic attacks became more severe over time. And nothing, it seemed, could change this dynamic between us.

It was becoming increasingly clear to me that this husband who was so right for me on paper was wrong for me in reality. Still, I blamed myself—for the mistakes I made, of course, but also for being a perfectionist—instead of also blaming him for not meeting me halfway on the things I cared about deeply. I fought and fought against leaving. I would not get divorced, as my mother had. I was *committed* to my husband, for life.

But by the time he was ready, finally, to be a father, a few years after what I think of as My Begging and Crying Year, I had lost my passion for him, my trust in our union. My heart had been broken by his refusal. My body and soul had been ready before, but now it was too late. Because I couldn't change anything but refused to leave, I withdrew and recoiled and seethed with suppressed anger. Finally I had a brief affair and then ended it and left my marriage, but after three months of separation I went back to my husband, unable to cope with the loneliness of life without him. However, the following two years of weekly marital therapy served only to underscore how insoluble our problems were, at least for me.

In the end, the two things that gave me the freedom to finally leave my marriage—and therefore to find Brendan, the man with whom I *do* have that deep connection and compatibility, the man who happens to be twenty years younger than I am—were the same two reasons I'd stayed. The first was children, or, as it turned out, lack of them. Though I obviously can't know, I imagine that having them would have helped dispel my loneliness and would have given my husband and me that deep shared bond I was so hungry for. Undoubtedly I'd have wanted our kids to have a secure and stable childhood with two loving parents in the same house, and I would have done my best to make that happen. I can't imagine that, if we'd had kids, I would have left. But we didn't have them.

The second reason I was able to leave my marriage was the same reason I'd stayed for so long: my mother.

• • • •

Though she'd chosen to be with all her partners, all four of them, for what at the time seemed like very good reasons, my mother also had the grit and strength to leave each of them when the relationship became untenable—regardless of the disruption it would cause to all our lives, regardless of how poor we would be. My mother taught me, by example, never to stay in a situation that wasn't working, and never to be afraid of change. And if I once thought that wasn't something to admire, in my forties I changed my tune about that.

"It's always better to be lonely alone," my mother told me more than once, "than to be lonely with someone else." She was right.

Now seventy-eight, busy, healthy, and happy, my mother—single and, yes, still sometimes wishing she had a true love and life companion, but with peers and close friends, both male and female—has lived a life of accomplishment, courage, joy, and fun. In her professional life, she was a Juilliard-trained cellist and a clinical psychologist with a successful private practice; since she retired, she's become a writer. She travels, reads, and throws dinner parties, visits her daughters and grandchildren. She lives well and loves her life.

By leaving her difficult marriages and telling me why she'd left, my mother gave me, by both example and advice, the ability to do whatever it takes—to make any sacrifice and give up any and all security—in order to be true to myself. And once I stopped worrying about "turning into her" and realized what she had given me, I was able to leave a marriage that was no longer working. Leaving was wrenchingly painful. No one should ever have to get divorced. But I survived.

In fact, I more than survived. I found the compatibility and deep connection I'd been yearning for in Brendan, who I met two weeks after I left my husband, though we didn't start dating until seven months later, when he asked me to have dinner with him. I went on a lark, since he was too young for me to take seriously as a potential partner: It was my first date since my marriage, so I figured it would be good practice, if nothing else. The joke was on me, of course.

These days, Brendan and I own a house that we furnished and decorated, together, to reflect our compatible tastes; we have a dog, and we're committed to each other. We'll probably get married someday, when we get around to it, but we've felt married in the truly authentic sense of the word for years now. Brendan doesn't want kids—never has—and this time around, that's a blessing. I make more money at the moment, as well I should; I'm twenty years ahead of him career-wise. But he likes to joke that he's my retirement fund.

At the beginning, though, our age difference felt insurmountable to me. It was bad enough that I'd left my marriage, my thinking went; now I'd be seen cougaring around with a guy young enough to be my son? It didn't help that many of the men I knew who were my age reacted to Brendan's presence in my life with arrogance and what felt like competitive annoyance. "Does he even know what to do in bed at that age?" asked one, a married man with two kids who'd repeatedly hit on me over the years. "I wouldn't tell anyone how old he is if I were you," advised another, a serial womanizer whose last girlfriend was not much older than Brendan. My ex-stepfather (twice divorced and currently single and lonely), in front of Brendan, advised us against the relationship, proclaiming, his voice dripping with condescension, "Katie, men like young bodies, you know, firm tits and a tight ass. Brendan, what'll you do when her ass is wrinkled?" (To my joy, Brendan answered, "I'll love her wrinkled ass.")

Brendan's parents, who are only eleven years older than I am, were hostile to me at first: What was their sweet young secondborn son doing with a middle-aged not-yet-divorcée? And vice versa? And while their concerns were understandable, and not hypocritical like those of my same-age male friends, that didn't make them any easier for me to tolerate; until then I had always enjoyed the uncomplicated approval of my boyfriends' parents. Among other things, all these comments brought home how weird our relationship looked from the outside, no matter how natural, obvious, and wonderful it felt to us. "Brendan and I are the same age inside!" I wanted to tell them. "We're perfect for each other! Sometimes he even seems older than I am."

But I couldn't say all that, of course. I had to let them see for themselves. And they have. Over the years, they have seen both Brendan and me as a couple and Brendan as I see him: as a mature and responsible man, not their sweet, shy little boy. At the memorial in Boston recently, they treated me as a daughter-in-law—as part of the family—and it hit me that afternoon that they'd finally accepted me as fully as if Brendan and I were the same age.

But I'm also aware these days that I look suddenly older and that Brendan still looks young. I haven't been conscious of looking so far apart in age since the beginning of our relationship, back when men my age were making insulting comments and I was worried about our age difference in a wholly general sense. Suddenly here it was again, visibly—but now I seemed to be the only one bothered by it or even fully aware of it.

"So why do you wonder what you look like suddenly?" Brendan asked as we drove north from the memorial, rain beating against the windshield, our dog snoozing in the backseat.

"You're not going to really start aging for at least another decade," I answered. "And I suddenly feel my age. I feel fifty-two. I look in the mirror and I think, *Yup. Middle-aged.* It's weird, it makes me feel *older* when I look at you, not younger. I truly have no idea what I look like these days."

"You mean you feel . . . outside of age," he said. "And if you were married to that guy back there, you'd be more anchored because you'd be looking at someone your same age. You'd get old together."

"Yes," I said. As usual, he knew exactly what I was talking about.

He looked over at me. "But you did that already, remember? Married the guy the right age?"

I nodded. I had.

"It doesn't matter what we look like," he said, reassuring me once again, as he had so often in our early days. "What matters is how we *feel*. So stop thinking about it. You're gorgeous and you're perfect for me and I will always think so no matter what."

I smiled, then leaned over and kissed him on his beautiful thirtysomething mouth. He kissed me back, laughing at my sudden burst of passion, his eyes steadily on the road.

It's almost a joke, how happy and contented we are with our shared routine, our quiet, settled New England life, our bright, uncluttered house—cooking meals, taking walks with our dog, working hard, sleeping side by side every night. I've never felt lonely with Brendan. Even if I say something oblique and out of the blue, he takes a leap of willing and curious comprehension toward me, and I do the same for him. When I'm angry, I say so. When I want something, I ask for it. He gets angry sometimes, but in a calm, low-key way. And we meet each other halfway, all the time.

I think that, in some ways, this is what my mother was missing and yearning for in all her own marriages. And maybe someday she'll find it, though she'll also be okay if she doesn't. That's my mother; she's always been able to find happiness in autonomy and solitude. As for me, I feel grateful every day to be able to love another person so fully and wholly, without being blocked or stymied, without having to suppress any part of myself. This, for me, is true love. And while in some ways my relationship with Brendan is anything but conventional, in another way, this is the conventional marriage I have always dreamed of.

Of course, I do realize this: We're both still young (or youngish, in my case). His friends and siblings don't have kids yet. My friends and siblings are still healthy and vital. In twenty, thirty years, our age difference will be even more pronounced than it is already; my recent landslide into aging is just the beginning. Possibly quixotically, possibly because after all these years we know ourselves deeply and well, neither of us is worried now about what will happen when his peers are raising children at the same time that mine start grappling with the realities of old age.

But who knows what will happen? If, when he's forty and I'm sixty, he suddenly realizes that his life won't be complete without children, or that he's unhappy being with an older woman now that he sees the reality of it—or both—I feel that I would owe it to both of us to acquiesce to these feelings without resentment or anger. Of course I'd be heartbroken, devastated. But I also want him always to be happy, to have what he wants and needs. After all, I have spent the happiest years of my life with him.

So I'm enjoying this as it comes, without taking him for granted or expecting that he'll never leave me. And, thanks to my mother's example, I know I would be just fine alone—in my case, knowing I'd once had this splendid and effortless love.

# What Was in It for ME

## Saying Yes, Saying No, Leaning In, Leaning Out

**RABIA HUSSAIN**

'm thirty-eight years old but I might as well be twice that, for all I've been through. For one thing, I have eight children—all biological, all with one husband—the oldest twenty-one, the youngest still a toddler. For another, I've been married for twenty-four years; I was wed at fourteen, to a man who was twenty-three—a marriage arranged by my mother. (Admittedly, I was divorced for three of those years, but since I remarried the same guy, it seems fair to combine it all at this point.) On the trip to meet my chosen husband and complete our *nikah,* or marriage contract—in Pakistan, where he was born and raised and finishing his graduate degree in Islamic studies—I put seventy-two packs of Juicy Fruit in my suitcase. What can I say? I was a kid. I liked gum.

I grew up on Long Island, but my parents came here from India as teenagers, and in our family arranged marriage was the norm: Both of my sisters were arranged at sixteen, my brother at eighteen. Friends, cousins, uncles . . . ditto. Still, when our relatives—both in New York and "back home" in India, a country I've actually never visited—heard the news about me, they were shocked. *Fourteen?*

Even my father objected. Besides my being too young, he thought my husband didn't have the credentials to support me. A *maulana,* or Islamic scholar, isn't exactly a cash cow; most South Asian fathers prefer a doctor or engineer son-in-law.

But my mother was determined. My prospective husband was the brother of an acquaintance, and when she saw his picture and heard about his studies and devotion to his widowed mother, she loved him for me: an intellectual guy who was religious *and* hot (my suit-wearing father, in comparison, probably didn't have "hot" on his short list). We were on the plane before I knew it. First stop, Saudi Arabia for the annual Hajj pilgrimage (a grueling five-day ceremony of rites—every Muslim is supposed to do it at least once), then on to Karachi for the marriage itself.

My mother had one thing right: My husband was very good-looking. But we were nine years apart, and all I saw was a grown-up man from a world completely different from mine. Two days before the ceremony—preparations in full swing: catering, henna, garlands of roses and jasmine—I told my mother I didn't want to marry him. Mostly I was just giving her a hard time; I knew I really had no choice. But word spread, because my cousin in Pakistan told her father I was being forced, and her father called my father in New York, and my father called me and asked if he should put his foot down.

I said no. For one, I didn't want to waste the money my parents had laid out for the travel and wedding. But also, I didn't think my father could persuade my mother. Although he was a highly qualified engineer, the big boss at work, my mother was the dominant force in our home, and I didn't want him to experience another nasty trampling by his wife.

Then, the night before the marriage, my male cousins sent me a message asking if I wanted *them* to stop the wedding. How? They'd kidnap the prospective groom until the marriage day passed.

Amused, I thanked them for their kind offer, then declined. Even if I escaped this marriage, my mother would hustle me into another. A highly educated woman with no attachment to domestic life, she wanted to shackle me to marriage before I could make the same mistakes she had: namely, getting too educated to want to devote my life to what she believed the more worthwhile pursuit—motherhood.

So I wore red and gold to my wedding and chewed gum onstage, and my husband slipped my ring on while we stared, embarrassed, at opposite walls. Then my mother and I went to my aunt's, and my husband returned to his Pakistani home. I wouldn't be expected to live or sleep with him until I turned sixteen and he finished school and came to the United States.

Before we left Pakistan, my husband's mother, a die-hard romantic despite her utterly unromantic life (widowed at forty, with twelve children—several of whom she tried to abort, she told me, by walking up and down stairs with buckets of water), asked my mother if my husband and I could go out together. I wasn't thrilled—I wanted to hang out with my cousins from Saudi Arabia—but soon I was off to dinner, the beach, the bedraggled Karachi Zoo, perched sidesaddle on the back of my husband's motorcycle, the folds of my abaya tucked up under my legs.

"Hold on tighter, please," he said at one point. "I don't want you to fall off."

I sighed, bored with this serious, distant old man. I didn't know then that despite his Islamic studies student exterior, my husband was a former motorcycle-racing "bad boy"; I also couldn't know, so young, how truly handsome he was, a curly-haired, well-muscled guy who'd been the captain of both soccer and cricket teams. That is perhaps the greatest loss in an arranged marriage so young; by the time I caught up to him maturity-wise, he was already like an older brother who's sexy to other women but not to me.

He later admitted he'd been bored with me too—this little girl from America who dropped her cheap ring and made him stop for two hours to help search for it through dirt and dust. He thought I must be scared riding on a motorcycle, and at one point he asked, "Would you like me to go slower?"

"Faster," I responded.

That, he said, made me a little more interesting, but still not above the yawn-worthy mark. Still, operating under his mother's orders, he was resigned to life with me.

* * * *

Two years later he arrived in New York, and our real married life began. First the giant reception: nearly a thousand guests. Then, suddenly, we were alone in a bedroom together. When people ask about that first night, I say: It was a disaster, yet a resounding success. Or perhaps the other way around.

My cousins and sisters had told me, *Don't tell him "hands off" for too long; the sooner you get it done, the better the relationship.* And my husband's sister's husband told him: *Do it the first night, or the in-laws will think you're impotent and probably demand a divorce.* So we spent the first night trying to "do it." He was a virgin too. Needless to say, it was an awkward, painful, long night.

The good thing was, we talked—a lot. By morning, we'd told each other our life stories and developed actual affection for each other.

I applied myself to the marriage as if it were a chore or my studies. *Got to get an A in this!* Manage the house, the meals, the almost immediate pregnancy (age sixteen), the money. Manage the sex, trying to make it exciting for him—something I considered my responsibility. Read, read, read to get it all right. What was in it for me? The question didn't come to me then, but would much later.

* * * *

A significant part of the "disaster" of our marriage was financial. My husband, the first son to leave Karachi, was expected to contribute to his birth family *and* support me, all with no training for a "regular" U.S. job. (If he'd stayed in Pakistan he'd have been the equivalent of a professor, but his education there didn't lead to that here, plus his English wasn't great.) So he worked doing odd jobs—in factories, or delivering newspapers. But there was never enough money, especially once our first child arrived.

There were good moments too, though, and—interestingly—many of them had to do with our love/sex life. Having never been in romantic relationships before, neither of us knew to say *This is not really love*. We accepted it, and we worked to make each other feel special: I'd leave him doughnuts and a note when he came home late at night, or he'd surprise me by taking me somewhere he knew I wanted to go. We fought—hard—sometimes, but never talked about our fights publicly or criticized each other to family or friends.

And soon we became very close. My husband, despite his age, was like a kid in some ways: He'd pick me up and drop me into the pool, then jump in; he got silly-happy when someone admired his muscles. He helped my uncle fix his car, my dad spruce up our neglected yard. He missed his family terribly, which made him cherish me more, and he'd give me massages even after working all day, leave parties the moment I got bored.

Our sex life improved, and we spiced it up however we could: stripteases, tying each other up, role-playing. I did it out of duty, but I had fun too. As for my husband, his professors had taught him in madrassa that the way to be satisfied with your woman was to look at no other. And he did always make me feel like the most beautiful woman, even after I'd birthed eight children and, at 108 pounds, barely had any breasts left at all.

• • • •

As those initial years passed, however, and I (literally) grew up, I began to feel I'd gotten the short end of the marriage stick. With sex, for instance: After a few kids I found it tedious, and in the absence of desire and attraction, it seemed more for his sake than mine. I continued to "make a good show of it" because I wanted my husband, who I knew made an effort not to look at other women, to have a good time. But when I hit my mid-twenties and began to feel drawn to other men, I resented having been deprived of a chance to feel desire in a relationship.

Also, having grown up in relative middle-class comfort thanks to my father's job, I was suddenly poor. Sometimes, after paying bills, I couldn't afford even a package of Chips Ahoy! cookies; once, we brushed our teeth with salt until his paycheck. We lived near my parents, but I hid our problems and never asked for help; I didn't want to insult my husband. And we never applied for state assistance, mostly because the thought never occurred to me.

Then there was education. My sisters and I were math whizzes—one year, both my eldest sister and I received the highest math scores in our state—yet marriage had stunted my schooling, which struck me as outrageous. After two years as The Wife, I announced I wasn't going to just sit home, have babies, and cook; I wanted to go to college. My mother discouraged me—*Who will watch the baby?*—and my husband balked. But eventually he helped me. *She's not housewife material,* I heard him tell his sister. *She might as well do something else.*

I was pregnant with our second child when I started college nearby. I worked my classes around when my husband and mother could watch my son, and once I started, he continued to support me, both financially and otherwise: through my bachelor's, then my first job (teacher's aide), and eventually through my master's and Ph.D. coursework.

As usual, though, a negative side arose. Suddenly—now teaching and maintaining a 4.0 in college—I was pegged as the future breadwinner. Meanwhile, I'd had two more children (one planned, one not). By twenty-two, I had four kids and was directing a non-profit, and life was frantic. Meals, laundry, errands, work, kids' homework, dishes, sex . . . everything was on a schedule (yes, even sex, at least three times a week), and everything, in my estimation, had to be perfect: the kids' and my schoolwork, the house, my job. Otherwise people would say, *She had all those kids* and *decided to work, and now her life is a mess.*

· · · ·

I spent much of my twenties and early thirties "doing everything": mother, earner, housekeeper, bill-payer, student . . . and—yup—the Bitch in the House. "Why are you sitting on the couch while I'm bathing the baby?" I would snap at my husband. "I worked all day too. Why is the house such a freaking mess? Am I the only one around here making sure we have milk?" He was building a business with his brothers—one that eventually would bring in more income—but still, his life was a hundred times less harried than mine. And though I loved working and earning and accomplishing my dreams, when I saw him reading the paper while I exhaustedly rocked a congested baby to sleep, I resented the difference in our lives. I resented *him.* He had become comfortable with my pulling in a paycheck—expected it, even—while not changing his own life much, it seemed to me. It wasn't fair. I'd gotten a traditional Indian marriage where love/attraction was sacrificed, yet a husband not traditional enough to earn enough to support us—and not *un*traditional enough to do at least half the household duties.

But despite the resentment, I wouldn't have given up my job or my studies for the world. People said, *Super-achieving mom!* and I smiled. People said, *You go, girl!* and I thought, *I already have.*

· · · ·

But things couldn't go on this way. In the final stretch of my Ph.D.—the dissertation half-written, pages piled on a desk littered with my awards, service and otherwise—I discovered that one of my daughters, barely a teenager, had been molested (groped, harassed, and flashed). Formerly a sweet child, she was suddenly fighting with siblings and mysteriously bursting into tears.

It was someone we knew, and, rightly or not, I blamed myself—and my husband. I was angry we'd missed what we should have known, angry he hadn't protected my daughter (though I wasn't sure how he could have done that), and angry, honestly, that he didn't just kill this guy. I was angry at not being able to fix the unfixable.

At first I focused on damage control, dropping everything to help my daughter.

And then I did the unthinkable: I dumped my husband.

I was thirty-two at the time, with half a dozen children, ages three to fifteen. Why, you might ask, did I keep having children? It's a good question. Two were IUD failures, another a failure of timing. But also, having married so young—as kids, really—we tended to always act that way with each other. We were responsible on the outside, but sloppy about birth control. And once I'd had one child, I couldn't consider abortion. I wanted to meet and cherish the new child growing inside me.

Anyway, at that point—without consulting anyone—I told my husband I was divorcing him. My parents, his mother . . . they were all horrified. But I wanted out.

• • • •

Divorce is generally easier in our religion (Islam) than in our culture (Indian). For the most part, in Islam, marriage is like a contract. Divorce can happen if either party isn't pulling their weight, or if marital problems make things ugly. An ugly marriage messes with one's fundamental goodness, and there's no stigma in divorce.

But in the Indian culture? Watch out. People were telling me my girls wouldn't get husbands because I had messed up my marriage.

Ultimately, the divorce didn't fix things on the technical level anyway. The kids were with me, and it was harder being a single parent than it had been with a husband, even one who wasn't doing his share. At least before, he'd hold a baby if handed one, or be dispatched to pick up bread or eggs. But now, with his business in New York City and his family all there, he moved into his mother's cramped apartment, two hours from our home. So there was no chance of sending over my children even if I'd wanted to. And while I did see another guy for a while—this time with real physical attraction—I was so determined not to neglect my kids that he got little of me in the end.

It was during this time that I realized how much my husband had contributed to our lives. Though I hadn't loved him in the "in love" way, I did love him, miss him . . . there was much grief. When I was informed one day, by my department chair, that I had been unanimously chosen for an award, I ducked into a restroom and cried. My husband always had been the most proud of my accomplishments, and now he wasn't here to share this with.

But while I was discovering what I'd taken for granted, I also was seeing, from the distance of divorce, why my faith in our marriage had failed. It wasn't a knee-jerk reaction to my daughter's molestation, or resentment that the marriage was arranged. It was that my husband and I had mashed all our decisions and desires (and yes, accidents with birth control) into one container, ignoring that the mixture wasn't working. My husband wanted both incomes; he also wanted a wife and a mother for his kids. I wanted to work and go to school, yet we had so many children. We didn't want to use babysitters or hire help—too expensive, for one—yet neither of us liked housework or cooking regularly. So I did most of the cooking and cleaning, but resentfully.

A large part of the problem, I realized, was that my husband had become accustomed to my doing everything. He leaned on me as if I were incapable of tiring—and I complained, but I also allowed this, by getting things done myself rather than asking and expecting him to help.

But the crucial thing I came to understand was this: While I had invested my body and best years in this marriage, I hadn't invested enough in my children. Sure, I'd fed them, clothed them, supervised their education, but had I recognized them as not just part of *my* life, but people in their own right who needed a mother's attention to truly ground them? I had built onto the situation created for me a certain life for myself, but that life left little room for the children I'd created, the *responsibilities*. My husband had been a good enough father, but he couldn't step in and provide what my children were losing—had already lost—by my being gone so often, so involved in my own pursuits. Some fathers might have it in them to be both mom and dad. My husband did not.

Initially, my family thought my divorce resulted from guilt at my daughter's experience. But really that was only the catalyst. My guilt was mostly at all the other things I'd left undone, or done sloppily. I kept remembering when my sixth child, then a kindergartner, walked up to me to say something, and I, on the phone with a student, held up a finger, mouthing "Later." She lingered awhile, then walked away. The "later" never happened. Yes, it's okay for a child to learn she can't always have her mother's full attention, but when the norm is seeing your child approach and then walk away because she knows you'll be too busy to talk to her . . . that wasn't okay with me.

And my children missing out wasn't all of it. *I* was missing out too. I had everything—kids, paycheck, a hubby truly proud of my success—but time was spilling away like water from an open spigot, and my kids' growing up was a blur. With all the commitments I'd piled on myself, I barely had time to cook for them and help with their homework, let alone soak them up and *enjoy* them. Every day passed like an arrow speeding by, too quick to catch it.

These flashes of illumination—that I was a sloppy mother, that I was losing my kids' childhoods—figured into my decision to remarry my husband. His mother had been calling regularly, and I'd told her he should marry someone else. But he didn't, even though, according to the grapevine, women were pursuing him. (His role as a *maulana* who volunteered regularly for clergy duties gave them ideal access.) In my culture, generally, it's easy to get married: no dating, no waiting years for the proposal that never arrives. So once we divorced, he could have remarried anytime. But he waited for me.

And we still shared money. Besides separate bank accounts, we had a joint account into which we deposited most of our income, because it was, well, necessary. I kept paying his credit card bills, because I knew he'd forget and ruin the perfect credit he needed for his business. Since he lived with his mother, our expenses remained roughly the same. They'd grown exponentially from our too-poor-to-buy-cookies days, but so had our income—especially from my end. At that point, we were each contributing just about half.

• • • •

Before I decided to remarry my husband, I told him, "If we remarry, I'm not working."

He stared at me. "Are you kidding? You want to throw all that education out the window?" When I didn't budge, he shook his head. "Relying on just business income is risky," he said. "Remember, I'll be contributing to the household work again. We'll divide it."

I rolled my eyes. "You've never done enough, and you never will." It was the old rehash. Because while I knew he was happy to be back together, I didn't think he really would change his ways—so

I was determined to change mine. If I was going to do everything at home, or even most of it, he would have to be responsible for the income. I was *done* with doing it all, all the time, at the expense of myself and the kids.

• • • •

Let me be clear: If we had depended on my job for food and shelter, I wouldn't have quit. But what was I buying with the time I was losing? A nicer rental home? Cuter clothes? A faster car for my husband? We'd have more money for the older kids' college if I worked . . . but we'd also get less financial aid. And—yes—if I stopped working, I'd give up more accomplishments for myself, advancement of my career. But were these worth the moments never spent with my kids?

The career question was tricky. I had always believed, despite my mother's efforts to thwart the idea, that a woman is supposed to break out of the housewife role and achieve; that this was—*is*—something to be proud of, not to regret. But in that moment, in the particular life I'd been given and myself further molded, I knew that proceeding with my career was something I might regret. And I wasn't about to stick around until it was too late and see.

"In the Qur'an," I told my husband, "it says that the believers are 'those who are to their trusts and promises attentive.' We talked about this before we got married. And you're an Islamic scholar. You know that in Islam, the man is responsible for supporting his wife and children." I looked him in the eye. "You had these kids," I said. "I'm taking care of them, for the most part. So start supporting us fully. Do whatever it takes."

I dragged him before a mufti (a religious authority higher than a *maulana*) who told my husband basically the same thing. My husband huffed and puffed a little. But after that, there was—and has been, for three years now—no more discussion of my working outside the home if I don't want to.

. . . .

These days, though my husband and I carve out time as a couple, my life revolves around my children. We watch movies, attend community functions, Rollerblade, clean together, discuss books. Often we just sit on the couch and, on weekends, talk until late at night. Once a week I teach a girls' *halaqa* (a talk group, this one focused on life as a Muslim girl in America); two of my daughters fell into the age bracket that had no teacher, so I volunteered. Meanwhile, I have slowly finished my Ph.D. dissertation. And I've written this essay. I'm not doing "nothing" outside of my home. I'm just doing much, much less.

While my kids have undoubtedly benefited in the years since I've been home—I've witnessed the decrease in catfights and "fine" responses to *How was school?*, the improvement in moods and grades, the way the girls now seek me out to discuss clothes and their classes, the way the younger ones sit down with me after school instead of tramping upstairs—the rewards in my own life are apparent as well. I often sleep in now, and my older children take care of the younger ones at night while I read or take a bath. Staying home hasn't made me a perfect mother. But my younger kids receive much more from me than my older ones ever did. Maybe even too much! But better too much, I say, than not enough.

My husband, who now runs his end of the business remotely, usually makes me breakfast. I cook dinner, but sometimes, for the first time in my life, I have an hour or two to lunch with friends. Although we've sacrificed certain luxuries because of our slashed income (no more eating out often or visiting relatives far away), and though I miss forging up the career ladder—and though there are occasional moments of panic at the opportunities I'm missing—I think I am the most content I've ever been. Sitting down to dinner sometimes on a weeknight—no papers to grade, no meetings to prepare for, my *mind* present as well as my body, all my children around me, the food something I've cooked myself—I can't stop smiling, even when the kids bicker or juice gets spilled. We have time, plenty of time, to clean it up and work it all out.

# Stepping Off the Scale

**ANN HOOD**

My doctor's assistant motioned me toward the scale, clipboard in hand. This was my third visit in less than a month—first for the swine flu, then for a mole that appeared suddenly beside my belly button and changed shape just as suddenly, and now for an earache that had kept me up all night. Each time, she had weighed me. But standing there now, I wondered what my weight had to do with my sore ear. Or my mole. Or the flu, for that matter. Standing there now, the last thing I wanted was to take off my winter boots and big puffy coat and watch as she slid that bar up and up, past the 129-pound mark, where for years it had settled, perfectly balanced.

"I don't want you to weigh me," I said.

The truth was, I didn't want to be weighed ever again if that bar was going to keep creeping upward, past 130, past 140, into territory I never imagined my weight would reach. God*damn* it! I was a thin person! The woman who people asked how I could eat so much and still be so skinny. The woman who fit into her size 4 jeans, even after two babies.

The doctor's assistant frowned at me.

"I mean, I have an earache," I explained.

She began to write on my chart. In red.

"And I was just here last week," I reminded her. "Remember? The mole?"

She blinked at me. "The doctor will be in shortly," she said, and left.

I immediately picked up my chart to see what she'd written. "Refuses weigh-in." At first I felt embarrassed. I hadn't exactly "refused," had I? It just seemed silly to get weighed again so soon. So frequently. But as I climbed up on the examining table, the strangest thing happened: After years—a lifetime, really—of worrying about and taking pride in my thinness, I suddenly didn't care that I was no longer a skinny size 4. And the reason I didn't care was that I was happy. Happier than I'd been since I was a teenager. I don't mean happy in that my life was perfectly in place; in fact, in many ways it was the opposite—messy and sad, confusing and frantic. Rather, I mean happy with *me*, with who I was and how I felt about my place in the world.

I'd been that way years ago, a girl who knew her mind and her heart. And now here I was, squarely in middle age, finally certain again of those very same things. Finally happy with myself, despite all the mistakes I'd made, all the bad decisions and wrong turns and enormous losses that marked my life. Despite, I realized with something—I swear—akin to wonder, the added twenty-plus pounds I carried.

• • • •

Some girls are raised to be the first female president or an astronaut. Some girls are raised to find a cure for cancer or to battle social injustice. Or to be a perfect wife or mother or hostess or chef. I was raised to be beautiful.

To my mother, beautiful meant tall and blond and—perhaps most important—thin. She spent most of her life embarrassed by her Italian looks. Unmanageable dark hair, brown eyes behind thick glasses, a large nose with a bump at the bridge like all the Masciarotte clan had. She dreamed of being a cheerleader, a girl who could easily be lifted onto the shoulders of football players. She dreamed of being homecoming queen, lovely in a pale dress with a sweetheart neckline that cinched a tiny waist. But she'd inherited the peasant-farmer genes of her ancestors: broad hips, large breasts, short stature. And so she was doomed to playing the sidekick to pretty girls, like Eve Arden in the old movies, all sass and sarcasm as she planned school dances but didn't get a date. Or at least not one with the boys she wished for. Her dates were neighborhood kids, also Italian immigrants, also short and squat and tough.

For me, her only daughter, she dreamed of a different life. A charmed life that she believed beautiful girls led. As a baby, I had big blue eyes and a winning toothless grin that made strangers stop and compliment my mother, who dressed me in elaborate matching outfits and used egg on my few strands of pale blond hair to make them stand up enough to hold a bow. One afternoon a man with a camera passing by our front yard doubled back, pointing to me in my stroller. "Your baby could win the Beautiful Baby of the State of Maryland contest," he said. "She could?" my mother asked hopefully. The man nodded and offered to take my picture for free if my mother split the cash prize with him should I win. She agreed. I won. And my mother got her wish: She had a beautiful daughter, and a certificate from the state of Maryland to prove it.

The problem was, I didn't care about being beautiful. I cared about the March family in *Little Women,* and poetry, and why the leaves changed color every autumn. As I sat squirming in pain while my mother wrapped my now long blond hair into rags to make perfect banana curls, I yammered on and on about the things that mattered to me, that kept me up at night. "How do you pronounce the name of the country spelled *I-r-a-q*? Why isn't there a *u* after the *q*? Why is *y* sometimes a vowel? Can I carry a baked potato to school to keep my hands warm like Laura does in *Little House on the Prairie*?" My mother twisted another thick hank of hair into a scrap of cotton and sighed. "No, you cannot carry a baked potato. You'll wear your new mittens that match your hat and scarf. Why do you have to be so weird? You're beautiful. That's all that matters." This last was always said with a sigh, resigned or grateful or both, I'm not sure.

Although I'd inherited the traits my mother valued from my midwestern father, I often felt that my mother believed I looked this way because of some kind of divine intervention. She had prayed for a beautiful daughter, a blond daughter, a *thin* daughter, and now she had one. Her prayers had been answered. I would fulfill all the dreams she'd had dashed because she was overweight. The fact that I didn't like being onstage or primping or shopping didn't matter. "If I'd looked like you when I was young . . ." she'd say as she exhaled a lungful of cigarette smoke. There was no ending to that sentence; it was implied. If she'd looked like me, she would have been happy.

I wasn't happy, however. I was a frightened, anxious kid who overthought everything. As soon as I learned the Earth was rotating, I worried that it would spin off its axis. After seeing a child die from a botched tonsillectomy on *Ben Casey*, I worried that I would die if and when I ever had my tonsils removed. When my brother showed me a flake of my skin under his microscope, I convinced myself that we were all actually microscopic and that a larger species was looking at us under *its* microscope. I wouldn't stop reading a book on a page that ended with a 3 because I'd heard that bad things come in threes. I was blond. I was tall. I was skinny. And I was miserable.

As I smiled my way through beauty pageants, collecting trophies and getting to ride in convertibles in parades and having my picture splashed across the local newspaper, inside I was all nerves and queasy stomach. For my talent in pageants, I recited a poem: *I have ten little fingers and ten little toes, long blond hair and a turned-up nose, big blue eyes and a cute little figure. Stay away, boys, until I get bigger!* This was recited wearing a leopard-print bikini that my auntie Julia had sewn for me, with matching leopard-print sandals. By the time I was ten, I asked if I could recite a real poem: Joyce Kilmer's "Trees." "That poem is so depressing!" my mother told me. "Why are you so weird? If I'd looked like you when I was young ..."

• • • •

Like all things associated with beauty, thin is relative, a subjective idea, a subjective *ideal*. In countries like Tonga and Tahiti, fat women are considered beautiful and desirable. Here in the United States, however, thin is usually equated with beauty. And, just as my mother believed, beauty is often equated with happiness. How interesting to me that a 1993 study conducted in rural Jamaica associated thinness with sadness and heaviness with happiness. Of course it took me decades to believe that such a notion could even be possible.

As a teenager, I stayed on the track that pretty girls move along. Although too uncoordinated to make the cheerleading squad (the one thing I failed at in my mother's eyes), at the age of fourteen, I became a model for Jordan Marsh, the local chain of department stores here in New England. Throughout high school, I did fashion shows from Boston to Maine as well as special spreads in *Mademoiselle* and *Brides*. I modeled at the mall, standing perfectly still for hours in the store window, dressed in the hottest teen trends. My modeling got me noticed by Bonne Bell cosmetics, and I modeled for them as well, my face washed in their Ten O Six lotion, my lips and cheeks glossy with their makeup. Then for two years I won a coveted spot as a special teen "correspondent" for *Seventeen* magazine, which primarily meant appearing in both print and photo spreads.

But this was the early 1970s, long before Kate Moss's heroin chic. Our icons were women like Cheryl Tiegs and Jean Shrimpton, who, though certainly still thin, had curvy bodies and good-sized breasts. To model back then, I didn't have to be super skinny, and I wasn't. Neither were the girls I worked with. Don't get me wrong, we were far from overweight. But we had breasts and hips and round cheeks. We looked, I daresay, like healthy American teenagers, which is exactly what we were.

When I wasn't working, I was starring in school plays or writing for the school newspaper. I was dancing to Van Morrison songs at sandy bars on the beach, kissing boys in Mustang convertibles and tiny Fiats, riding waves and eating fried clam cakes. Although I had my share of teenage angst, much of what I'd felt so anxious about as a child disappeared. I worried about more concrete things: the war in Vietnam, losing my virginity, the environment. But mostly I was happy. I had friends to share my dreams with. I had creative outlets. I had boyfriends, lots of them. I used my brain all the time. And I was doing something considered valuable in my family: putting on clothes and makeup and walking down a runway. I didn't love it, but I was used to it by then, and it conferred a certain status that I now understood—not to mention providing me with extra money.

Somehow, everybody was happy with me. But even more important, *I* was happy with me. I knew how I felt about politics and love and art. I was confident as I moved through the world, as small as my world was then, its borders reaching only from Rhode Island to Maine, and most of it contained in Jordan Marsh, the mall, and West Warwick High School.

My freshman year of college, I went from happy to, frankly, miserable. I roomed with a girl from high school who I didn't know well. I'd never shared a room with anyone, and the ins and outs of now accommodating someone baffled me. School baffled me too. Did I fit in with the pot-smoking dorm kids or the large Greek community with its keg parties and formal dances? Neither, I feared. When I went on dates, boys suddenly wanted sex, not just making out, and I was confused about these new expectations. Previously an effortless straight-A student, I floundered under the burden of syllabi and no roll calling. I skipped classes frequently. When grades for that first semester arrived, I was shocked to find myself on academic probation.

Although many first-year college girls succumb to the Freshman Fifteen and gain weight, the opposite happened with me. Pounds fell off, not because I was dieting or starving, but because I was anxious. That first winter break, I had to take all my Christmas money and buy new, smaller jeans that fit. The more unhappy I felt, the skinnier I seemed to get, until people were commenting on how thin I was. Through college, the weight stayed off and I stayed, in many ways, unhappy. Even though I had friends and boyfriends and served in student government, I never believed I truly fit in anywhere.

As graduation approached, fellow classmates bought suits and took résumé-writing classes. Even though I felt confused about who I was and where I belonged, I understood that I didn't want what they wanted. My childhood dream of becoming a writer had not faded, even though I never shared it with anyone. Alone in my room, I scribbled stories and poems in notebooks that no one ever saw, read every book I could get my hands on. I needed to run with the bulls, I decided! To jump naked in fountains and live in a garret in Paris! A girl raised differently might have bought a Eurail Pass and headed for Europe after college, or applied to graduate writing programs. But I was a girl raised to be beautiful. I decided to become a flight attendant.

· · · ·

In 1978, weight restrictions still existed for flight attendants. Along with the application came a weight chart. If you were above the maximum weight, you were told not to bother to apply. For my height—almost five-foot-eight—the maximum I could weigh was 135 pounds; I was around 123. But so desperate was I for this job that would take me away from Rhode Island and allow me to have the experiences I yearned for that I went on a binge diet before my interviews and managed to shed four more pounds, leaving me a skeletal—and weak, famished—119.

At training in Kansas City for TWA, we were told that if we went above our *hiring* weight, we would be fired. Routinely, when we got off a flight a supervisor was there waiting to weigh us. One of my roommates was fired for weighing six pounds over her hiring weight, though still five pounds below the maximum weight on the airline's chart. So for the first time I began to starve myself. Dinner—my one meal a day—might be steak on a stick from the appetizer menu at TGI Fridays, or a shared salad at Crickets or Lily's in Boston's Faneuil Hall. For years, I survived mostly on coffee and wine. My size zero uniform was loose enough that I could slide my skirt entirely around my waist, easily.

Then, in 1982, my brother, Skip, my only sibling, died in an accident. The grief that followed took over my life for the next decade. At the same time, I fell in love with an actor and moved to New York City to be with him. Of all the things he gave me during our time together—and there were many—that he fed me, that he satiated my actual, physical hunger, was one of the most important. He brought home Chinese food late at night after work and took me for Indian food on East Sixth Street, cooked me soft-shell crabs, elaborate breakfasts, spicy noodles. I was happy with him, truly happy, but also grief-stricken—so much so that I didn't even worry about gaining weight and losing my job. And I needn't have anyway, because, once again, and despite my loving boyfriend, I was horribly anxious; afraid to be alone on layovers, certain that someone I loved had died in my absence. So even though he fed me, constantly and well, I stayed skinny. Too skinny.

• • • •

Out of the grief of that period, I wrote my first novel. By the time it was published, the actor and I had broken up—partially, I see now, from my own inability to deal with my sadness. A man who had been a good buddy confessed he'd been in love with me all the time I'd been in love with someone else, and without pausing I stepped immediately into a new love affair, even though it had none of the passion I'd felt before. If such a big love failed, I reasoned, perhaps I should not wait for that again but opt instead for companionship. That we had in abundance, staying up until all hours playing Scrabble or watching old movies. Reading together and sharing each other's writing. Best friends. So we married, even though in my heart I knew that I didn't love this man the way he should be loved, the way I wanted to love someone.

As I grappled with this over the course of years, my weight once again dropped, this time lower than ever. Here I was, a successful writer, living the literary life I'd dreamed of . . . and unhappier than I'd ever been. In pictures from that time, I see gobs of long blond hair hanging down a too-skinny body. I see an unhappy woman. The relationship ended, and again I jumped right into a new one. This time, I felt all the corny things someone in love says they feel, but the man—who would become my second husband—lived in Rhode Island. So I found myself packing up my New York City apartment and moving back to the place I thought I'd never live again. We wasted no time in starting our family, and before I even knew his morning routine or favorite color, we had our son, Sam, and then our daughter, Grace. Getting to know my husband, figuring out how to raise children, and trying to keep my writing career afloat took all my time. No longer a flight attendant, I no longer had to focus on my weight, and I ate again, now with abandon, and wrote, and took care of my kids. And one day I looked up and realized that I was truly and fully happy.

When, in 2002, Grace died suddenly from a virulent form of strep, this new world of mine fell apart in ways I never could have imagined. Not only was my grief all-encompassing, but I also couldn't read or write, the two things that had never failed to comfort me. Eating for pleasure was a distant memory; my body, at that time, was not something I thought of or cared about.

I wrapped myself around Sam, worrying over his every move, unable to be calm when I couldn't literally see him. I learned to knit, and I knitted constantly. Crowds made me nervous. I was unable to speak on the telephone. During the day, I took small bites of food, but I had no appetite for more. After I'd had my babies, my weight was a healthy but still thin 129 pounds. Now it once again plummeted.

It seems to me that I crawled out of that abyss of grief slowly, slowly. I remember tasting food again, and then actually enjoying it. I remember marveling at a tree whose leaves had changed color. I remember breathing in my favorite smell of salty air and really smelling it, as if for the first time. I read *The No. 1 Ladies' Detective Agency* and remembered the joy a good book can bring. We adopted a baby girl from China, and Annabelle reminded me how a child's arms lifted to you for a hug can make your heart soar. One night I had Sam asleep on one side of me and Annabelle on the other, and I understood how sadness and happiness can live side by side in our hearts.

When, during this time, did those twenty pounds begin to accrue? I don't know, because I was too busy reminding myself of what mattered, of what made me happy . . . of how to *be* happy. I wasn't noticing numbers on a scale. I was just trying to find my way back.

I am still a person who goes to the doctor a lot, partially because I have a touch of hypochondria and partially because I frequently get mild illnesses and strange pains. But the doctor's assistant no longer tells me to get on the scale. She knows I won't; I know I don't need to. Because whatever that scale says, it can't tell me what I already know. Skinny isn't beautiful. And thin or not-so-thin really doesn't matter. What matters is how you *feel* in your body, regardless of what you weigh. And what's beautiful is being in this sad, messy, lovely world and liking who you are in it—and knowing that the people you love are right here in it with you.

# Getting It Right the Third Time. Or Wrong. You Tell Me.

**KAREN KARBO**

*When Karen Karbo was a child, her mother, holding
forth from their gold-and-white Formica breakfast bar,
proffered advice and wisdom to her daughter about
marriage, including not just that she should marry
someone older, smarter, taller, and richer, but also that
marriage was possibly "life's greatest achievement."
Unfortunately, Mrs. Karbo died at forty-six—long
before Karen, then seventeen, could carry out the advice.
And so, much later, when she did marry—and then
divorce, not once but twice—she always half wondered
if the problem was partly that she didn't follow her
mother's advice. "Mom, you were right," she wrote in*
The Bitch in the House. *"If I had fallen in love with
the rich man who was older, taller, and smarter, this
probably wouldn't have happened. Or it would have."*

*At the time of that writing, fifteen years ago, Karen had
recently moved in with a new boyfriend—only negligibly
taller, and considerably younger, than even the first two.
Here's how it unfolded, and what she believes it all means.*

L ately I've had a fantasy about buying a house in the South of France. That I do not have enough money to hire someone to prune the tree in front of our house in Portland, Oregon, much less purchase a terra-cotta tile-roofed cottage on the Côte Vermeille, is immaterial. I dream of buying this house, and based on absolutely no evidence, I've come to believe that becoming a citizen of the European Union would ease this fantasy real estate transaction. Poland would be my country, as my father's people are from there, and—happily—Poland awards citizenship based on bloodlines (as opposed to the United States, which of course does so based on where you're born, more or less). Once I obtained my Polish citizenship, and then my house in France, I would want to import my boyfriend, Jerrod, my live-in love for the past fifteen years. And at that point, it seems, it would only be right for me to marry him, so that through matrimony he too would be a European Union citizen, with all the benefits—a sort of reverse green-card marriage.

A therapist might suggest I'm generating some ludicrous precursors to marrying my longtime partner, and she wouldn't be entirely wrong. The reality is, I've already been married twice, and neither time ended well, if you consider "well" something other than divorce. I suppose I could be one of those people who just keeps getting married, cycling through husbands until I'm on life support, but as I actually don't want to break up with Jerrod, I'm thinking we should simply avoid the whole thing, since it appears I just don't have long-term marriage in me. Literally. I'll spare you the science, but my recent findings have led me to believe that my cavalier attitude toward matrimony may be caused by my DNA—my genes.

Delving into my Polish background—which I've been doing at the suggestion of my online Polish lawyer (speaks English, no fees up front)—has revealed a pair of wayward grandparents who were about as uninterested in the rules of marriage as I appear to be. My grandfather, Viktor Karbowski, of Warsaw, dragged his poor wife Emilia, of Krakow, to Chicago to give birth to my father, and then promptly decamped for Mongolia (where, rather than sending back money to help support his family, he forwarded pictures of himself on horseback). Eventually he "remarried." Meanwhile, back in Chicago, Emilia then had another short-lived marriage to someone named Wisniewski before carting my young father off to Hollywood in the 1930s and changing her name back to Karbowski.

As for my mother, she had her own irregular heritage, the truth about which she took to the grave. She probably never dreamed I'd become not just a wage earner—and the higher one, at that!—in both of my marriages, but a woman who fails pretty spectacularly in the domestic arena, something she held dear.

As I stare down the barrel of sixty, I feel the same about marriage, or about me and marriage, as I always have. As with foreign languages and piano playing, I simply have no aptitude for it. This is not to say I'm against it. In fact, I envy the successful marriages of at least some of my friends. Still, I myself subscribe more to Mae West's famous comment that "Marriage is a great institution, but I'm not ready for an institution." Not now, and maybe never.

This—prepare for an understatement—is not how I was raised. As I've said, my mother had firm opinions about matrimony. Unlike my friends' mothers, who all treated it as a fait accompli—one day you'd simply "get married," probably to whoever was standing there when the music ended, sort of like in musical chairs—my mother seemed to believe I would have many choices in potential husbands and their attributes, from height to economic standing. I was to marry "up" in terms of both; *she* had, after all. The only thing she didn't seem to believe is that I had a choice about *whether* to marry. Marriage was a given, and everything I did, from participating in sports (on the one hand, exercise burned off calories, a necessary weapon in the battle of the bulge, but on the other hand, those muscular thighs were just the kind that my future Rich Man might not find appealing) to how I treated the boys in my life (I was to "play hard to get," let him open all doors, and make him pay the tab), was toward that aim.

As for me—already, at twelve, taller, smarter, and more well-off than most boys I knew (and certainly than the ones I liked), and without exactly a long queue of "suitors" anyway—I listened, and I observed. My parents' marriage seemed good, if good is defined as "not many fights, some laughs, and the ability to enjoy the holidays." It was a mid-century marriage, divided firmly along gender lines. My mother wasn't expected to mow the lawn or tug a weed, and my dad did no laundry or vacuuming. (In a pinch, he could fry up an overcooked steak.) On the other hand, he made all the money—something that, at least back then, did not seem unenviable to me.

Privately, I thought my mother didn't deserve to be trapped in a tract house in Whittier, California. She was hysterically funny and smart enough to do the crossword in pen. She liked people and could get them to confide in her. She'd been the first female executive at Holley Carburetor Company in Detroit (Peggy Olson of the automotive sector!), though she'd quit her job a month before she married my dad, a designer at Ford. So then, instead of working, she could alternately do chores and sit at the breakfast bar smoking a cigarette and drinking a beer—and, a few years later, in California, staring out the patio door at the bougainvillea, waiting for me to come home.

When I did—late afternoon, after sports—she'd ask about my day, but I wanted to hear about *her* day. Observing her life, I came to believe that after high school, after college, after I chose the Tall Rich Man over the Poor Short One, my life would turn into doing the same soul-crushing tasks she assigned me during school vacation: cleaning bathrooms, vacuuming, shag-rug raking. Was this the price of love?

No, I decided, but it was the price of marriage, as confirmed by Carly Simon, my idol in junior high. On my stereo with the automatic repeat feature, I played the crap out of "That's the Way I Always Heard It Should Be," about the slow-mo heartbreak of matrimony. Every third song sung by a *guy* stressed how love ties you down, babe, but this was the first one I'd heard by a woman that (therefore) spoke straight to *my* soul about the wages of marriage.

In contrast, my life's ambition was to be the glamorous, carefree girl in the Joni Mitchell songs. I knew the lyrics to "California" and "Carey" and sang them to my bedroom mirror, crooning into my hairbrush microphone. I longed to be the girl with beach tar on my feet, toasting to nothing and smashing down my empty glass—or at the very least the confident, footloose chick in Bob Dylan's "If You See Her, Say Hello," whom he respects for leaving him—for "busting out and getting free."

This idiotic life goal aside, I also had, and still have, a practical nature; I knew I couldn't be a "free man in Paris . . . unfettered and alive" without money. So I secretly decided I would support myself as a foreign correspondent after I made my mother happy by going to college, where I'd pretend to keep an eye peeled for the tall rich brilliant husband. Everybody wins!

The problem was, before I even made it through freshman year, she died. My father sold the house, bought a beach condo, and started courting an old girlfriend. And I lost confidence in both myself and my big plans.

• • • •

As I wrote in *The Bitch in the House,* I met my first husband (H1) in film school at USC. He had black hair and a black beard and looked like a nineteenth-century Russian author. He came from Portland, Oregon, and drove a vintage faded-red Land Cruiser. Exotic, right? We fell in love, and it was good for a number of years. We were companionable. We traveled well together. We made each other weep with laughter. I moved in with him when, after a summer where I'd gone from house-sitting gig to house-sitting gig, everyone came home and I suddenly had nowhere to live. Not particularly romantic, but so what? We lived well together. We shared the housework—already a huge change from my housewife mother and her wage-earner spouse—and he did most of the cooking. (I washed and dried.) We both contributed, about equally, to the family income.

We had been together for a dozen years when it became clear that if we were going to have a baby, we'd better start trying. However uninterested I was in marriage, I wanted a baby. This presented a quandary. Would I have a baby and we would just be, what, like the common-law couples that seemed to show up as regulars on *America's Most Wanted*? I was from Whittier, California, daughter of a stay-at-home mom and an industrial designer dad. I wasn't *that* much of a free man in Paris. I felt able to get married when I was doing it for the sake of my unborn kid.

What went wrong? I've moved through the reasons over the years, trying to choose. We drifted apart. We loved each other but were no longer "in love"—that is, nothing more than roommates. A friend who's knowledgeable about love addiction guessed that we were both love avoidants, terrified of being hurt, so we could never fully commit, even though it *felt* as if we had. (In shrink terms, this is *avoidant attachment*—when you can't tolerate the vulnerability of being intimate with someone on whom you depend, so you create a self-protective distance around them. This explanation would make sense to me, except I'm not at all like this with Jerrod. More on that in a bit.) Or maybe nothing went wrong, but the relationship reached its expiration date. Friendships run their course, working associations become unprofitable, and love affairs self-immolate, so why can't a marriage end without being deemed a failure?

At any rate, our marriage went into a slump when our daughter was around three, and rather than seek counseling or suck it up and wait it out—or simply stay in a marriage that's not sexually passionate (as a friend's mother puts it, "The way to stay married is to not get divorced")—I told him the marriage was over. I went straight into therapy, but didn't invite him to join. Why couldn't I have given it some time? An inspirational saying popped up on my Facebook news feed recently: "Suddenly all my ancestors are behind me. 'Be still,' they say. 'Watch and listen. You are the result of the love of thousands.' " I privately amended this to, " 'Be like us!' they say. 'Get the hell out!' "

But I didn't learn about my ancestors' predilections until later—my quest for Polish citizenship, remember?—and so, at the time, my therapist and I decided that I am motivated by a colossal existential fear. The great takeaway from my mother's sudden, brutal demise was that anyone could die tomorrow. *I* could die tomorrow. Therefore, terror prevented me from giving it time, seeing how it would go. I needed to move on, live like I was dying, carpe diem . . . etc.

Perhaps for this reason, as cautious as I was about getting married the first time, I dove into it the second time (again, note my family). Why not? The second husband (H2) was as different from the first as night is from day. H2 was warm (verging on hilariously so, with his penchant to cuddle all night—and all day) where H1 had been cool (verging on withdrawn). H2 had relatively little ambition (best reward for a job well done: pizza and a new video game), where H1 was all ambition (best reward for a job well done: an Academy Award). And H2 was tall, blond, broad-shouldered, and right-leaning—exactly the opposite of H1, who was dark, barrel-chested, and a lefty. As a couple we were a disaster, although—again—very good at cuddling, which took our minds off our problems. Indeed, we were so busy cuddling, I didn't realize until much later that I was love avoidant in this marriage too.

This time my therapist and I concluded that H2 reminded me of my mother, only without the ability to do the crossword in pen. Or even pencil, come to that. But he'd grown up just two suburbs over, could get people to confide in him . . . you get the gist.

This marriage proceeded to explode in a fashion worthy of an overwrought romance novel turned Lifetime movie. He activated my inner crockery-slinging shrew. For our three wedded years I was like a woman in a Tennessee Williams play. All I needed was a satin slip and a highball. Put another way, I never thought I was one to throw a drink in a man's face or engage in a wild-eyed screaming match on a busy sidewalk . . . yet there I was. This husband did me a favor by first pushing me into a bookcase, then trying to choke me. I served him with both divorce papers and a restraining order the same morning.

Then came Jerrod. Basically the third husband, only without being an actual husband (shall we call him $NH3$?), Jerrod is sixteen years younger than me. I'm sure this should bother me. I'm sure I should refuse to have sex with the lights on, lest he realize he's getting it on with a middle-aged woman, but somehow the thought never occurs to me. Sometimes I think I chose Jerrod at least in part because our age difference inoculates us against marriage: six years younger (H2) was one thing, but *sixteen*? My mother is shaking her head from her grave. When we first began dating, he was baby-faced, with center-parted floppy brown hair, long-lashed hazel eyes, dimples, an earring, and a goatee.

When we moved in together I sat him down and asked whether he was okay with having no biological children. My daughter would be his informal stepdaughter; would that be enough? He said yes, though I realized he might change his mind someday. He wouldn't be the first guy to hit forty and suddenly panic that his genes aren't being gifted to the next generation. We've passed that milestone though, and so far, so good. Over the years we've "talked about" marriage, but in the same way you lie around on a summer afternoon drinking gin and tonics and idly remarking that you really should clean out the garage. On some level—if not all levels—I must be glad we never pursued this.

I know how irrational this sounds, but part of me suspects marriage is what killed my mother, though I allowed with my therapist that perhaps it wasn't marriage per se, but being a housewife; had she continued her glass-ceiling-busting trajectory at Holley Carburetor instead of scrubbing bathrooms on Monday, cleaning the oven on Tuesday, and so forth, then sitting around all afternoon smoking her head off, her life might have been . . . there the logic ended and the tears began. Even I had to admit that hiring a housekeeper probably wouldn't have saved her from an aggressive brain tumor.

· · · ·

Officially married to Jerrod or not, I do married-woman things with him and for him. I make him risotto, I listen to him complain about his job, and I pick up his dirty socks, even though he drops them right in front of the hamper. Women are born with a finite number of eggs and loads of laundry and I've about reached my limit, but still, I do more than my share. I'm guessing there's a perfect storm of reasons why this doesn't make me stomp around swearing the way it used to.

The obvious reason—or obvious to me, anyway—is that we can both walk away at any time. Sometimes, when that pile of hamper-adjacent dirty socks gets too big and I think I cannot live like this another moment, it calms me right down to think, "Hey! I don't have to!" In other words, the idea that there is nothing forcing us together is, at least in part, what has kept us together. A long-married friend once told me she thinks the task of the happily married is to keep picking each other, again and again. To that, I say: H1 and H2 each gave me exactly what I needed at the time, but neither one would now, whereas Jerrod, who does, I couldn't have picked when I married H2, because he was in grade school. One more good reason not to tie any knots. Not that I'm planning to leave Jerrod any time soon, but again, it's nice to know we stay because we want to, as opposed to because we have to.

Here's another reason we stay: The societal expectations and nonstop domestic burden that accompanies the role of Wife (as defined by my mother, long ago) now have nothing to do with me. Nor does the label Husband with Jerrod. I get to be me, and he gets to be him, without struggling also to embody some culturally sanctioned role that nobody can live up to.

Furthermore, without quite knowing why, I just don't give a fuck about a lot of stuff anymore. I'm well on my way to being one of those women who don't care about how they look in a bathing suit, drink too much at weddings, and speak their minds with impunity. It's one of the few advantages of not being a hot twenty-five-year-old, and fortunately, it's a big one. The laundry issue? The occasional all-night video-gaming session or too-ardent love of *Star Wars*? The serious aversion to manual labor? I just don't care, writing it all off to the wages of living with another human being—one who cracks me up, listens when I talk, and wants sex just when I do. Speaking of which, unlike with H1 and H2, I am now, with NH3, no longer "love avoidant." Is it age? The man himself? All that therapy finally paying off? Who knows? But I know this: From my two marriages and two divorces, I've learned that as long as my partner is *in it with me*, I'm able to be in it too. When Jerrod and I fight—and we do—it always ends when he reassures me that I'm not alone in this, whatever *this* might be. And even though it somehow never includes picking up the socks, it's good enough for me.

• • • •

I haven't lost sight of my initial thesis here—that I am the way I am in part because of certain propensities passed down from my forebears—nor have I forgotten that we inherit our genes from both sides of the family. It turns out I am homozygous in my disrespect for the sanctity and strictures of marriage. The secret my mother was so ashamed of—and, I now believe, what motivated her devotion to marrying up, gaining security and status—was this: After a lifetime of pretending otherwise, it turns out she was not the daughter of Maud Sharkey, the woman I was told was my grandmother and who died before I was born, but in fact Maud's *foster* child. My *biological* grandparents—this set—were two teenagers in love who didn't even try to make a go of it, instead handing my mother over to Maud, who ran a boardinghouse in Ypsilanti, Michigan. (It's possible they even left her on the doorstep.) My seventeen-year-old grandfather, Calvin Rex, listed his profession on my mother's birth certificate as cab driver/poet. My grandmother didn't list one—unsurprisingly, as she was sixteen.

So my mother was not Maud's menopause baby, the child of old loins, as family lore held, but a love child of two sexy teenagers. This explained why she didn't look anything like the rest of her family. Also how I came my by facility with language, not to mention my preternatural ability to parallel-park.

• • • •

Once, when I was a small child, I stayed with Emilia, my father's mother, at her house in North Hollywood. She went by Luna of California then, and had become a dress designer for the wives of movie producers. She worked from home (her clients changed clothes behind a carved wooden screen in her living room), with a cigarette stuck on her lip, the long ash dangling perilously (not, actually, unlike my mother's at the Formica counter, though my mother ashed hers more frequently, but still—perhaps some of the attraction between her and my father?). She wore strapless sundresses with high heels, a gardenia tucked behind one ear. She had wood floors and a cleaning lady. No toilet scrubbing or shag-rug-raking for Luna. I found her to be terrifying and desperately glamorous.

Luna had a Russian gentleman friend who would take her out to eat at Chasen's. He wore dark suits and had a long pale mustache. He sat in her red brocade chair, legs crossed. I asked her if they were going to get married. She, who rarely smiled, opened her red-lipsticked mouth and laughed. "I have no need!" she said in her heavy Polish accent. I was fascinated. I had no idea then what she was talking about, but now I think I do.

• • • •

Uncovering my family history, both sides, has actually helped me feel better about how my life has turned out—as though I'm not so much defying my mother's dreams for me as simply living out what, based on my genes, I'm destined to be. Turns out it wasn't my mother's untimely death or Carly Simon or possibly even the men I chose that was responsible for my failings on the matrimonial front. Lack of interest in going with the program is part of who I am; Reader, I was *born* this way. My grandparents on both sides? All free men in Paris. They didn't give a shit, or at least not enough to not do exactly what they wanted. I feel great relief.

But when I explained all this to Jerrod, he was dubious. And he has some authority, because he's been studying genetics. He's decided he wants to become a doctor, and like the good wife I'm not, I've been shouldering most of the financial burden while he takes the necessary prerequisites (chemistry, biology, physics) in addition to genetics, embryology, and statistics. He believes that while genes might have imbued me with a certain impulsiveness or hardheadedness, this doesn't extend to a specific attitude toward marriage, which is, after all, a social construct. He did say, however, that he is very much looking forward to becoming an EU citizen, which is as close as he's come to proposing.

The thought is cozy, in the way that being part of the herd is always cozy, but in the end, I hope he doesn't. My relationship with Jerrod—approximately my height and equally smart, but much younger and currently poorer (see above, re: medical school)—has now outlasted both of my marriages, and is the best long-term relationship I've had. Why would I mess with that just to gain . . . frankly, at this age, I don't know what I'd gain. A better income-tax bracket? A diamond ring I'd snag on sweaters and drop down drains? The approval of acquaintances and strangers? No thanks. We've finally reached a time in society when it's no longer scandalous to choose *not* being married—at least where I live. I am happy my gay friends can now marry, and just as happy I don't have to. Sometimes I even hope, if my mother can see me today, that instead of shaking her head in dismay, she's raising her beer glass in a toast saying what mothers the world over always say: I just wanted you to be happy. And now you are.

# Yes

## SUSANNA SONNENBERG

You're *what?*" my best friend says. I'm getting married again, I've phoned him to announce, and I want an explosion of congratulation, but he points out that my divorce was settled just fourteen months ago. I know it's soon. Partly drunk in love, I don't care. Rob and I live thousands of miles apart, as we have for years—through September 11, when it took me the whole day to reach him in New York; through his career triumphs, the birth of his child, his silence during his wife's illness and the garrulous relief of her recovery; through my elopement in Montana, pregnancies, parents' deaths; through the long spasm of my marriage's end. We've written books, bought houses. He was my first friend, in the early nineties, to visit Missoula, a gesture of gratifying faith when I myself was uncertain of the choice I'd made for new love. It's been three decades since we lived in our noisy studio apartments in New York, yet when I return to the city we settle into a relaxed knowing that has no equal in my life. In Rob's presence, all our rowdy past selves evoked, I'm always surprised that we're also, right now, constant, mature professionals and parents. We have cheered and commiserated and teased.

Not this time. He's taken aback, has barely heard of the guy. He knows *me,* forty-nine, two and a half years single, and he reminds me of my impulsive decisions that did not always work out. The time you quit that job! The time you moved to England! I want to talk about love. About the wedding, which will be my first, and about the man I'm marrying. But no wonder my friend is surprised. For a year and a half I've been wrapped in ardent isolation with this lover, greedy for his details, eager to reveal my own. My friends, Rob included, helped me to sustain the terribleness of an ending marriage, of divorce, but in my recent elation, I've been unavailable. And to Rob, my oldest and most sensible friend, I haven't said much. I have not risked being talked out of David.

• • • •

I don't know David, not really. I know facts, some biography: He married young, was widowed five years before we met. He has a grown son and a daughter still at home, he's limitless in his passions, yells at NPR, likes copious hot sauce. That's not *knowing*. We are still testing limits, unearthing irritations. When you've been with someone for twenty years, as I was with my former husband, you're used to an indelible intimacy that can't be willed or fashioned in a few months. I have not locked eyes in the delivery room with David. I haven't met his mother. We are at the beginning of ourselves together. If I were twenty-seven, no one would worry that a year was too short a time to decide on marriage. But today I am almost fifty, and a year seems paltry, a single Halloween.

In that first month of delirious obsession I joked to David that he'd risen to the top five of my concerns, but not to number one. So much else occupied me. My children, mainly, and their experience, mysterious and fragile, of the divorce. As suddenly as I'd become a parent when my first son was born, I was, the weeks the boys were at my place, a single parent, their schedules and dirty clothes and brief emergencies left to me. Alone, I changed the beds, made the breakfast burritos, cleaned the toilets. Alone I sat in the kitchen, hoping the boys would want to talk (they didn't). Also, right before I met David I'd bought a three-bedroom place, so I had a mortgage, a garage door opener, an unknown neighborhood. He had appeared, a pleasure, a source of glee and magical thinking, as falling in love is, but I had to rally and be unmagical too, because divorce is a practical matter. In financial terms, it's a mistake, and I was swamped by perpetual reckonings, trying to have order once more—Internet plan, car insurance. Without my husband's income I faced a stark reliance on savings and scant earnings as a writer, which I knew couldn't sustain me. And the sticky bureaucracy of divorce was time-consuming. I was angry or exhausted or grieving much of the time. At forty-seven, I was blessed by this new affair, by David, but I held a large store of myself in reserve from him, so that my sons got my real energy and so I could try to earn my solo living.

. . . .

We met online. *She's a 100 percent match,* the website's algorithm told David, encouraging him to write to me, and he did, to say, "99 percent I'd believe, but 100 percent is absurd, isn't it, so let's meet." I laughed, and we met. I'd been out plenty, dressed for dates, armored myself with optimism. It was thinning. I'd learned to schedule coffees in low-key places. I'd had flings, checking my wrecked heart each time to see what had healed. It was slow going, and I was cautious, nearly indifferent. What's the point, I asked myself, if you are led to *this*—wounded, derelict solitude and the unanswerable *What happened?*

At the end of our first date, he leaned toward me and said, "I need to know, do you want to see me again?" I'd been considering the polite deferral. His gaze hooked me, but what if his intensity was overwrought, unfit? "Yes," I said. I didn't know if I meant it, but I thought I would seize the dare, risk yes. We had a date every day for five days: sunny patios for lunch, shaded benches in small parks. He came to dinner. I roasted eggplant with caramelized onions and chopped lemon and forgot to think, *What's the point?*

He took me to his cabin outside of town, where he poured us wine, grilled game hens, walked me to a waterfall. I watched him leap into a blue pool from a high rock. Enticed, appreciated, desired, I felt the health of the stirring heart and the forgotten body.

Later, a December evening when we'd been dating a few months, the boys at their other home that night, I was driving to David's after teaching a class, tipsy with the endorphins from constant lust. He had saved dinner for me, I knew, and his teenage daughter, whom I adored and who adored me, was waiting too. He opened the door, smiling hugely, and my heart roused, rose up. His two German shepherds nosed past him to herd me in, the house smelled of roasted meat, the living room lamplight forced back winter. Yes.

When I scanned for reasons to end it—there were some—my closest girlfriend said, "Enjoy this, can you?" She pointed out that I was happy. I *was* happy, falling more in love, even though David could get angry fast and fight, could be petty, didn't get some crucial things about me, making me miss my ex so badly. And I was used to sorrow, quiet and central within much of my marriage, then devastating at the end. But with David I laughed freely and hard, welcomed silliness, let him call me on my arrogance. Even fighting, which I hated, was an unexpected lesson for me, who'd always avoided conflict. He welcomed my anger, handled it. We found passion everywhere.

• • • •

Who can say how a marriage ends? The metaphors fail. Our sons, then eleven and fifteen, came and went in the kitchen. They finished homework and ate vastly, left to shoot baskets in the park. What did they find when they got home? Our battered silence, our pale, unacknowledged war. We'd reached the point where it was impossible to tidy these things away. Those brittle months at the end I tried to rouse myself, show them a mother intact, but pain flattened me. Instead of working on our marriage, we were now deliberate about its unmaking. It took concentration to dismantle the mutual reliance, the healthy compromises and neurotic self-deceptions, the tolerant blind spots. We'd worked with the optimistic couples therapist, an endeavor long over. We'd watched the demise of our sex life. We'd endured his unexplained failure to join me in New York the week my father was dying. We'd had the revelation of my affair. I tried to make it right. He tried. But we could not see each other anymore, or love as we wished to, or be loved, our paths blocked by dread and loathing. We were changed people, and I hated who I was, a mean tormentor kidnapped by disappointment. God, I wanted not to be married.

When we met, twenty years earlier, we'd each understood something of the other right away, that we'd both been scared witnesses in difficult families. The relief in finding each other—discovery and discovered!—felt so great that it *had* to be a benediction. We could ease sadness in each other and make a soft kingdom, undisturbable. I wanted to root this solemn friendship and to secure, for my unmade children, a solemn, peaceable father who would honor their bruises and believe in their ambitions. A father I had not had. With him, also, I could be the mother I had not had—instead of wildly adorned and striving, charismatically dishonest, voracious to seize and flick off lovers, I would be steady and attentive and truthful. Maternal. Sex would quiet in me, and my adventurous history would be left behind. I would nest with this kind man so that my future children would feel loved firmly. So that we all would.

I think we did that. My husband and I made a pact not to replicate bad childhoods. We had studied the pernicious habits of the unconscious and tried to make sorrow as visible as daylight, our defense against heedless mistake. We committed, I think, to a sacred contract of parenting. I cannot regret this. I'm grateful for the man who taught me the value, foreign until then, of tranquil love and structure, of generous solitude. From me, he took moxie, lilacs, parakeets, hand-mixed red paint for the living room. With him I wrote books. With me he earned a doctorate. We completed stalled development in each other. "Not us. We won't be like them," we whispered, and for half my life nothing was more important than becoming un-them.

Then, when I was forty-four, my father died, and a year later my mother. Orphaned, I didn't have *no* to cling to anymore, the un-them. A flagrant impulse shot forth and took hold, a raw inspection of the self that would alter our marriage, alter everything. I craved the force of a fierce *yes*. The marriage did not end because my parents died, but I balked at the staid bond I'd tended so assiduously.

The bed told the story. The hostile expanse of the queen we'd long slept in grew unbearable, our bleak separate territories staked out. I asked him to sleep in another room, and he did, but we maintained our parental routine, reading to the boys in their beds or ours. After they fell asleep, my husband would find his way in his robe to the extra room in the basement. At five he rose, dressed in runner's clothes, and left the house for an hour. I'd wake to the sound of the front door shutting behind him, and I'd breathe sadly, glad he was gone. Before the boys woke, he was upstairs again, showered, drinking coffee with me on the bed as we watched our northern mornings spread daylight. I knew, uneasily, that we had begun to invest in a fiction, but I didn't know what to do about it.

A few months later I couldn't stand the bed, the room, the house at all, and I started to spend nights in our carriage house, which served as my office and our guest room. *He snores*, I told the boys, to explain. I couldn't tell them we were in trouble; I didn't know any words yet for this trouble. After dinner I crossed the back garden and slipped into the dollhouse of a room, turned back the quilts and slept a miserable dark sleep. Nothing felt right. Winter started, the carriage house unheated, uninhabitable. My husband and I sat down with our boys for a conversation I cannot bear to recount, and then I moved to my best friend's spare room while I looked for a new home.

• • • •

David was painting my bedroom. I'd refused his offer twice. Five months in, it felt too boyfriendy. But he'd listened to me bemoan the wall color, a Realtor's careless beige with pink undertones, and he knew I couldn't afford to hire painters. With kindness and persistence, he persuaded me to let him help me. I sat on the bed he'd pushed into the center of the room, watching him train his brush along the baseboard trim. I felt happy watching my new love do me a favor. It had been an awful week: meetings with a lawyer, my financial papers spread in their disaster across her desk; harsh e-mails between me and my husband; and two days ago, the divorce made manifest by our signatures. This all hurt so much, but I was concentrating on the immediate gift David bestowed of a lemony color and a bedroom made homey. With his back to me, arm raised to a ceiling corner, he said, "Do you think you'll get married again?"

I pretended his question had no bearing on us. He'd had five years since his wife's death, and he'd had a short relationship and then a longer one, and then a year alone. *Ahead of me,* is how I thought of him. I said, "I cannot imagine it," but really I felt the bile of disgust. God, no—why would I face again the disintegration, the torn spirit? I'd said good-bye to the glassed-in front porch, to the certain light in known rooms, to my adored garden. I thought, *Let me just choose new dish towels, fold them in thirds, as I like to.* I wanted to pace days according to my rhythm, to work, read, negotiate my own pacts with my children, give sudden, delicious parties. I was delighting in my new kitchen's drawers, which glided; in the walk-in closet, where I'd hung every dress and coat, trousers, skirts, even T-shirts, because I had the space. Never mind the walls' bad color, the B-grade wall-to-wall carpet that was (dear God) almost the same color. I was in love with emptiness and this blank stare of potential.

• • • •

I broke up with David after eight months—three rank days of fury on both sides and incredulous hurt (he didn't *listen,* he didn't *see* me, so *stubborn!*) until we met at a trailhead, walked into the woods, sat staring in the same direction and revealed our early resentments and bare fears, our anxieties . . . all the real stuff that had gotten pushed under the tidal swell of fresh love and new sex. This was work I wasn't certain I could do, I told him. But here we were, doing it; we were happening, every day a new way to feel each other. We wanted that, and we started again, delicate, brave, and keenly aware that the stakes had just rocketed higher.

• • • •

Every other week the boys came to me with their small duffel bags. Finally, one of them hung a couple of posters in his room. The other one didn't bother. I'd imagined I would feed them foods they loved, except I'd forgotten what I liked to make and what they wanted to eat. We were all in pain. I tried to hide my list-lessness, but anyway they spent their hours in their rooms, doors closed. Sometimes I stood in the hall, waiting to hear the static of exclamation as they played Team Fortress 2 with online friends, headphones firmly planted. I longed for my boys, but I never knew when to knock. When they went back to their father's, emptying the house and taking with them all routine, I did not have friends over or throw parties. I made popcorn for my dinner and took it and a glass of bourbon to my bed with my cat, where I watched five, six hours of streaming TV, until my body shut my sad, sad frantic mind down, and I slept.

My closest friend in Missoula celebrated my upheaval with enthusiasm and unexpected presents that reminded me not to be always sad—a set of champagne flutes, a red linen tablecloth. She herself lived alone, her rooms painted glossy purple or shocking orange, her kitchen impeccable with rows of clean glass jars for flour and nuts and various rices. I would be like her. She sent me Craigslist postings for cool lamps or dining chairs—"$50 for all four!"—which I'd procure within the hour, loyal only to my own tastes (I still thought of such money as "only $50"), and she'd come right over to see. When she called and suggested wine, I'd be at her house in ten minutes. She kept me company with devoted interest, a salvation. Except for the one time I sobbed, unable to stop, and she held me hard in her arms for a long time, we focused on the *fuck yeah* of domestic freedom and independent choice.

But without beloved others to share intimate space and daily experience, I was stranded. I missed those who cared and made noise and brought life to all the rooms at once. One week I set a single bag of trash in the Dumpster, which embarrassed me, as if I'd be discovered in the smallness of my days. I could not write because I could not establish routines, could not think because I couldn't risk inspecting the consequence of my choices. I sat on the couch, texting my sons at their other house—*what did you have for lunch today? how was rehearsal?*—and waited for their curt answers. I did not miss my husband or the outgrown marriage, but I missed my family. A refugee from a savaged homeland, I missed all I'd known.

David made another offer. You could live with us for a while, he said. Your cat too. He was not, he made clear, saying we should live together, but he was sensitive to my financial struggle. Why not rent out your place, come stay, get your feet under you? I heard: Give up. I had some dim instinct that this personal revolution I'd started would have no meaning unless I took care of everything myself and stood alone. My kitchen looked like my friend's—glass jars of steel-cut oats, loose black tea—and David's kitchen teemed with sink clutter and scattered pellets of dog food on the linoleum. I refused to admit that I was unable to write or earn. Every night I pretended that in the morning, the *next* morning, I would be up early to work—and I couldn't do *that*, obviously, if I was packing again and moving in with David and his daughter, if I had to nego-tiate domestic compromise. Alone, afraid, tired, I did not count the nightly meals I was fed at his table, or every free minute I spent at his house, each night embraced and sheltered. Still intimate with my compounded losses, with the awareness that whatever my sons endured was opaque to me, I didn't count that with David I was healing and thriving. I didn't take us seriously.

A week before my forty-ninth birthday, my sons left Missoula—one for college, the other for boarding school. The next day I began to move out of the three-bedroom I could no longer afford and into a converted garage rented behind someone's house. Two tiny bed-rooms, one for me and one for the boys' visits and my desk. David helped. He loaded his truck with my books, hefted my blue pots planted with lavender. I sold off big furniture on Craigslist ("$100 for all four!"), dropped boxes at the thrift shop. Most of my better belongings would have to go into a storage unit. David lent me the lock, unspoken between us the knowledge that I couldn't spend $13 if I didn't have to. When I dragged down the aluminum door and snapped the padlock, I didn't care if I saw the glass coffee table or the velvet chaise again. Just things. I'd cut my expenses by two-thirds and finessed a little income from renting to tenants. Good-bye lemon-yellow bedroom, hello landlord beige, yet again. I felt both defeated and exalted in every gesture. I bought one box of butter and stashed three sticks in the freezer. Alone and in charge; alone, and alone.

Days I worked in my converted garage, and in the evenings I drove to David and his daughter, the dinner and the dogs, my robe that had its hook in their bathroom, my clock I'd put on one side of his bed. "Our bed," he said. On school mornings, my children too distant to feed, I made sandwiches for his daughter, and when he couldn't take her to doctors' appointments I did, where once, in a moment of registration hassle and complex grace, she referred to me as her stepmother. I loved and felt loved and could stand up because of it. Writing returned. We fell into a shape, a new family. In the mornings I left them for the little house, arrived to my cat's disapproval and the chill of a low thermostat, until finally I realized this was silly, a posture of independence when what I really wanted, how I really knew to be, was in the embrace of a lively home. I packed again and brought the cat and moved into David's.

We struggled, adapting. David and his daughter made room in their long-decided spaces, and the well-meaning dogs hassled my outraged cat, and I was never sure on the phone with my kids how much to describe. But what I felt was *right*. Alive, loving, not fully settled but open to each day, to each turn of David's complicated, bountiful heart. Six weeks in, many of my boxes still lined against the walls, I was stunned to realize I wanted to marry David. To marry again. All that effort—getting out, copping to the fictions, undoing the mixed identity, claiming artistic space—only to find . . . that I'd loved being married. I loved the joint venture, the daily concern for the other person's back. Here it was again, the matched commitment that meant we would try, and try. My strength came this way, not from the composed kitchen counters and closets. I checked my motivation: Do I want to marry for company, for health insurance, for the privilege of being this girl's stepmother? Well, yes. Those things matter. But more: love, right now.

One day six months later I wondered to David if he might like to be married to me. He kissed me and said yes. "You realize we're both crazy, right?" he said, our scarred histories readily available. We were laughing, kissing, giddy. I thought, *Why?* Because our first marriages ended? Because we'd each lived decades in relationships that shaped us, held us, gave us insight into ourselves and glimpses of the insight we didn't yet have? These were not failures but educations, not mistakes but the natural tides of life.

• • • •

Who can say how a marriage begins, how gossamer and personal and whimsical we might be as we launch into unexpected places? When I call Rob, I'm not surprised he wants evidence and explanation, but I don't have them. I can't reassure him or myself. To marry again, after decades with one husband, after divorce, is, it turns out, an act of faith. I don't know if this will work. How could I? Maybe it is a bad idea, impulsive and rash, and Rob's right to be concerned for me. But, equally, impulsive and rash and glorious, there's wonder here, and I am brightened, called to *yes*. David and I may have a few years, or many. I will live them brightly, willing to show up for each honest night, every wide-open day. In marrying again, in marrying David, I say *Why not?* and *Who knows?* I touch the flame and grow taller. I say *Now*. I say *Yes*.

# A New Life Under the Ladder

## CYNTHIA KLING

*In "Erotics 102," her piece in* The Bitch in the
House, *Cynthia Kling wrote about holding on to
passion—of all kinds—in her marriage by remaining
mysterious to her husband and by keeping certain
parts of herself private; also, sometimes, by purposely
deceiving him or by doing something "forbidden."*

*Fifteen years later, Cynthia is on to other
adventures, bigger and loftier.*

*Read her story. Get inspired. Make the world
better. Live your life, live your life, live your life.*

I remember when Buzz Bissinger, author of *Friday Night Lights*,
wrote an article in *GQ* about his shopping addiction. Eighty-
one leather jackets (including a Gucci ostrich skin for $13,900),
seventy-five pairs of boots, $5,600 leather pants—you get it.

For two years he was afraid to add up how much he'd spent. Finally he made himself do it: almost $600,000. Although he admit-
ted he had a problem, he also was clearly proud of his front-row seat
at the European fashion shows with the editors from *Vogue* and of
getting the "royal Gucci treatment" (free plane tickets and hotel

rooms, Italian salesmen sucking up to him abroad). Back home, consults with his stylist kept him busy.

My friends snickered. Here was a successful, sixtyish guy admitting to a habit that one expected of some Manolo-shopping trophy wife. Some wondered: Was Mr. Lights announcing a newly burnished gay vibe?

With me, his actions hit a different chord. I felt he was talking about getting to that point in your life when you are set—you've hit some of your career goals, know you're tumbling down the other side of success mountain and don't really care anymore. Your age shows—face, neck, all over—no matter how hard you work to stay young; and you've settled into a relationship with your spouse that would be too expensive and complicated to end, even if there are days when you wake up thinking, *Him?* Put another way, the early struggles are over, but the Big Adventures may be too. And you think, *So now what?*

By the time we reached that place, my husband and I had had sex approximately 2,200 times. If there were any exciting positions left, we didn't know them. (I refused to do Reverse Cowgirl—use your imagination.)

But maybe that wasn't the point.

• • • •

When I was in my twenties, a friend told me to marry the person I wanted to talk to at the kitchen table at 3 A.M.—someone whose mind interested me, because the rest fades. I took the advice. For years I came home with stories, almost like little presents—lunch with some B-list celebrity, jacking up a corporate bigwig for a decent paycheck . . . or even just saying something stupid and feeling humiliated.

By midlife, my husband had heard all my stories, and I'd heard his. In fact, he barely listened, knowing he could fake a response while never taking his eyes off the game on TV. I think he'd gotten it down to three phrases: "No way." "Really?" "Great!" He used the third after I told him I'd been fired.

Outside marriage, life was "fine." We owned a house with a reasonable mortgage; I had enough work not to worry (too much) about money. In other words, like Bissinger, I could have gone to a dark place to fill my life, because I was bored and am not without my own vices (wine, gossip, and if there's a Valium in the vicinity, I will find it and swallow it).

Then one night a friend and I were discussing a prison program where professors from Yale, Princeton, and other colleges teach a small, elite group of inmates subjects like calculus and transcendentalism. Volunteers were needed to help students write their thesis papers.

I am not a do-gooder by *any* stretch; in fact, close friends and family would call me a shit-stirrer. But I was curious: What went on behind those high prison walls wrapped in concertina wire? Who was there? This was one of the few worlds I'd never managed to get a good sniff of.

This volunteer program was so tony I couldn't even get hired to work for free without a connection. But one of the few benefits of old age is that you can always scrabble one up. I did, and after an interview, found myself at a maximum security prison, like Attica, where the violent criminals are housed. I met my students in a simple cinder-block classroom: some fourteen black and Latino guys convicted of murder, robbery, assault, drug dealing. I am thin and white, and was raised in a nice Philadelphia suburb; if ever I had told myself I was "color-blind," I now realized I'd been full of shit.

I was expected to help guys who hadn't been past eighth grade with grammar, punctuation, and word usage. Though well educated, I'm a terrible speller and can never remember certain grammar rules. (Affect? Effect?) But I did my best, and we got through the first night.

When I got home, my husband was standing in the driveway waiting. I would have waited for him too if he'd spent the evening chatting with murderers, but still, it was nice. Inside, I told him how I'd been a little freaked out with all these guys waving their papers at me until one of them, Alex—a thirty-one-year-old former gang member on year ten of a fourteen-year sentence for manslaughter—began organizing the men. Alex was Dominican, with brown eyes and a soft but commanding voice. If it hadn't been for his green prison scrubs, I told my husband, I would have assumed he was a TA from one of the elite colleges, because the guys immediately deferred to him.

After that, I went to the prison once a week. It took twenty minutes to drive there and twenty-five to get to the tutoring room: metal detector, hand stamped, ID checked, then the walk down the long, dark, mazelike tunnels, escorted by a guard with a billy club. The prisoners marched on one side, tight single file. We walked on the other. Sometimes the guard stopped to talk to one of the inmates—invariably a Mafia hit man or some Important Bad Guy, the guard would tell me afterward. I could tell he was proud of this relationship. (Later, Alex would tell me that the guys who committed the most despicable crimes got the most respect. You can imagine what they thought of the geeky prison students.)

At the final checkpoint, there was a blocky blond guard with an old-fashioned crew cut who loved to lecture me. "Why waste your time with these guys?" he'd say week after week. "If they get out, they just end up right back here. Why not help a *good* person?" The first time, I tried to explain—these were men who'd been dealt a bad hand; I wanted to give them a chance to start over, so maybe they *wouldn't* end up "right back here"—but he just repeated himself. So I learned to shrug, not engage, each week when he ranted.

One time, he made me wait as he checked off the prisoners coming up for educational courses, AA, religious meetings. He'd tell an inmate that his name wasn't on the list, even though I could see it. "Back to the cell," he'd say. "Try again next week." Then he'd smirk. The prisoners left fast, because the wrong look or words could land them in solitary confinement, or "the Box." I knew enough to keep my mouth shut. The backyard bully had found his perfect job.

• • • •

Quickly the inmates moved out of a blur and I got to know them and their situations. Jake, a gangly man with a huge laugh, was in for life. Three strikes—the first, he told me, in fifth grade when he brought a water pistol to the playground that the teachers thought was a gun. (No mother around to explain.) Mow-Mow, a short, bouncy twenty-two-year-old, talked about his grandmother's big house down south, about how he wanted to set up a school when he got out—in twenty years. Alex was in for fourteen, because, he told me, he'd been on the street with a friend from his crew when the guy shot and killed a man. If he'd turned state's evidence—testified as a witness for the state, against his friend—he could have had a much-reduced sentence . . . and probably would have been dead on the street a week later. He chose the time.

As a middle-class white woman, I knew I'd probably never wind up in prison for being with a friend who shot someone. Or for three strikes that started with a water pistol. Every week driving home, I'd realize how lucky I was. My sagging boobs and receding career now felt like ridiculous problems.

Selfishly, I was happy Alex was there. He made deeply gifted arguments and loved language, often sneaking words like *sesquipedalian* and *palimpsest* into his papers just to see if I knew what they meant. As the Yale philosophy professor told me, he was the

ideal mix of "a brilliant and creative thinker with real scholarly
potential."

• • • •

My husband now waited up each week to hear my report. One
week, the guys prepared five-minute speeches on contemporary
topics. Mow-Mow talked about the word *nigger,* and there was a
heated debate about whether or not it should be used. "Can I *ever*
use it?" I asked, meaning "I" as a white person who heard the word
tossed around by these guys, rappers, comedians. "Only if you're in
a crew," Mow-Mow said. "And then never when your crew meets
another."

Jamel, a thin guy with elegant hands and long dreads, talked
about the periodic table. Before its discovery, he said, we wouldn't
have been able to understand global warming or what happens as
a result of fracking because we couldn't know the science behind
how it worked. Now we can—yet many people get their information from politicians who don't know the science. Alex talked about
the value of owning *Webster's Dictionary*—especially if you're
brought up in a place like the South Bronx, where you kick crack
vials aside to get out of your apartment and school consists of the
teachers ducking spitballs.

When they finished, they looked at me. "Your turn, Cynthia,"
someone said. I thought about it for a second: The prison wanted
tutors to maintain distance because of the trouble that could ensue
otherwise. But how could I teach them unless I connected with
them? I also realized these guys were learning from me partly because they trusted me for exactly that reason: I *did* care. In return,
they were teaching me about a parallel universe I hadn't known existed: about the difference between "gangs" and "crews," and which
gang ran Rikers, and why you had to join a gang in prison—because
if you didn't, you wouldn't have protection and could get killed.

I decided to break the rule about distance and connection that night. I stood up and gave a five-minute speech about my own struggles: my lifelong insecurity, my fears about my intelligence and whether I could make it with those voices in my head scream-ing, "*You're stupid!*" I knew it wasn't anything like the shit they'd been through. But it was true and heartfelt and painful, and it was what I had.

They were fascinated. How could this well-dressed white chick have these problems? But we were finding our common humanity: We were all fragile, mortal, frightened of having no talent and trying to figure out how to make a decent life in this world. "You guys are behind these walls for a long time," I told them, "so I know you have stories, real stories about how you got here. Start writing them down so people like me can learn from you."

As I left that night, the guys said, "Be safe." No one had ever said that to me before, because I'd never needed that kind of good-bye. But they were used to it.

• • • •

Outside the prison, I did editorial consulting, maintained a yoga website, and continued with the occasional magazine assignments that had been my bread and butter for years. But my colleagues and I had reached the age where many of us were simply push-ing our career markers around the journalism chessboard trying to stay employed until someone younger and cheaper knocked us off. Now, though, I found that all this didn't sting as much, because I was riding an exciting new horse.

The things I talked to my friends about were changing too. It was no longer the crinkling of our under-eye skin, or how much—if any—sex this or that married couple was having, or who we looked down on because they'd just sucked their way to the top of some masthead. (We were too proud to admit our real feelings: envy.)

Now, I grilled my friends about whether they'd read *The New Jim Crow* so they could learn about why people like Alex were in prison, or if they knew that the United States has 5 percent of the world's population and 25 percent of its prisoners—more than any other country. When a well-known comic writer I knew told me she was bragging about my new prison work, my heart swelled with pride. Unlike other parts of the body, the ego, it seems, never dries up. I was alive again, curious and motivated.

• • • •

One night—about two months before the program inmates were supposed to graduate and move to a better prison with bigger cells, far fewer brawls, and less supervision—I got to class and noticed that Alex wasn't there. *Huh,* I thought. He'd missed class only once or twice in three semesters, because he loved a good conversation— whether about Viktor Frankl's *A Man's Search for Meaning* or his own favorite story, Plato's *The Allegory of the Cave*. (I had tried to read it but couldn't get through it.)

This particular night the guys were strangely subdued. When I pressed, I learned, through whispers, that Alex had been sent to the Box, and they thought he'd be there for a year—a *year!*—because an anonymous note had been slipped to the guards from a prisoner saying that if they checked, they'd find contraband in Alex's cell: a handcuff key, which ostensibly could be used to escape.

I was momentarily stunned. And then I thought, *Wait—Alex?* Ten years in prison and he hadn't gotten a single disciplinary infraction—almost unheard of—and he was the best student in the program, with a 4.0 average. It was ludicrous to think he'd risk hiding a key in his cell when he was so close to getting out.

I soon learned that getting framed in prison is common. A member of his former gang probably set him up, Jah told me, someone pissed that Alex quit to become a student and jealous that he was going to a better place.

The next morning, I called the volunteer program supervisor and asked what we should do.

"Nothing," she said. "It's happened before and it will happen again."

"But he got into this fix because he was one of our students!"

"It's a very tough tightrope we walk," she replied, and explained that if we didn't follow prison rules, we could jeopardize everything.

I shook my head. "Just how far does your 'look-away policy' extend?" I asked, using the term I'd heard during the recent Rikers Island horror: No one had spoken up when they saw guards beating kids, breaking elderly prisoners' arms for minor infractions . . . they were taught to look away.

She was silent.

I hung up, freaked out and confused. If I stood up for what I knew was right, I would not only lose this thing I loved doing but possibly imperil this program that been featured on *60 Minutes* and elsewhere because it did so much for a select group of prisoners. Yet if I didn't say anything, Alex could lose not only his chance for parole but possibly his mind. A United Nations expert had called on all countries to ban solitary confinement, which he considered torture and which has been shown to cause lasting mental damage after even a few days.

What should I do?

*Who was I?*

I thought of a Yeats poem I loved:

> *. . . Now that my ladder's gone*
> *I must lie down where all the ladders start*
> *In the foul rag and bone shop of the heart.*

Here in the final third of my life, no longer striving and climb-
ing, it was time—and a chance—to look carefully at what I was
made of.

An hour later, I picked up the phone. First I called the Innocence
Project. Then the ACLU. Then a few lefty lawyers I knew. People
listened, then gave me numbers of criminal lawyers and even ex-
cons who might help.

One former inmate who had actually escaped from the prison I
taught in told me you don't do it with a key, but by bribing someone. (The guards had let him escape when he was being taken to
the dentist. Two years later, he was found in his apartment and
brought back to serve his time.) Now a private detective, he told
me that Alex would have an in-house hearing (no lawyer), tried by
prison employees. To me, that sounded like he was screwed.

It was important, I learned, to have a lawyer write to the prison
and let them know there were people out there paying attention.
After talking to a few more lawyers, who agreed to take the case
for $20,000 to $40,000, I called everyone I knew, raised the money,
and put together my own killer team: two lawyers and one university law professor—all women—who would work together to try to
get justice for Alex.

Predictably, I was fired from the teaching job when someone I
contacted called the program to ask if "what Cynthia Kling said"
was actually true. I then received a letter from the prison's super-
intendent saying I was barred from the prison "effective immediately" because I had been accused of breaking guideline 11: "Care
should be taken to avoid becoming emotionally involved with
inmates." I would be investigated, the letter said, because I had
"allegedly commenced a personal relationship with an inmate."
Following that came a request from a prison investigator that I
"provide a written copy of the events surrounding this." A former

D.A. told me this was a legal maneuver meant to embarrass me and keep me quiet; evidently, they considered me a threat.

When I told a good friend, she laughed and said, "That's great, Kling! You're still in the game." But for me, the "game" was no longer something I was doing for excitement or fun—though there were funny moments. Alex had no idea what I was organizing until one day, after about two months in solitary, when he was escorted from the Box over to a blond stranger in her forties—Norah, one of the lawyers I'd hired to help him. When she told him who she was and why she was there, Alex told her he was speechless. That made me laugh.

• • • •

The lawyers and I worked hard, but there were always setbacks. It was another dark day when Norah and I drove seven hours to see Alex at the prison where he'd been transferred. Farther upstate, it was nicknamed "the Human Kennel."

I was worried about his mental state, especially because he was being double-bunked here, in the tiny, isolated room—something that happens often in "solitary," despite the name. Violent inmates tend to fight in the claustrophobic spaces—who wouldn't? (Imagine being locked in the bathroom with a stranger for five years.) And I'd heard that Alex was in with a guy who'd been there ten years, was mentally deranged, and had had about four hundred "roommates."

When we got there, the guard wound us through the hallways, telling us how dangerous these inmates were—people like Joel Steinberg, who'd beaten his six-year-old daughter to death. We arrived in a room filled with thick plexiglass boxes. There was Alex, sitting behind a partition with a two-inch opening at the bottom. He held his hands down so we wouldn't see his arm and leg irons.

I saw them anyway. I also saw that he was now impossibly skinny.

But despite my horror, he was the same thoughtful Alex. When I asked about his bunkmate, it was clear he was sympathetic to this poor man, someone in obvious need of psychiatric help who'd been dragged from cell to cell and would probably die alone in one of their cages.

A guard brought over Alex's lunch: two shriveled slabs of white bread with a plastic cup of hazmat-orange glop they called tuna fish. (Lawsuits have started in several states over the hideous quality of prison food.) Norah and I got potato chips and candy out of the machines. Even that we weren't allowed to give Alex.

Driving home, I thought of his emaciated face, the deep circles under his eyes, and I felt anew that I was doing the right thing. I was exposing an egregious wrong and helping save a young man's life in the process: a man who had never committed a violent crime, who I believed was kind and moral and intelligent. And maybe, in my small way, I could help save some other lives, too. I could make a difference. Me and my wrinkles and my past-its-prime married sex life . . . none of that mattered now. My life wasn't so much about *me* anymore. It felt glorious.

And yet, this all also *was* about me, at least in part. Because if I hadn't been middle-aged and bored and jaded, if my ladder hadn't been gone—and if I hadn't had the wisdom and compassion of my years, the lack of caring so much about my career future combined with the drive to stay in the game that is *life,* all of it resulting from years of success and of failure, from having been young but not being young anymore—I would not be doing this. I wouldn't have wanted to, and I wouldn't have known how. It was exactly the state of having nothing left to lose that had given me, once more, everything to gain.

• • • •

That night, as usual, my husband was waiting when I drove up the driveway. He hugged me as I got out of the car and ushered me into our kitchen, handing me a bowl of soup. "Tell," he commanded. And later, in the bedroom, it was different too. But really, things there had been changing all along in recent months. Before this, we'd become almost like brother and sister, caring but also carefully avoiding that huge elephant called married sex. But my new life fascinated him, and in bed and out, he wanted to know and touch this person I was becoming. We weren't rooting around for the old hormone-driven feelings so much as connecting with each other in that deepest, most ancient human way. And while that isn't the point I've been making all this time, I'd be lying if I said it didn't matter.

• • • •

So here's the end of the story. After nine months of working every spare minute—making calls, writing letters, having meetings to get other people involved who also might help Alex—I asked the three lawyers to write to the acting commissioner of the New York State Department of Corrections to explain the situation. We also sent Alex's 4.0 transcript from the college program. Then I nagged—and nagged, and nagged. (Isn't that what "old women" are good for?) I made friends with his assistants and called them every day, making them so sick of me that they couldn't *not* force him to read it, if only to get me off their backs.

Two weeks later, the commissioner dismissed the charges against Alex. His record was expunged, and he received a letter saying he was cleared of having contraband and was being moved back to the prison where he was headed when he was framed.

• • • •

As for me, at the moment I'm still barred from returning to the prison where I taught. In the meantime, I've moved on to another prison and am starting to get my feet wet there too. That's all I'll say—I don't want to jeopardize anything—except for this: I feel lucky to have found what I did under my fallen ladder; to find what really matters at this point in my life. And if I can't ever go back to the old prison, or I get thrown out of the new one? There's always another, and another after that. They can keep pushing me out, and I'll keep coming back, until one day they might just have to wheel me out, white hair flying.

# CONTRIBUTORS

**JULIANNA BAGGOTT** is the author of more than twenty books, published under her own name as well as under two pen names. Her novel *Pure* was a 2012 *New York Times* Notable Book, and *Harriet Wolf's Seventh Book of Wonders* was a 2015 *New York Times* Notable Book. Her most recent release is *All of Us and Everything*, a comedic novel about an odd family, written under the name Bridget Asher. Baggott's essays have appeared in the *New York Times* Modern Love column, the *Washington Post, Real Simple*, and the Best American Poetry series, as well as on NPR. She teaches in the film school at Florida State University and holds the Jenks Chair in Contemporary American Letters at Holy Cross.

**JILL BIALOSKY** is the author of three novels—*House Under Snow, The Life Room*, and *The Prize*, a 2015 *New York Times Book Review* editor's choice—and of four volumes of poetry: *The End of Desire, Subterranean, Intruder*, and *The Players*. Her memoir, *History of a Suicide: My Sister's Unfinished Life*, was a *New York Times* bestseller and a finalist for a Books for a Better Life Award and the Ohioana Book Award. She coedited, with Helen Schulman, the anthology *Wanting a Child*. Bialosky's poems and essays have appeared in *The New Yorker, Harper's, O, T: The New York Times Style Magazine, Real Simple*, and *The Atlantic*, among others. She lives in New York City.

**JENNIFER FINNEY BOYLAN,** author of fourteen books, is the inaugural Anna Quindlen Writer in Residence at Barnard College of Columbia University. Her novel *Long Black Veil* is forthcoming from Penguin Random House in spring 2017. She serves as the national co-chair of the board of directors of GLAAD, the media advocacy group for LGBT people worldwide. A contributor to the op-ed page of the *New York Times* since 2007, in 2013 she became a contributing opinion writer for the page. She also serves on the board of trustees of the Kinsey Institute for Research on Sex, Gender, and Reproduction, and as a special advisor to the president of Colby College, in Maine. She lives in New York City and in Belgrade Lakes, Maine, with her wife, Deirdre Grace, and their two sons, Zach and Sean.

**VERONICA CHAMBERS** was born in Panama, raised in Brooklyn, and writes often about her Afro-Latina heritage. She is best known for her critically acclaimed memoir *Mama's Girl* and for the *New York Times* bestseller *Yes, Chef,* which she coauthored with chef Marcus Samuelsson. You can reach her online at Veronicachambers.com and on Twitter @vvchambers.

**KATE CHRISTENSEN** is the author of six novels, including *The Epicure's Lament* and *The Great Man,* which won the 2008 PEN/Faulkner Award for Fiction, as well as two memoirs, *Blue Plate Special* and *How to Cook a Moose.* She writes essays and reviews for numerous publications, most recently *Elle,* the *New York Times Book Review, Bookforum, Cherry Bombe, Vogue, Food & Wine,* and the *Wall Street Journal.* Christensen lives in Portland, Maine, and in the White Mountains of New Hampshire. Her new novel, *The Last Cruise,* is forthcoming from Doubleday.

**SARAH CRICHTON** has had many chapters in her life. She's been a magazine editor (*Seventeen, Newsweek*); a writer and cowriter (with

Mariane Pearl, *A Mighty Heart*); and a book editor. She is now publisher of Sarah Crichton Books/FSG, where she edits a broad variety of writers, from Cathleen Schine (*They May Not Mean To, But They Do*) to Ishmael Beah (*A Long Way Gone*), Roy Blount Jr. (*Save Room for Pie*), Dominic Smith (*The Last Painting of Sara de Vos*), and Brigid Schulte (*Overwhelmed*), as well as crime thrillers. She lives in Brooklyn.

**LYNN DARLING** is a writer living in New York City. A veteran of the *Washington Post* Style section, she has since contributed to *Esquire, Harper's Bazaar, Sports Illustrated,* and the *New York Times,* among other publications. She is the author of the memoirs *Necessary Sins,* published by Dial Press, and *Out of the Woods: A Memoir of Wayfinding,* published by HarperCollins.

**HOPE EDELMAN** is the author or editor of seven books, including the bestsellers *Motherless Daughters, Motherless Mothers, The Possibility of Everything,* and *Along the Way.* Her books have been translated into eleven languages, and her articles and essays have appeared in many publications, including the *New York Times,* the *Los Angeles Times, Huffington Post, Real Simple, Writer's Digest,* and *Parade.* Over the past two decades she has taught writing workshops and lectured all over the world, from Australia to Italy to Dubai. She lives in Los Angeles with her husband and two daughters, and teaches writing every summer in Iowa City.

**KERRY HERLIHY** is a high school English teacher living in southern Maine. Her essays have appeared in multiple publications, including the *New York Times* and *Good Housekeeping,* as well as in the anthologies *Toddler: Real-Life Stories of Those Fickle, Irrational, Urgent, Tiny People We Love* and *Motherland: Writings by Irish American Women About Mothers and Daughters.* In addition, her story has been featured on the BBC's program *Witness*. Currently she is working on a memoir about love, loss, and motherhood.

**ANN HOOD** is the bestselling author of the novels *The Knitting Circle, The Obituary Writer,* and *The Red Thread* and the memoir *Comfort: A Journey Through Grief,* which was chosen by *Entertainment Weekly* as a Top Ten Nonfiction Book of 2008 and was a *New York Times* Editor's Choice. She has won two Pushcart Prizes, two Best American Food Writing awards, a Best American Spiritual Writing Award, and a Best American Travel Writing award. Her new novel, *The Book That Matters Most,* was published in summer 2016 by W. W. Norton.

**PAM HOUSTON** is the author of five books of fiction and nonfiction, all published by W. W. Norton: *Contents May Have Shifted, Cowboys Are My Weakness, Waltzing the Cat, Sight Hound,* and *A Little More About Me.* Her stories have been selected for volumes of *Best American Short Stories, The O. Henry Awards, The 2013 Pushcart Prize,* and *Best American Short Stories of the Century.* She directs the literary nonprofit Writing By Writers and teaches in the Institute of American Indian Art's Low Rez MFA program and at UC Davis. She lives on a ranch at 9,000 feet in Colorado near the headwaters of the Rio Grande.

**RABIA HUSSAIN** is the pseudonym for a Muslim mother of eight with a Ph.D. who has worked as both a college professor and a nonprofit director. She currently stays at home with her children.

**CLAIRE JOHNSON** is the pseudonym for a marketing and sales executive who grew up in New York City and also has lived in California, New England, and elsewhere.

**KAREN KARBO** is the author of the bestselling "Kick Ass Women" series: *Julia Child Rules; How Georgia Became O'Keeffe; The Gospel According to Coco Chanel;* and *How to Hepburn.* Her 2004 memoir, *The Stuff of Life,* was a *New York Times* Notable Book, a *People* magazine Critics' Choice, and the winner of the Oregon Book Award for Creative Nonfiction. Her three adult novels have all been named *New York Times* Notable Books, and she is a recipient of a National Endowment for the Arts Fellowship in Fiction. Her essays, articles, and reviews have appeared in *Elle, Vogue, Esquire, Outside,* the *New York Times,* and Salon.com. Her new book, *In Praise of Difficult Women,* will be published in 2017.

**CYNTHIA KLING,** a former staffer for magazines ranging from *Newsweek* to *Domino,* has happily left that world. These days she's writing a book for HarperCollins about creativity; running The Plantagenet Group, a garden design business in the Hudson Valley; working with prisoners for criminal justice under her own 501(c)(3), Transforming Lives (www.transforminglives.org); and finding ways to make trouble—but only when necessary.

**SANDRA TSING LOH'S** most recent memoir, *The Madwoman in the Volvo: My Year of Raging Hormones* (W. W. Norton), was selected as one of the *New York Times*'s 100 Most Notable Books of 2014. Inspired by her Best American Essay in *The Atlantic,* to which she is a contributing editor, the play version of *The Madwoman in the Volvo* received its world premiere at South Coast Repertory Theatre in 2016. Her Pushcart Prize–winning short story "My Father's Chinese Wives" appears in *The Norton Anthology of Short Fiction.* She is the writer/performer of many original solo shows, and her weekly personal commentary, "The Loh Life," and daily science radio minute, "The Loh Down on Science," are heard on KPCC FM in Los Angeles. The latter is also syndicated on over 150 stations. Her education includes a B.S. in physics from Caltech.

**ANNA MARCH'S** writing has appeared in numerous publications, including the *New York Times* Modern Love column, *New York Magazine*, *VQR*, *Tin House*, *Hip Mama*, and *Bustle*, and she writes regularly for *The Rumpus* and *Salon*. Her novel, *The Diary of Suzanne Frank*, is forthcoming, and she is at work on an essay collection. She lives in Los Angeles with her husband and is the cofounder of The Lulu Fund: Supporting Racial and Gender Justice. Follow her on Twitter @annamarch or learn more about her at annamarch.com.

**HAZEL MCCLAY** is the pseudonym for a writer of fiction and nonfiction born and raised in the Midwest.

**GRACE O'MALLEY** is the pseudonym for a financial advisor in the Northwest.

**ROBIN RINALDI** is the author of the 2015 memoir *The Wild Oats Project*, which has been published in twelve countries and translated into eight foreign languages. An award-winning journalist, she has written on feminism, psychology, sexuality, and culture for publications such as the *New York Times*, *The Atlantic*, *O*, *Yoga Journal*, and others. Formerly the executive editor of 7×7 magazine in San Francisco and a food columnist for *Philadelphia Weekly*, she now lives in Los Angeles. Visit her website at www.robinrinaldi.com.

**LIZZIE SKURNICK** is the author of *That Should Be a Word*, a collection of neologisms, and *Shelf Discovery*, a memoir of teen reading. A regular contributor to the *New York Times Magazine*, NPR, and *Jezebel*, she's also the founding editor of Lizzie Skurnick Books, which reissues classic YA novels. She lives in Jersey City with her son, Javier.

**SUSANNA SONNENBERG** is the author of two memoirs, *Her Last Death* and *She Matters: A Life in Friendships*, both *New York Times* bestsellers. She is a recipient of fellowships from the MacDowell Colony, the Corporation of Yaddo, and the Djerassi Resident Artists Program. Her personal essays have appeared in a wide range of magazines and several anthologies, and she reviews books for the *San Francisco Chronicle*.

**DEBORA L. SPAR,** the president of Barnard College, is the author of numerous books, including *The Baby Business: How Money, Science, and Politics Drive the Commerce of Conception* (2006), and the 2013 *New York Times* bestseller *Wonder Women: Sex, Power, and the Quest for Perfection*. Prior to taking her position at Barnard, she spent seventeen years on the faculty of Harvard Business School, teaching courses on the politics of international business, comparative capitalism, and economic development. A member of the American Academy of Arts and Sciences, a director of Goldman Sachs, and a trustee of the Wallace Foundation, Spar, a political scientist by training, has focused her scholarly research on international political economy and, more recently, on issues of particular importance to women.

**KATHY THOMAS** is the owner and head cleaner of Cathy's Cleaning Crew. The single mother of five sons, with three grandsons and one granddaughter, she lives in Greenfield, Massachusetts.

**ERIN WHITE'S** work has appeared in the *New York Times, Creative Nonfiction, The Morning News, The Rumpus,* and *Killing the Buddha*. She lives in the foothills of the Berkshires with her wife and two daughters, and is at work on a memoir.

**CATHI HANAUER** is the author of three novels—*Gone, Sweet Ruin,* and *My Sister's Bones*—and the editor of the #10 *New York Times* bestselling essay anthology *The Bitch in the House.* She has published articles, essays, and/or criticism in the *New York Times, Elle* (where she's a contributing writer), *O, Real Simple, Self, Glamour,* and other magazines. She lives in western Massachusetts with her husband, writer and Modern Love editor Daniel Jones, and their daughter and son. Visit her at www.cathihanauer.com.

# ACKNOWLEDGMENTS

Without the enthusiastic support and astute feedback of Kate Christensen, Dan Jones, Amy Hanauer, and Bette Hanauer, my books might well be lying in drawers, mountains of pages gathering dust. I'm deeply grateful to all four of you.

The twenty-five bold and brilliant contributors to this anthology, like the twenty-six who wrote for its prequel (nine appear in both books), have shared their stories and lives, their humor and wisdom, so that we all might be moved, amused, and enlightened by them. They worked graciously and patiently, with me and without, to make these essays pristine not only in and of themselves but also as part of this book. Heartfelt thanks to every one of you.

In addition to providing their essays, several of the contributors also helped me with other aspects of this book, notably Julianna Baggott, Cynthia Kling, and Sarah Crichton; also Veronica Chambers, Lynn Darling, Anna March, Robin Rinaldi, and Susanna Sonnenberg. Other people who were helpful: Cindy Chupack, Robbie Myers, Laurie Abraham, Lisa Chase, Susan Squire, Amy Maclin, Lauren Mechling, Jim Baker, Laura Marmor, Elizabeth Kaplan, Sarah Chalfant, Jin Auh, Dani Shapiro, Abby Thomas, Bethanne Patrick, Vivian Gornick, Elissa Schappell, Rory Evans, Ted Conover, Brendan Fitzgerald, Sari Botton, Elizabeth Benedict, Karen Mockler, Kate Bernheimer, Monica Holloway, Jen Marshall, Karen Axelrod, Deb Bernardini, Deb Denhart, Judy

Spring, Lonnie Hanauer, Vera Jones, and, of course, the walkers: Carrie Baker and Renee Wetstein, Shelley Zimbalist and Sarah Belanger. Gretchen Jennings said something to me years ago that I taped above my desk and still look at every time I need inspiration. (I won't reprint it, but it has to do with there being a need out there for something I might provide.) Deb-Jane Addis and the Tucson crew supply dreamy hikes and riveting conversation when I'm lucky enough to get there. Phoebe Jones and Nathaniel Jones have been my favorite sources of distraction and comic relief all their lives, but now they're old enough to offer real insight and wisdom too. It's a cool and miraculous thing, and I cherish and adore both of you. I also thank Phoebe for the author photo(s).

Marjorie Braman took a leap when she bought *The Bitch in the House* back in 2000, and I thought about her almost every day I worked on this sequel. I was privileged to spend an afternoon with her not long ago, in the final months of her life, and although she was very ill, she was, as usual, both great fun and a mentor. Her spirit and wisdom pervade this book, and I miss her.

Luckily for me, the exceptional Jennifer Brehl had the task of filling Marjorie's big shoes. She and Lisa Bankoff make up my other team, and we've happily come to refer to ourselves as Team Bitch. Thanks to both of you, and also to the lovely Berni Barta, and Anna Will. Also at Morrow/HarperCollins I am grateful to Laura Cherkas, Andrea Molitor, Mumtaz Mustafa (for the excellent cover!), Bonni Leon-Berman, Tavia Kowalchuk, Kelly Rudolph, and the many others who worked hard to create and launch this book.

Finally, and again, I thank the readers of the book. The world moves at a dizzying pace these days; we all have endless things to cram into our time, and, in our rare free moments, endless options for what we might do. I'm grateful that you chose to read a book, and especially grateful that it was mine. Thank you.